1989

W9-CLJ-760

ABUNDANCE OF LIFE

Columbia Studies of Social Gerontology and Aging,
Abraham Monk, General Editor

Columbia Studies of Social Gerontology and Aging
Abraham Monk, General Editor

HARRY R. MOODY

Abundance of Life
Human Development Policies for an Aging Society

COLUMBIA UNIVERSITY PRESS

NEW YORK

1988

To Elizabeth and Carolyn

Columbia University Press
New York   Guildford, Surrey
Copyright © 1988 Columbia University Press
All rights reserved

Library of Congress Cataloging-in-Publication Data

Moody, Harry R.
Abundance of Life.

(Columbia studies of social gerontology and aging)
Bibliography: p.
Includes index.
1. Aged—Government policy—United States.
I. Title.   II. Series.
HQ1064.U5M66   1988   362.6'0973   87-32654
ISBN 0-231-06592-2 (alk. paper)

Printed in the United States of America

Clothbound Columbia University Press editions are Smyth-sewn
and printed on permanent and durable acid-free paper

Contents

Acknowledgments

I began this book as a "policy framework" prepared for the *National Aging Policy Center on Education, Leisure, and Continuing Opportunities* of the National Council on Aging, Inc. (NCOA). The NCOA Policy Center was created by a grant from the federal Administration on Aging (AoA) in 1980 as one of six such centers charged with examining emerging issues of aging policy across a wide spectrum. From the beginning the NCOA Center was faced with an anomolous mission. It was easy to see that retirement, health care, or income policy were matters of clear importance for the welfare of America's aging population. But what about the more intangible issues addressed by the NCOA Policy Center? Indeed, why should education, the uses of lesiure time, or quality of life be matters for public policy at all?

The six Policy Centers were established in the last year of the Carter Administration. With the coming of the Reagan Administration, and with the intensification of public debate over Social Security, Medicare, and economic policy, it was clear that hard times had arrived. It often seemed that social welfare policy now had best concern itself with survival needs, not with "frills" such as the NCOA Policy Center was commissioned to examine.

In fact, I believe it was a far-sighted decision of the federal government to establish the Policy Centers and to assign them a mission based, not on day-to-day political crises, but on examination of long-range impli-

cations of public policy for an aging society. During its three years of op-
erration the NCOA Center did turn out a body of work in fulfillment of
that broad mandate. The present book is in no sense a summary of that
work, but it represents an attempt to think through the issues that an
aging society must face when survival needs are assured. Of course to separate survival needs from other aspirations is already to make certain assumptions and beg crucial questions. It will be evident in this book that
I do not accept any such watertight distinction between "hard" issues and
those that pertain to quality of life. The dichotomy may be part of the
problem in the first place. In any case, there is abundant evidence that
quality-of-life questions are becoming inescapable. Public policy may not
be able to answer them in any definitive way but we ignore them at our
peril.

Portions of different chapters in this book were prepared and published
separately. I am grateful to many people and institutions who have made
it possible for me to work on the ideas set forth in this book. First, Jack
Ossofsky, NCOA Executive Director and Edmund Worthy, Co-Director
of the Policy Center, were supportive of my work during the life of the
Policy Center. The chapter "Aging and Quality of Life" was prepared as
a background statement for the Policy Center. An earlier version of "The
Specter of Decline" was prepared for a conference sponsored by the Aging Society Project supported by the Carnegie Corporation of New York.
I am grateful to Alan Pifer, Carnegie President Emeritus, and Lydia Bronte,
Staff Director, for their continuing support. The Aging Society Project
has been decisive in shaping my own thinking on the issues in this book.

Portions of "Late Life and The Uses of Time" appeared in a paper prepared for the Board of Directors of Elderhostel and at a conference on
aging convened by the Provincial Government of Alberta. A different
version of it appears in *What Does It Mean To Grow Old? Views from the
Humanities,* edited by Thomas Cole and Sally Gadow. An earlier draft of
"Ideology and The Politics of Aging" appears as a chapter in *Gerontological Social Work Practice with the Community Elderly,* edited by George
Getzel and Joanna Mellor. A portion of "Mutual Self-Help" appeared as
an article in the March 1985 issue of *Aging* magazine published by the
Administration on Aging. Parts of "Late-Life Education" and "Retraining Older Workers" appear in an article in the book *Education and Aging,*
edited by James Birren, David Peterson, and James Thornton, and also
in an article "Education and the Aging Society" from *Daedelus* (Winter
1986). Portions of "Culture, Leisure, and Lifespan Development" appear
as an introductory essay in John Balkema's *The Creative Spirit: An An-*

notated Bibliography on the Arts, Humanities, and Aging. The chapter "Mediating Structures" incorporates work done under the "Mediating Structures and Aging Project" supported by a grant under Title IV-A of the Older Americans Act from the federal Administration on Aging to the Brookdale Center on Aging of Hunter College.

At the Brookdale Center on Aging I have benefited in more ways than I can acknowledge from the inspiration and advice of my colleagues Rose Dobrof and Sam Sadin. I acknowledge support from the Brookdale Foundation for grants that established the Brookdale Center and have made possible its work over the years. I am also grateful for appointment as a visiting Fellow of the Andrew Norman Institute of the Andrus Gerontology Center, University of Southern California, where I enjoyed the collegial support of Dr. James Birren and Dr. David Peterson. This book was begun under support from the AoA grants to the NCOA Policy Center and finished on sabbatical as a Mina Shaughnessy Scholar of the Fund for the Improvement of Post-Secondary Education, U.S. Dept. of Education. Needless to say, the views set forth in the book are my own and do not reflect the views of the institutions who have supported my work.

Finally, I have the deepest gratitude to my wife Elizabeth, who encouraged me to write this book.

ABUNDANCE OF LIFE

"I came that they might have life,
and have it abundantly."
                —Jesus of Nazareth

"Richness does not lie in the abundance
of goods but in the richness of soul."
                —The Prophet Muhammad

1

Introduction: Abundance of Life

"The settled pessimism of so much of the culture of the late 20th century is in effect an absolute loss of the future: of any significant belief that it can be both different and better."
—Raymond Williams, *The Year 2000*

The title of this book suggests an optimistic note. The achievement of advanced industrial societies of the twentieth century has been a demographic revolution of unparalleled scope. In brief, we have created societies in which most human beings born can expect to reach old age. In 1900 life expectancy in the United States averaged 43 years; today it is 77 and still rising. Astonishingly, two thirds of all the gains in life expectancy since the emergence of the human species have occurred in the twentieth century. For the first time in history, most people can expect to live out the full course of the human life cycle from childhood through old age. These advances in longevity will certainly be remembered as an achievement of world-historical importance in our time.

Along with this achievement of individual longevity, another trend has been visible through virtually all advanced industrialized societies: the aging of populations. Population aging means a shifting balance of age-groups in the population: a larger proportion of old people, a smaller proportion of children. It is lower fertility, more than biomedical technology, that has brought about the phenomenon of population aging.

This advance in individual longevity, combined with population aging, constitutes the theme of this book. Together, they comprise a demographic challenge for social policies, a challenge few societies have even begun to face. The coming of an aging society is a new historical event, and the problems created by this new state of affairs are unprecedented.

Yet in stressing the problems, one must never lose sight of what is positive in this new historical situation. It is understandable to become preoccupied with problems of an aging society. But in this book I am concerned with the opportunities created by an aging society. The demographic revolution promises an abundance of life whose possibilities still remain largely unexplored.

THE FAILURE OF SUCCESS

When we think about old age as the most tangible evidence of this new abundance of life, we are likely to think not of triumph but of defeat or disaster. Our image of old age is commonly an image of decline and decay. Loneliness, nursing homes, crime against the elderly: this has long been the public image of old age in America. But preoccupation with the problems of late life can blind us to its triumph and to its unexplored possibilities. We lose any confidence that the future could be both different and better.

Public policy repeats this error. This is partly a matter of what Herman Kahn dubbed the "failure of success." We have created a world enjoying mass consumption, an open society, or sustained economic growth, and immediately we come to take the achievement for granted and bemoan the new dilemmas that success now presents us. The successes of longevity are followed by new problems. But an attitude that equates old age with a "specter of decline" is itself profoundly destructive of the quality of old age itself. The negative image of old age becomes a self-fulfilling prophecy. A more balanced point of view would include attention to the unexplored positive possibilities of the last stage of life.

This book is concerned with policies for an aging society, and it addresses both the problems and the possibilities opened by the new abundance of life. One of the principal arguments here is that policies that address the deficits of old age without attending to opportunities are in fundamental error. It is an error that leads public policy, and in particular the contemporary welfare state, into a blind alley. We offer old people help with their needs but do nothing to nurture the strengths that might allow people to solve their own problems. We ignore latent strengths and respond only to dependency or failure.

It is difficult to reverse the assumptions on which policy has been based. We have too long maintained yesterday's largely negative image of old age. The image itself is a kind of false consciousness that is increasingly out of touch with improvements in income and health status in America's older population. The image of old age as a specter of decline is ill adapted to the unprecedented abundance of life found in an ever-growing proportion of our population. The negative image means two things: first, our social policies for helping older people tend to overlook contributive roles that older people can play. And, second, our policies for developing and nurturing strengths are skewed toward childhood and youth. Later life is ignored, as if growth or change were impossible. Again, this self-fulfilling prophecy forecloses contributive roles we have not begun to imagine.

The result of this failure of imagination is a condition in which our public policies for old age generate contradictions. During the Great Depression large numbers of people witnessed the paradox of poverty in the midst of plenty: crops were burned and milk was dumped in ditches while people went hungry. The paradox was inescapable. Abundance co-existed with poverty, and public policy was helpless to cope with the contradiction. These contradictions helped spur changes in government policy, above all the New Deal, including the Social Security Act (1935) that remains the cornerstone of U.S. policy on aging to this day.

But the domestic social policies for old age in the welfare state have not abolished contradictions. The paradox of abundance in the midst of need has not diminished today. This is nowhere more evident than among advocates for the aged as a group who speak the language of interest-group advocacy while failing to acknowledge the differences and contradictory interests within that 11% of the American population over the age of 65. The aged as a group cannot be labeled uniformly poor or needy or frail unless we deliberately overlook the dramatic gains that our social policies have themselves brought about. This false consciousness ignores the failure of success and so breeds pessimism about the future.

The failure of success brings us to the heart of the contradiction. There lies the central challenge of American liberalism today: how to maintain commitment to active government responsibility in a period when the historical conditions of liberal politics have changed, partly because of the very success of liberalism itself? The thesis of this book is not that liberalism is discredited in aging policy nor that we are losing ground because of its failures. On the contrary, it is precisely the hidden success of liberal policies for the aging population that now generate new contradictions that conventional liberalism seems poorly prepared to address. This failure of imagination is more disturbing than the failure of success.

NEED FOR HUMAN DEVELOPMENT POLICIES

The failure of imagination is not confined to old age or to aging policy. Our society has generally lacked human development policies on any broad scale. But the failure eventually comes home to roost. In the last stage of life, we encounter the cumulative impact of all the life events occurring in the earlier course of a lifetime. The cost is not avoided, only postponed. That cumulative cost can be reckoned back to childhood and never stops being counted. Increased life expectancy means that we pay for a longer period of time. Failure to invest in child nutrition means schoolchildren have trouble learning in school and so fall further behind. That early failure to invest in child development is echoed by high school dropout rates a decade later; then in crime rates, unemployment, and ill health; and finally, in the poverty and dependency of old age. The cost never stops being counted.

The failure to support human development policies over the entire adult life course will be echoed in the condition of old age. But there are no professions or institutions that look at human development in *lifespan* terms instead of responding to problems of specific age-groups: children, adolescents, the elderly, and so on. Each interest group advocates for its own constituency, and the life course remains divided into separate segments. If aging policy must address conditions arising over an entire lifetime, then a life course perspective on policy is indispensable.

Thus, for example, problems of retirement income and older workers need to be seen in this context. The displaced or unemployed older worker enters old age with no pension, no savings, and no job. Still others will face different problems. Some well-to-do retirees with time on their hands may see new-found leisure as a curse instead of a blessing. The elderly widow suffering from arthritis or diabetes may not realize that self-help initiatives can benefit those with chronic health conditions.

None of these cases are beyond help, but present policies are not well designed to help them. Work, leisure, and health care policies fail to address these issues. Few institutions in our society systematically encourage people to develop the strengths and skills needed to help them solve their own problems. In retraining of workers, in creative use of leisure time, and in self-help groups we have only a few examples of what aging policy might be concerned about. But these examples point to a common set of concerns. When we speak about developing strengths and skills from a lifespan perspective, it means nothing less than giving people the tools to cope with both predictable and unexpected transitions faced in later life. A policy for lifespan development means thinking boldly about how the unprecedented abundance of life could be mobilized for the benefit both of older people and of society as a whole.

If this point of view sounds utopian, consider the alternative. Failing to attend to human development means an aging policy that responds only to problems. When policy is defined in this way, it is easy to fall into the habit of thinking of old age itself as one big problem for society. That mood contributes to a pervasive pessimism, the specter of decline, and the paralysis engendered by it. Not only is this "fire-fighting" approach to the needs of the aging inadequate in itself, but also it fosters continuing depreciation of the strengths and capacities of older people by professionals and by the public as a whole.

THE PROMISE OF HUMAN DEVELOPMENT OVER THE LIFESPAN

Will this problem-focused approach to old age persist? There is evidence to think it may not. There are reasons to believe we are now at a historical turning point in our view of late life development, a change in our concept of the kind of growth or development that is possible in the last stage of life. A theoretical foundation for a new view of late-life development is now emerging from studies of lifespan development psychology. These studies demonstrate that the human capacity for learning and growth continues well into later life, provided opportunities and incentives are available. Research also shows the devastating effects that poorly designed interventions can have in fostering dependency among the old.

But the driving force for a developmental policy toward old age will not come from new ideas alone. The policies of the past are simply too wasteful and too inefficient to continue in the path marked out to date. The basic argument of this book is that we are living today through a demographic revolution of unprecedented scale that can in turn make possible a new, developmental view of positive growth potential in later life. The historical basis for a new developmental view of old age and for policies of lifespan human development can be found in changes in family structure, in life expectancy, in health status of the aged, and in the postindustrial economy. In order to appreciate the historical significance of this change, we need to look at a comparable, but earlier, historical transformation: what Philippe Aries describes as the "invention of childhood" over the last two centuries.

Aries, in *Centuries of Childhood*, notes that the idealized image of childhood as a protected period of psychological growth and development first arose among the urban bourgeoisie. In this class there first appeared radically new values such as tenderness with children, a lengthening of the period appropriate to childhood, and most important, an appreciation of the long-range, *lifetime* consequences of the quality of childrearing itself. This attention to quality of life in childhood was linked in turn to a developmental view of childhood and to the identification of long-range effects of the early period of life: elements we take for granted today. Yet a century or two ago, when child labor was common, or in the Middle Ages, when a child was treated as a grown-up by age 13, our contemporary "developmentalist" ideas would have been incomprehensible.

At first, the new perspective was embodied in the family itself. But before long, the developmental perspective found its systematic expression in public policy: namely, in the public school system. Children and youth were kept in school for ever longer periods of time. The justification for this prolonged educational dependency was the belief that skills and knowledge would pay off from a long-range, lifespan perspective.

As public policy increasingly took over responsibility for developmental tasks, the family itself experienced a loss of functions, such as education, carried on earlier. But with loss of some functions came the addition of new possibilities, particularly in the realm of leisure and the private uses of time. The result was to separate ever more sharply the private and public spheres of life. The family became a "haven in a heartless world." For both adulthood and for youth, the public sphere was dominated by the competitive values of a political economy that controlled both work and education in the name of productivity and developing the capacities of children and young people.

There is an irony in the triumph of the developmental perspective through the spread of schooling. The developmental ideal, now extended into adulthood through adult education and worker retraining, increasingly fell under the domination of a political economy that defined development exclusively in terms of the marketplace. It was only retirement and old age—the last of the three boxes of life—that remained outside the framework of development and productivity and so remained an arena of freedom. But the price of such freedom in old age was an image of leisure time that was utterly privatized and trivialized. The developmental ideal did not seem to apply to old age. Old age became a period of empty time, its cultural or psychological possibilities drained of meaning.

Today this image of old age as empty time is being challenged from a number of directions. First and foremost there is the economic abundance that has lifted many in the older population above the poverty level and has given millions of others a margin of affluence and leisure. Second is the dramatic improvement in health status and life expectancy. Old age, especially for the young-old, has become a period when new modes of fulfillment are possible. Third is the rise in levels of education and in opportunities for participation in cultural life and in active roles in later life. This abundance of life will make possible a developmental image of old age in the future. With a margin of material security, with better health and education, more and more older people today enjoy possibilities for quality of life unavailable before.

The parallels with the discovery of childhood are evident. Just as there arose a new tenderness toward children, so today we are seeing a new discovery of positive growth potential, such as adult education or artistic creativity, that persists in old age. This new sensitivity is presently limited to elite sectors, just as the bourgeois ethic of tenderness toward children was once limited. But the positive view can be expected to spread, and there must be attention to the kinds of institutions that can nurture growth and development in later life. In addition, we are seeing a lengthening and differentiation of old age itself, including the demarcation of specific subsegments (the "young-old" versus the "old-old" and so on), just as, earlier, distinctions arose between infancy, latency, adolescence, etc. With more careful differentiation comes a new appreciation of the developmental possibilities of the different stages of life, including the last stage. Increasing longevity, accompanied by improved health status, means that it makes more sense to invest valuable time and effort in helping older people. The developmental perspective on old age now responds to material possibility, as well as to social necessity.

Most important, we now begin to understand that it makes no sense *not* to adopt a developmentalist outlook. Just as the bourgeoisie first insisted on the long-range consequences of the quality of childhood, so we too will discover that the cost of *not* developing capacities of older people is far greater. The cost of health and social services in caring for old age dependency is far greater than modest investments that might reduce dependency through strategies of self-help, education, and building on latent strengths and abilities.

POLICY IMPLICATIONS

What specific policy guidelines follow from this prodevelopmentalist point of view?

1. Wherever possible we should prefer policies that reduce unnecessary dependency while nurturing latent strengths. Incentives for this new style of professional intervention must be built into human service policies for the older population.

2. We must have better definition and more accurate measurement of the scope of contributive roles of older people. Contributions include nonmonetized economic transactions, as well as the noneconomic continuing contributions seen in self-help and volunteerism.

3. If we seek policies that build on strength, not weakness, then those policies must involve some commitment to the lifelong development of human capacities through education. Such a lifespan perspective on education would carry with it the potential of older people for greater self-sufficiency and contribution to the wider community. Education then would not merely be a private pursuit of leisure-time activities in old age. Instead, lifelong learning would be anchored in a vision of continued social productivity and personal growth.

Enumerating these principles makes it clear how far aging policy has fallen short of its challenge in the area of education, voluntary action, culture, and leisure. Not only have these quality-of-life issues been neglected, but also programs developed have often contradicted the goals set forth here. Education for older people has evolved into a form of private leisure-time entertainment. Volunteerism has been brought under the domain of professionalized human service specialists. Self-help and mutual aid among older people have been given scant encouragement by public policies. And in the development of initiatives in the key areas of aging policy—work and retirement, health care, income maintenance— we have failed to recognize the role of quality-of-life concerns in enhancing the contributions of older people.

This analysis underscores the failure of both liberal and conservative policy prescriptions in the area of aging. The conventional liberal solution to the problems of old age is the expansion of the welfare state: more services, more professional intervention, greater dependence on government. The conventional conservative solution is reliance on the private marketplace: on production and consumption of goods and services mediated by the cash nexus of monetized transactions.

But there is a third policy alternative: government acting as an enabling force. This third alternative is equivalent neither to "getting the government off our backs" nor to expecting government to provide all desired services. Both liberals and conservatives are too quick to monetize the problems and to use one yardstick to measure the needs or the productivity of the old. If old people are a "problem," it is because they live too long, grow dependent, cost too much money, and so on. The solution? Keep people on the payroll longer, encourage them to save their money or turn their assets (e.g., home equity) into cash. A still harsher version of this scenario demands cuts in entitlements and proposes market incentives in health care, hoping that "voluntarism" will take up the slack. Liberals reject these solutions, of course, but conventional liberal solutions are no more persuasive, since they usually involve promising more public services at a time when public provision is in retreat.

Both the liberal- and conservative-style solutions are mirrors of one other, each emphasizing opposing sides of the problem. Both share the same root assumptions: in general, "monetized" solutions. Either let the marketplace solve problems or get the taxpayers to pay more. Like American defense policy, the loudest voices in the debate speak only the language of quantity: are we spending more or less than the Russians? But in military matters as in domestic policy, what is *not* measured—troop morale, tactical leadership, net assessment, and global strategy—count for much more than quantity of weapons or military appropriations. Clearly, money matters, but the greatest failing is in the absence of overall strategy. This failure means "redoubling our efforts when we've lost sight of the goal" —a danger as evident in social policy as it is in military affairs. In the largest single category of our domestic budget and policy—namely, programs for the aging—liberal advocates for the aging are in danger of falling into the same trap as conservatives fell into on defense policy: namely, overmonetizing all the problems and solutions and so losing sight of the goal.

In our preoccupation with exclusively measurable components, we have lost sight of the quality-of-life issues that can best answer to the ultimate question about old age: namely, why survive? This concentration on measurable components has led to an exaggeration of the weaknesses and deficits of aging without appreciation of latent strengths, contributive roles, and continuing opportunities in later life. In this way, policy development in the field of aging has been narrowed, and single vision has fostered a self-fulfilling prophecy: what Townsend calls the "structured dependency of old age." The purpose of this book is to provide a vantage point for policy analysis that would reverse that trend. In this way we may hope to see how America's growing population of older people can be mobilized as a growing national resource rather than be seen as a burgeoning problem in the decades ahead.

PROSPECTS FOR THE FUTURE

Over the last twenty years we have lived through a period where aging issues have moved from earlier neglect to a position on center stage of the domestic policy agenda. This prominence has had beneficial results. But in the process, a neglect of human development has persisted and grown worse. We have not really answered the question, Why survive? This neglect has meant that, despite enormous expenditure of public money, in the public mind at least, the problems of aging only seem to get worse. A policy pessimism affects both liberals and conservatives. Conservatives have, of course, a certain vested interest in claiming that public dollars have not cured poverty, redeemed old age, or solved other social ills. But liberals, too, acquiesce in a widely felt view that the problems of old people are worse than ever.

This view is as deeply mistaken as it is commonly held. The impulse to dwell on failure is understandable: how else are advocates for the aging to gain public attention for the real problems that persist? But this line of negative thinking, supported by liberals and conservatives alike, is deeply destructive. Insistence on failure erodes our confidence that, given the right kind of help, people can solve their own problems. That confidence was for generations a deeply felt American tradition. It is in short supply today. But pessimism erodes our confidence in vigorous public action. This is no less true in old-age policy than it is for foreign policy or economic policy. It is an abandonment of the American style of confidence that, given the right kind of help, people can solve their own problems.

But confidence requires two elements: first, a belief in the basic strengths and capacities of older people themselves; and, second, a commitment by public policy to assist people with the right kind of help. Over the last generation, aging policy has neglected both sides of this equation, with the result that aging policies today foster dependency and fail to nurture basic strengths. We need to return to the older American tradition with a proper balance between personal responsibility and public provision.

In part, this message, which is the essential framework of this book, is deeply conservative: suspicious of professional imperialism, doubtful about the culture of modernism, insistent on the need for self-development within small-scale communities that have traditionally been sensitive to the human experience of old age. On the other hand, the thrust of the book is also radical: a critique of ideology and vested interests of the political economy, a call for grass-roots activism, an appeal for widened opportunity for the poor and the least advantaged elderly. But ideological labels are less important here than an understanding of how the advent of an aging society calls for a critique of our accepted ways of thinking about the last stage of life. That critique is necessary if the future of the aging society is to fulfill the promise of an abundance of life.

2

The Specter of Decline: Fear of an Aging Society

"The progressive state is in reality the cheerful and the hearty state to all the different orders of society; the stationary is dull; the declining melancholy."

—Adam Smith

AGING IN THE COUNTRY OF THE YOUNG

Aging means acknowledgment of finitude: of limited time, a limited span of organic life. Just as individuals grow older, so do societies. In both cases there is often a self-consciousness about belonging to a particular epoch of life: youth versus age. In our own time, newly established states of the third world identify themselves as young countries, often with implications of hope and optimism for the future. But in the late eighteenth century America was the first of these new nations. America, the young Republic, was founded in a revolutionary act consciously breaking with the past. The "New World," from the beginning thought of itself as a young country. As such, it possessed the attributes of youth: above all, an open future bright with possibilities.[1] That national self-image of youth persisted down to John F. Kennedy's appeal to youth, to a new generation taking over leadership toward a "New Frontier." Even Ronald Reagan, our oldest President, projected an image of youthful vigor and insisted to Americans that "Our best days are ahead of us."

From the beginning America held out a promise of escaping from the common destiny of aging and decline associated with European societies, with the Old World. As Noah Webster put it, "For America in her infancy to adopt the maxims of the Old World would be to stamp the wrinkles of old age upon the bloom of youth. . . ."[2] American exceptionalism meant that America would defy the common destiny of decay by the virtues of youth and self-renewal. The roots of this youthful self-image run deep in the origins of the Republic. The Great Seal of the United States (*Novus Ordo Seclorum*) announces the beginning of a "New Age." Vestiges of the old world were to be swept aside. Indeed the American Revolution was only the first of the great upheavals that would pit young revolutionaries against an established order.

This early mood of youthful optimism flourished from the Revolution on throughout the nineteenth century. The same mood also entailed a devaluation of old age and aging. In the new, young country it was youth and the image of future progress that were increasingly exalted.[3] But after the tragedy of the Civil War and particularly by the end of the nineteenth century, the myth of American exceptionalism had became tarnished. Writers such as Henry Adams and his brother Brooks Adams became preoccupied with the loss of American innocence, with the specter of decadence and cultural decline. Brooding on the passage of time from the founding of the Republic, they were not alone in their forebodings of a pessimistic future.

The pessimistic forecast of things to come has had a history of its own. Other civilizations have been fascinated by metaphors of organic growth and decline, youth and old age. In earlier historical periods of catastrophe or decline, the feeling has taken hold that a society as a whole has grown too old. One catches the mood in the Roman Empire at the time of Augustine and again in the calamitous fourteenth century with the waning of the Middle Ages.[4] The aging of an entire society—the Roman Empire or medieval Christendom—was felt as an exhaustion of the original energy that inspired its birth.

The aging of society as a whole is understood by comparison to the individual life course: birth, maturity, and decline. Berger and Berger, commenting on societal decadence, use the metaphor of senility: "A decadent society . . . is one embarked on the decline of old age; decadence is the societal equivalent of senile debility."[5] The analogy with individual organic life seems irresistible: aging means exhaustion, decline, and collapse.

We need to disentangle three intertwined yet distinct ideas: (1) individual aging—the normal aging of the organism, a process studied by gerontology as a scientific discipline; (2) population aging—that is, a demographic change in the age composition of a population to include more older and fewer young people; and (3) societal aging—that is, the chronological age of collectivities, such as the United States or the Roman

Empire. The crucial question is how the three levels are connected with one another. It is by no means an easy question to answer. Whether aging at any of these levels must involve decadence or decline is of course, equally important. The answers to these questions will come from a historical examination of attitudes toward aging as we think about how those attitudes shape our image of the coming of an aging society in the future.

AGING AND THE AMERICAN SELF-IMAGE

There is a restlessness in the American character that has never been comfortable with old age, no more than with limits on individual aspirations for achievement. Progress for the individual meant surpassing one's origins: children were expected to rise about their parents' position in life. Progress for the nation meant a similar expansion. In both cases, the pattern meant turning away from the past: going West, turning away from the old settled ways.

For a hundred years or more after the founding of the Republic, the self-image of America as a young country coincided with geographic realities and with real possibilities for social mobility. Well into the twentieth century, the story has been much the same. The individual denial of old age was tied to a collective self-image of American exceptionalism, of America as a youthful country blessed with unlimited opportunities. The worship of youth and belief in progress were two sides of the same coin. But the same attitudes prompted an increasing cultural separation between the young and the old, since the future, after all, belonged to the young. A generation gap was already visible in the 1920s, and the word "teenager" appeared in the 1930s.[6] During the 1960s, the Baby Boom generation captured the headlines and reinforced a public image of the youth culture that was influential far beyond sheer numbers of young people in the population.

By the 1970s a different mood began to prevail. America increasingly came to recognize itself as an aging society. The announcement was usually made in a tone of crisis and, often enough, with deep pessimisn about the future of such a society. Burgeoning numbers of older people and popular magazines made it a cliché to speak about the "graying of America." The clichés and popular images did confirm a very real demographic trend. The proportion of people over 65 in the American population was increasing steadily: up from 4 percent in 1900 to more than 11 percent in 1980. The contrast could not be sharper with what America had been when George Washington became President, when half the population was under age 16 and only 2 percent were living beyond the age of 65. Now forecasters were telling us to expect a tidal wave of elderly by the beginning of the next century. By 2030 close to 20 percent of the American population would be over 65. The young country was growing old.

This awareness of a demographic shift paralleled another development, perhaps more profound: namely, a sense that America *as a society* was growing older, was on the defensive, was being forced to cope with limits. During the 1970s, the American self-image began to change. Oil shortages and military debacle in Vietnam brought home the limits of American power and self-sufficiency. On the positive side, more people became interested in historic preservation, in recycling natural resources, and, in general, conserving what was old instead of discarding it. As America began to recognize itself as an aging society, it confronted limits in every direction:

> **A Clouded Economic Future.** Low industrial productivity, persistent high interest rates, lack of capital for future investment, and short-range management orientation: all these factors have contributed to a slowdown in economic growth apparent since the 1970s. Few people had confidence of a return to the buoyant economic climate of the 1960s.
>
> **Environmental Constraints.** The environment now puts limits on economic growth and has forced a new awareness of the need for caution and conservation. With higher energy costs and expenses for pollution control and cleanup, the limits of growth became the most obvious signs of finitude.
>
> **The Decline of Mobility.** A young society is a society on the move, but an aging society finds that geographic and social movement slows down. By the 1970s, for the first time, parents could no longer count on their children's surpassing their station in life. People were moving less frequently because of high mortgage rates and high housing prices. At the same time members of the Baby Boom generation were finding promotions blocked.[7]
>
> **Suffocating Credentialism.** For generations of Americans, educational opportunity has been central to an image of upward mobility. But as more and more people acquire credentials, degrees and diplomas lose competitive value. Expanding educational requirements for entry into professions have erected a new set of guild bar-

riers that restrict entry and curb opportunities. The credentialized society introduces new rigidities into occupational mobility.

Seniority and Tenure. In universities, labor unions, and civil service systems, layoffs take place on the basis of seniority: a practice with adverse impact on the young. Increasingly, we see the spread of two-tier wage systems and the tenuring in of older employees in many sectors of the economy. The result is a growing sclerosis in major institutions, particularly in slow-growth sectors of the economy already plagued by lack of innovation.

Security, bureaucratic cautiousness, the management of decline, and a sense of running up against limits—these factors arise from historical developments in foreign policy, in the economic system, in the adverse impact of new technologies. In themselves they have nothing to do with an aging society. And yet, taken together, they confirm for us an unconscious image of what it means to grow old: to become overcautious, to lose creativity, to preside over declining powers, and finally, to face death and disaster. If our society as a whole is moving in these directions, while, at the same time, America is becoming an aging society, does not this confirm—at the unconscious level at least—the inevitability of aging as decline?

THE REAGAN YEARS

In 1980, as if to refute the notion that aging means inevitable decline, the American people elected Ronald Reagan, the oldest man ever to occupy the Presidency. The 1980 election of Ronald Reagan was a protest against the notion that America was decadent or in decline. Instead of Jimmy Carter's preaching about an American malaise, Reagan insisted that our "best years are still ahead of us." This optimism and upbeat message, including a promise of economic growth, was welcome news, but it was based on a paradox. The message succeeded by looking forward and backward at the same time: by returning to traditional values of the past, we were promised an advance into a brighter future.

The results were something else again. Reagan's first term brought the worst recession since the Great Depression of the 1930s, while foreign affairs aroused fears about nuclear war in the future. In social policy concerned with aging, the first Reagan Administration witnessed a profound crisis in the financing of the Social Security system, a crisis resolved only by a bipartisan Commission when the Social Security issue became too hot to handle. Along with the immediate satisfaction over economic growth, there were fears of long-term problems tied to uncontrollable federal deficits.

By the 1984 election, the electorate was still fearful about the future of Social Security and Medicare: the two largest items of domestic expenditure. Democrats, sensing a political issue, played on those. There was also concern that Ronald Reagan, running for a second term at age 74, might be too old to be an effective President, regardless of his popularity. But as an elderly President, he paradoxically retained an upbeat, youthful image that refused to accept any pessimistic limits of growth for the American future.

The Sources of Pessimism

Our oldest President's youthful image was not merely a curiosity or a paradox. Aging evokes contradictory elements in the public mood. There is deep anxiety about growing old. After all, individual aging signifies threats to personal well-being: ultimately, loss of control, loss of the unlimited future. Today this *personal* fear of aging—of what will happen to *me* when I grow old—coincides with a massive loss of confidence in those institutions that might protect us from the vicissistudes of time and old age. If Social Security will someday be "bankrupt," how do we count on support in our old age? Where do we turn for protection? People are threatened by a fear of poverty, illness, and abandonment in old age. In the face of that threat we turn for protection to our jobs, to our families, and to our government.

But these sources of protection are now losing credibility. Job security is threatened by foreign trade and technological advances. Older workers can gain protection by seniority or tenure, but who can be sure how solid that protection will remain? Unemployment for older workers is particularly fearsome since, once out of work, it can be almost impossible to find another job. Family ties that might be counted on for protection in old age are eroding for other reasons. Increasing numbers of young and middle-aged people are unmarried, childless, or divorced. Even when families try to take care of their own, people realize that going into a nursing home could quickly wipe out their life's savings. Thus, along with job and family, people turn to government for protection.

But confidence in the future of government support for the elderly has been severely weakened. Headlines about impending bankruptcy of Social Security took their toll. Experts and Presidential Commissions gravely announced that these programs might run out of money. As government deficits pile up, it becomes evident that government has lost control of its own spending. There is fear that the deficits will continue out of control, forcing new cutbacks in unpredictable ways. Not long ago it was "unthinkable" to propose taxing Social Security benefits. But by 1983 what was unthinkable had become the law of the land. It is not unreasonable to fear that Medicare, like Social Security, could face further cuts in the years ahead. So a feeling grows that the three sources of protection— jobs, families, and government—can no longer be counted on. The personal fate of old age—*my* old age—confirms a broader pessimistic shift in public opinion.

The Liberal Turn to Pessimism

One of the most important ideological developments of recent years has been the way that contemporary liberalism has embraced a pessimistic view of the future. Early indicators included the Club of Rome's famous *Limits of Growth* Report issued in the 1970s, which forecast a dismal future of overpopulation, pollution, and environmental collapse. In the final years of the Carter Administration, the *Global 2000* Report struck the same gloomy tone. In both cases, liberal experts embraced pessimistic conclusions about economic growth, world population trends, food supplies, and nonrenewable resources.[8]

This pessimism of the liberals was a striking departure from earlier phases of liberal ideology. From nineteenth-century laissez-faire liberalism to New Deal interventionists, liberals had always held to an optimistic image of the future based on expanding economic growth. As Sheldon Wolin notes:

> During the past two decades . . . faith in progress has dimmed as liberals contemplated deteriorating cities, thickening pollution, increased racial tensions, widening social inequalities, the worsening of the competitive position of the United States in the international economy, and the puzzles of stagflation.[9]

Here lay much of the secret of Ronald Reagan's political success. At first, supply-side economics promised a return to the postwar levels of economic growth with no permanent pain or sacrifice. The Reagan economic program, like Reagan's presidential campaign in both 1980 and 1984, proclaimed a positive, optimistic image of the future. It was the liberals who had acquired a vested interest in a pessimistic image of the future in order to enlist social action in the present.

And this last point is, of course, the key. In a mood of disillusionment and diminished expectations, it is difficult to get public action unless dire consequences are predicted, unless an emergency threatens. Only when toxic wastes threaten to poison whole towns is it possible to get the Environmental Protection Agency to act. Only when Social Security is about to "go bankrupt" will politicians patch up their differences and save the system. But such crisis management erodes public confidence. Last-minute rescues, lurching from crisis to crisis, confirm a deep-seated public suspicion about the incompetence of government. The crisis reinforces the fear of an aging society.

AN AGING SOCIETY: A HISTORY OF FEARS

It is ironic that, in the short space of a decade or two, we have gone from fears of population explosion to the specter of an aging society. No sooner has a Malthusian terror of population growth subsided then the new gloom of a steady-state population takes its place. Yet as birth rates decline, as they have throughout the industrialized world, and as medical science allows a greater proportion of the population to live out a full lifespan, then an aging society becomes a certainty. There is no alternative to an aging society except expanding population with the much-feared population explosion.

There are, however, some legitimate reasons to be concerned about population aging, such as economic stagnation, societal character, reduced military manpower, and concerns about intergenerational equity.[10] Another fear is that, with an aging population and fewer young people, there will be a decline in creativity and innovation. Common experience suggests that older people are more resistant to new technologies, but in the postindustrial era, economic growth depends on technological innovation for productivity. The societal character of an aging population is likely to be conservative and uncreative,[11] so the outlook ahead is grim.

Before we accept his gloomy forecast, we should remember that there is a long history to the fear of population aging that can give some perspective on current anxieties about the future. Population aging is brought about primarily by low fertility, and this development is not recent. The trend toward lower fertility is well over a century old. Population aging began first in France, where fertility declines began as early as the eigh-

plications of theoretical knowledge: e.g., in quantum physics, molecular biology, systems analysis, etc. Major new growth industries in computers or biotechnology are founded in such theoretical understanding, not on life experience, age, or seniority. And innovation requires risk-taking. The founding of new businesses—entrepreneurship—is the engine behind economic growth and the diffusion of innovation.

With the coming of postindustrial society, Sauvy's observations take on ominous implications. Willingness to take risks would give way to a desire for security: "Owing to demographic stagnation, no sizable new businesses are started, so that enterprising young people must enter an inflexible, slow-moving machine, without hope of promotion to posts of higher responsibility until relatively late in life."[22]

This pessimism may be too extreme. Other economists reject such fears of an aging society, contending that the rising educational levels and workskills of the middle-aged population will improve the quality of the work force.[23] Numerous investigators have documented the positive attributes of older workers, including capacity for change and retraining.[24] An earlier Commission on Population Growth and the American Future (1971) concluded that the transition to a stationary (no-growth) population pattern would have no adverse affect on economic performance.

In some areas of American life the aging of the population has already become an element in the growing sense of declining opportunities. Examples are the relationships between age groups and occupational mobility, between credentialism in education and unemployment among young people, between job seniority and layoffs, between mortgage rates and home ownership. The baby boom generation has found job opportunities and home ownership more limited in comparison with the older generation.

A basic cause for fear of an aging society is the belief that more old people will limit the life chances of the young. This concern has been expressed in public in recent years. For example, in 1978, when Congress passed the law extending mandatory retirement from age 65 to 70, there was much discussion about whether such a move would prevent advancement of younger workers whose promotions would be blocked by older people who had not retired. Advocates for the aging initially rejected such concerns, arguing that most older workers would retire on schedule anyway. But Nathan Keyfitz has analyzed the result of the move toward a no-growth or stationary population. He estimated that the slowdown of U.S. population growth from its traditional increase could create a delay in reaching the middle ranks of most organizations by nearly five years.

Work and retirement is only one of the areas where it makes sense to see the changes in America's age structure as a factor in destructive competition, inequality, diminished opportunity, and, finally, a negative image of the future. If young people are forced into prolonged schooling, if they cannot afford mortgages, if jobs and promotions are blocked, then these inequalities cannot simply be ignored. All of this has its importance for how we think about what it means for America to become an aging society. For some groups in the population, the transition to an aging society will have a price: sometimes for young people, sometimes for older people. It does advocates for the elderly no credit to gloss over these negative realities.

POSTINDUSTRIAL GERONTOLOGY

But demographic change does not operate outside of history and political economy. In the long run, the transition to a postindustrial society may be more important than the overt and exaggerated images of a "war between the generations." Commentators make much of this specter of intergenerational warfare, but they fix their attention on only the most obvious battlegrounds: for example, financing the Social Security system. Other areas of competition in public policy—"graying" suburbs voting down school bond issues, policies favoring Medicare but rejecting school lunches—are actually tradeoffs that were never framed as direct competition between young and old at all. The tradeoffs "just happened" when budget cuts prompted cuts in benefits for the most vulnerable groups. The burden of those cuts has fallen disproportionately on the poor and on children. But this result was not a conspiracy by agents of gerontocracy.

The real problem is that the new competition among age-groups takes place in what Thurow described as a "zero-sum" society.[25] When older workers are locked in to declining industries or ownership of a home that is too big in a neighborhood that is no longer desirable, it is not obvious that the old have won when a young couple cannot qualify for a new mortgage. It is a game in which all parties, young and old alike, can lose ground, as each tries to hold on to what it has. This is the dilemma faced alike by advocates for the elderly and by proponents of generational equity. The problem is that interest-group liberalism in the politics of aging is still the dominant approach of advocates on all sides,[26] and this is a form of social protectionism that has not served us well in aging policy. In the war of all against all, the future cannot help but look threatening.

I have argued that the specter of decline image of an aging society is fundamentally mistaken. Yet at the same time, the coming of an aging society presents some very real problems, problems intensified by the fact that we are seeing the simultaneous coming of an aging society and a postindustrial society.

Today the U.S. economy is no longer the industrial economy it was when Social Security was first adopted, and new forces of production exacerbate the old contradictions. High unemployment is aggravated by introduction of new technology such as robotics or automated factories. These developments, among many, inspire pessimistic wages of future employment. With automation of factories and offices, jobs will disappear forever. Some older workers will try to hold on to their jobs through seniority, featherbedding, tenure, or other job-security strategies. But the result of that strategy will only be to further stifle productivity and mobility. Once displaced from jobs, middle-aged and older workers easily become unemployed or downwardly mobile, competing with teenagers for low-skill jobs in retail trade or the fast-food industry. Job retraining is one hopeful answer here, but retraining by itself will accomplish nothing unless jobs are created for the workers retrained. In light of pressures toward technological unemployment, the temptation will be to write off older workers and continue the practice of institutionalized retirement as the least threatening way to cope with the fact that we do not have enough jobs for everyone nor do we have social policies that encourage older people to be productive, contributive members of society.

SOCIAL WELFARE PESSIMISM

Instead of enhancing the productivity of an aging population, social policies have reinforced a condition where older people are viewed as consumers, not contributors, to common societal needs. Both liberals and conservatives have contributed to a mood of pessimism in different ways and for different reasons. Liberals have portrayed the elderly as the deserving poor. For two generations, the aged have been an ideological loss leader[27] for other liberal social welfare reforms. These reform measures in health care, income maintenance, and so on were originally intended to be universal but in the end were targeted at the aged as a matter of political compromise.[28] Conservatives defeated attempts to extend liberal benefits to the jobless, minority groups, etc. But the elderly, because they were the deserving poor, could legitimately receive public benefits. Thus, national health insurance became Medicare (1965), the Guaranteed

Minimum Income became SSI (1971), until today age-based entitlements have become the greatest single factor of the domestic federal budget.

While legitimating public benefits, the liberal ideology also played a role in reinforcing the pessimistic view of old age. Here ideology and political tactics worked hand in hand. Liberal advocates for the aged have played up the evils of nursing home scandals, elder abuse, and crime against the elderly. The result is that, during the 1970s, while the condition of the old in America progressively improved, public opinion of that condition moved in the *opposite* direction, believing that the old were becoming *worse* off over time. By 1985 a survey by the *Los Angeles Times* showed that two thirds of the respondents thought that poverty among the old was *increasing,* directly contrary to the facts. This liberal drumbeat has been successful in drawing public attention to the problems of some of the elderly. But it has also reinforced our pessimism about old age and an aging society.

In their campaign to curb entitlements the conservatives have made their own contribution to policy pessimism. Critics on the right constantly raise the specter of uncontrollable entitlement programs, attacking Social Security and Medicare in particular. They charged that a powerful "Gray Lobby" composed of advocates for old people had made politicians tremble in fear before the voting power of the elderly.[29]

This crisis rhetoric reached a peak in 1983 when it proved necessary to whip up a national mood of impending catastrophe—the imminent "bankruptcy" of the Social Security system. Only in such a crisis atmosphere did it seem possible for legislators to act, to "save Social Security."[30] They did act, of course, and the compromise was widely seen to be reasonable and judicious. But this successful crisis management came at a price. The fallout of that crisis atmosphere has been a serious diminishing of public confidence in the future of Social Security. Two years later in 1985, a Yankelovich national poll found that 71% of young professionals—an educated and well-informed segment of the population—had "little or no confidence in the Social Security system," while an astounding 40% actually believed it was likely that they would receive *no* payments from Social Security in the future.[31] Most young people came to believe that Social Security would no longer be there to pay out benefits when they retire. Once again ideology has reinforced an image that an aging society spells future disaster.

In sum, for both liberals and conservatives, getting public attention and political action for their favored policy agenda has meant exaggerating the problems of old age and reinforcing the pessimism of the public mood. The residue of that ideological deformation will remain with us as we continue to pay a price for years to come.

THE WORLD WE HAVE LOST

Liberals and conservatives have had their own reasons for supporting a pessimistic ideology of social welfare for old age. But their appeal to the public imagination could succeed only because of deeply held images about old age in modern societies. I have in mind the strange persistence of the Myth of a Golden Age of Aging: the idea that in premodern or preindustrial societies the elderly held a cherished position that is now lost.

Peter Laslett has characterized it as the "world-we-have-lost syndrome," in which he identifies several dogmatic beliefs.[32] First, there is the belief in a historical before and after: that is, old people were better off *before* industrialization and modernization. Second, there is the belief that before, three-generation families lived together and children cared for their parents in old age, whereas today, the elderly are abandoned by their children.

The world-we-have-lost syndrome has long been subjected to devastating empirical refutation by historians and gerontologists. The extended family, it turns out, began to disappear in the eighteenth century and was never as widespread as commonly believed. But the "decline-and-fall" theory is yet another pessimistic way of casting the elderly in a tragic role. Such moralizing pessimism carries its own prescriptions for social policy: children should take care of their aging parents; perhaps filial responsibility should be enforced. In any case, the villain of the piece is the collapsing family.

Those who subscribe to these beliefs are likely to see the future of an aging society in gloomy terms: more and more elderly, increasingly isolated from their families. Liberals and conservatives, for different reasons, tend to accept the world-we-have-lost syndrome. Liberals characteristically insist on the plight of the elderly. When pressed to account for it, they explain the diminished position of the elderly in terms of structural economic tendencies of modern industrial society. Their solution? More welfare state spending and more professionals to care for old age dependency.

But conservatives, too, find it useful to subscribe to the Golden Age image. Once upon a time, we are told, families took care of their own."

But today, government welfare programs have eroded personal responsibility. The solution? Enforce filial responsibility—insist that families take care of aged relatives and cut the budgets for programs that help anyone except the truly needy. The moralistic tale of the decline and fall of the family is more than a dangerous myth. It is part of the ideology of old age examined critically in a later chapter of this book. The conservative and liberal solutions differ, but the pessimistic picture of old age is strangely similar.

EXISTENTIAL PESSIMISM

A further element in the negative image of old age is rooted in the outlook of the modern world. The culture of modernity emphasizes change, novelty, and the fluidity of personal choice. In Robert J. Lifton's image of "Protean man," choices are always open and identity formation becomes a lifelong process. This entire cultural stance has definite implications for old age. The culture of modernity—the "modernization of consciousness"—in fact defines itself in opposition to time past, to tradition, to fixed boundaries of all kinds.

But the overwhelming fact of old age is that time is limited and the sense of unbounded freedom is, finally, an illusion. This fact about the human condition, the finitude of life, is unchanged by modernity:

> Modernity has accomplished many far-reaching transformations, but it has not fundamentally changed the finitude, fragility and mortality of the human condition. What it has accomplished is to seriously weaken those definitions of reality that previously made that human condition easier to bear.[33]

Thus, the culture of modernity is distinctly uncomfortable with old age as an existential reality—the reality of limit, finality, of our one and only life cycle. Society at large tends to deny or disparage values that previously assured the elderly some measure of meaning or dignity: religion, patriotism, the validity of wisdom earned by life experience, and the enduring appreciation of past institutions and achievements. As traditional values come under attack, this negative image of old age becomes more difficult to bear.

A final paradox of the modern ambivalence toward old age can be seen in the ideology and technology of medicine. Through biomedical technology all possible effort is expended to keep elderly patients alive as long

as possible. Thanks to the triumphs of public health and general affluence, an increasing proportion of the population now lives to experience
the last stage of life only to find that it has itself been progressively drained
of meaning. At the moment when the meaning of old age vanishes, we
find enormous economic resources are expended to prolong the lives of
those whose lives have been deprived of any purpose. This paradox is apparent to anyone who works among the elderly in our society. The contradiction is at the center of the modern despair over the meaning of old
age.

The problem is rooted in what Gruman has described the "modernization of the life cycle."[34] The modernized life cycle is characterized by a
twofold development: first, the separation of life into separate stages and
age-groups and, second, the displacement of death into old age. And the
simultaneous convergence of these two trends imperils the sense of meaning in late life. The modernized life course is divided into the "three boxes
of life," namely, youth, adulthood, and old age, which are correlated with
the activities of education, work, and leisure. The problem with this separation of life into segments is that it deprives us of any image of the
unity or meaning of life. Each stage of life has its own characteristic style
of behavior; work and leisure are divided from each other, just as the public and private sphere are set apart. There is no sense of the unity of human life above the separate spheres and stages that segment the life course.

The modernized life cycle, then, sets the stage for the contemporary
problem of the existential meaning of old age. Late life becomes the period when, freed from alienated labor, the real self can be fulfilled. The
modern world relentlessly seeks for the meaning of things in the future,
in the idea of continuing development. Work, savings, deferred gratification, all are striving after a goal located in the future, ultimately, in
old age. But upon arriving at old age, there are many who would agree
with Yeats that "Life is a preparation for something that never happens."

There is a strange contradictory experience of modernity to be found
in the condition of old age today. Old age is both loss of meaning and
greater opportunity for freedom. It is not simply that "modernization" has
weakened or transformed the status of the elderly or thrown previous values into question. More strikingly, old age itself, as a period of life, is no
longer felt merely as a climax, brief or extended, to earlier habits of life.
The enlarged time period of old age itself incorporates the dialectic, the
contradictions of modernity. Modern societies create economic and technical conditions that vastly enlarge the abundance of life for an ever larger
segment of the population. But this abundance of life is increasingly felt

as a void, a space emptied of traditional roles and behavior. Old age, like modernity itself, is the simultaneous experience of emptiness and fullness. It is the emptying of fixed values and, at the same time, the fullness of possibilities.

It is this very abundance of life that increasingly takes on the appearance of a life without purpose, of a technological process out of control. The dilemma is captured in the folktale of the sorcerer's apprentice. It was this very image that was invoked by Marx and Engels in *The Communist Manifesto:* "Modern bourgeois society, . . . a society that has conjured up such gigantic means of production and of exchange, is like the sorcerer who is no longer able to control the powers of the nether world whom he has called up by his spells." The image of the sorcerer is commonly invoked today in the case of nuclear energy and the dilemmas of its use and control. The existence of nuclear weapons, like the fear of population explosion not many years ago, feeds a mood of profound pessimism about the future. In just this fashion, the same medical triumphs that have led to advancing longevity and the coming of an aging society now begin to cause unease about the future.

IS THERE A TECHNOLOGICAL FIX?
BANKRUPTCY THROUGH LONGEVITY?

At a national meeting of the American Association for the Advancement of Science, data were presented to document the rapidly increasing life expectancy of the American population. A major cause is the fact that the death rate of older Americans is dropping rapidly. Since the mid-1970s, the Social Security Administration has revised upward by a full four years its estimates for life expectancy for men and women by the year 2000. As recently as the mid-1970s, the estimate was 69 years for men, and 77 years for women. Now projections call for 73 years for men and 81 for women.

But the reaction to this good news about falling death rates was not as warm as might have been expected. The President of the Gerontological Society of America was quoted in the *New York Times* as being skeptical about whether it was desirable to pursue technology that might extend the human lifespan. Why? Because even a modest increase in life expectancy of ten or twenty years might have absolutely catastrophic social effects by increasing the proportion of the elderly in the population. The mood of gloom and catastrophe was echoed by economists from the Federal Office of Management and Budget who saw the falling death rate of older Americans in terms of an "already ominous" potential for growth in expensive government programs for the elderly. In the tradition of the dismal science, these economists offered calculations that, in a recent year, if Americans had avoided premature death from cancer, heart disease, etc., then the net cost to the Federal Government would have been $15 billion.[35]

But not all biologists are gloomy about prospects for an aging society or further extensions of longevity. Roy Walford, one of the leading biological investigators in the field, for example, in *Maximum Life-Span*, argues for a coming "technological fix" that will rescue the problems caused by an aging population. Walford rejects any dismay about longevity: "Both our knowledge of preventive health measures and the bright outlook of the developing neurosciences signify that the fear that superlong life might be compromised by significantly deteriorated mental functions is unnecessarily pessimistic."[36] But Walford's argument boils down to hope for a vast technological fix: once we have new tools, values will change accordingly. Indeed, Walford, after spelling out the prospects for maximum lifespan extension, goes on to paint a glowing picture of what he calls the "long-living" society, in contrast to an old or aging society.

These bright possibilities for self-realization and an abundance of life are very distant from what we know today. What is missing in Walford's technological fix is some sense of how this distant utopia could be achievable in light of history, political economy, and the dominant order of today. Unless we have faith that a human mutation will occur inevitably, we will need to fashion more specific proposals for institutional change to adapt to an aging society.

If medical technology is successful in bringing about major gains in longevity, then the aging of individuals will only intensify a trend toward aging of populations. Any increase in individual life expectancy will lead to an even larger proportion of the population at advanced ages. Here lies the irony. It is precisely the most optimistic scenario that leads, in turn, to a pessimistic view on the same lines as earlier fears about population aging brought on by declining fertility. Whether any of those fears come to pass will depend very much on the specific historical response of social institutions as they adapt to a new demographic condition. Barring such a response, the aged will appear more and more as a burden, and prospects of further life extension will be ambivalent at best.

CONCLUSION:
ARE THE AGED A "SURPLUS POPULATION?"

It is ironic that this goal of an aging society—long sought by those who feared the population explosion—now becomes the basis for regarding the elderly themselves as a "surplus population." What does it mean to regard the elderly as a surplus population? Where has this idea appeared before and with what consequences? At one time, and still today in many parts of the world, it was children who were regarded as surplus population: that is, an unproductive group contributing to undesired population growth. But in the developed industrialized world, the picture today is different. As we approach population equilibrium, it is now no longer children but instead the aged who are the fastest growing population group. The elderly appear as consumers, not producers, of society's resources. In this scenario, the aging of the population threatens to "bust the budget" with rising costs for Social Security and Medicare. At the same time, the elderly are also seen as part of a sinister Gray Lobby, the elderly are a powerful group who control the allocation of resources.

The fear of an aging society mingles all of these strands in a way that is disturbing for those who remember the fate of other groups who were categorized as a surplus population. Even well-intentioned liberal advocates may inadvertently contribute to this unfortunate image: for example, by stressing statistics on the "tidal wave" of growth of the aging population or by exclusively emphasizing the neediness (i.e., unproductiveness) of the frail elderly population. Such images, often essential to the benevolent appeal of liberal ideology, nonetheless reinforce a picture of the elderly as a surplus population: as a "bundle of needs." The intent is benevolent. But the consequences for public policy may be quite different from what liberal advocates intend.

The source of the problem lies in two fundamental weaknesses of the liberal ideology of old age: first, separating need from productivity and, second, a pessimistic vision of the future. In aging policy, contemporary liberalism has fallen into the trap of separating needs from productivity. Liberals insist on meeting the needs of those who are weak, while productivity and growth are too readily conceded to conservatives.

In the case of the aged, the assumption is that older people are bound to be weak and, in any case, cannot readily become productive. Thus, the liberal approach to aging policy has followed the same pessimistic path as on environmental policy and energy policy: a specter of decline linked to dwindling resources. Based on this pessimistic outlook, the defensive response of interest-group liberalism seems unavoidable. The answer to such a specter is a new vision of human development and productivity over the lifespan: enlargement of the abundance of life to match the new demographic conditions of an aging society.

3

Aging in the
Postindustrial Society

In the previous chapter I examined the fear of population aging and the problems of transition to an aging society. In this chapter, attention shifts from past and present to the future. I examine the overarching political and economic environment of old age: namely, the emerging "postindustrial" society with its multiple shifts in technology, economy, values, and ideology.

A postindustrial gerontology will face different options, different trade-offs, different dilemmas, than policy options that have grown up in response to industrialization and the welfare state. To cite only one example, the value and distribution of free time over the life course will likely challenge presuppositions about the conventional life course divided up into a linear stages of education, work, and retirement.

Contemporary aging policy, with its focus on work and retirement, may be ill adapted to deal with new opportunities and new costs associated with this abundance of time. Neither the Left nor the Right is addressing the new choices, which are quite different from redistributive politics of either the liberal or conservative variety. While we cannot know or predict the details, the main outlines of the future are clear enough. That future will be characterized by the transition to population aging at the same moment as we are moving toward a postindustrial economy. The fact that the two changes are taking place *simultaneously* is what defines the new environment for aging policy.

SOCIETAL AGING

The coming of an aging society can be considered on three quite distinct levels: individual aging, population aging, and the aging of societal institutions. All three are related, but each is distinctive and needs analysis in its own right. Individual aging is the most familiar in the time-related biological changes, cumulative and irreversible, which are visible over the life course. Population aging is less familiar but is easily recognized. Population aging means a change in the relative age composition of society: an increasing proportion of elderly people, a diminishing proportion of young people.

This third level—the aging of societal institutions—is the most elusive. Societal or institutional aging refers to those changes—cumulative and irreversible—associated with the passage of time from the origin of major social institutions. One can speak of the "aging" of institutions or even whole societies by analogy with aging at the organismic level.

The force of the biological metaphor should not be pressed too far, as, for example, Spengler tried to do. Yet the passage of time has discernable consequences for institutions and societies at their own level. In that sense at least, social institutions, like individuals, may have a life course of their own: not defined by biological laws, but rather by a cycle of innovation, maturity, stagnation, and renewal. The rhythm is most evident in the product cycle of innovation in corporations or the marketplace. Something similar appears to take place at wider levels: companies, industries, regions, nation states, even civilizations. Some institutions fail to respond to new challenges in their environment and become extinct. Others prove more adaptable and find sources of renewal or growth. This cycle of growth or decline in societal institutions is the center of inquiry in this chapter.

A basic question for the future is, How will population aging interact with societal aging in the years ahead? In particular, how will the transition to an aging society affect the simultaneous transition to a postindustrial society in the years ahead? The pessimistic answer, which we considered in the last chapter, is that population aging diminishes a society's capacity to respond to new challenges, such as the challenge of postindustrial economic change. Larger proportions of older people mean a loss of creativity and productivity in precisely the period when these qualities are most called for. As the United States undergoes population aging, major social institutions will have to change and adapt to new circumstances.

Consider, for example, the history of the American automobile or steel industry during this century. Looking at those smokestack industries today, it is easy enough to recognize them as having aged, in contrast to young industries such as computers or biotechnology. Economists commonly speak of the life cycle of industries as those industries move through a phase of early rapid growth until they reach a state of maturity. The same reasoning can be applied to entire societies. In *The Decline of the West*, Spengler invoked a familiar organic metaphor, comparing the career of whole civilizations over time to the cycle of the seasons through the year. Growth in springtime would be followed by summer maturity and then the decay of autumn and winter extinction.

The Causes of Economic Decline

Serious historians have rarely given Spengler's ideas much credence. Yet his basic insight has recently been revived and recast into the language of comparative economic analysis. I have in mind here the recent work by Mancur Olson, *The Rise and Decline of Nations*. Olson's work, as the title suggests, is written partly in light of the familiar condition of economic stagnation that industrial economies have experienced since the 1970s. Innumerable explanations and policy prescriptions have been put forward in response to the economic problems of advanced industrial nations. But few analysts have been willing to consider that the aging of a society can be a basic cause for flagging economic performance. Is it possible that as a society as a whole grows older, it loses its creative energy and tends to decline? If so, what is the mechanism of societal aging that brings about this rigidity and decline?

Olson's thesis is that as societies grow older, more and more "distributional coalitions" arise to seek their own advantage. The passage of time allows special interest groups to mobilize control over segments of the economy and choke off innovation and growth. Over time, the behavior of both individuals and groups will channel self-interest away from economic productivity and toward redistribution of resources by collective action. The vehicle for such collective action will be dense networks of guilds, cartels, unions, monopolies, special-interest groups, and political lobbying organizations, all engaged in collusion that reduces economic efficiency and may even make societies ungovernable. The irony here is that the older and more stable a society, the worse off it becomes.[1] Olson's analysis enables us to understand the power of special-interest groups, those "dense networks" that make societies ungovernable and reduce economic growth.

The consequences of Olson's Time-Aging-Decline hypothesis are visible at a smaller scale as well. Older manufacturing industries such as automobiles, steel, or railroads are declining, while newer industries such as electronics or computers are on an upswing. Within declining industrial sectors, another kind of aging process is at work as well, this time tied to workers' protective response to economic decline. As industries decline, layoffs take place on the basis of seniority: older workers stay, while younger workers are let go. Labor unions understandably seek strict seniority rules to determine who will get the benefits from contracts negotiated by the union. The same reasons that led unions to favor seniority protection and work rules also led them for years to defend mandatory retirement as a result of collective bargaining agreements.

The effect of these distributional coalitions is that specific industrial sectors can age in two senses: first, more time passes from the period of initial formation and economic growth and, second, the age composition of the labor force is skewed by seniority toward more older workers. In the absence of retraining or other policies to promote renewal, both tendencies diminish the capacity for resilience and adaptive change to a new environment. In the short run, older workers may benefit, since they keep jobs that younger workers lose. But in the long run older workers lose, too. If the spiral of decline continues, then plant closings and bankruptcies cause older workers to be thrown onto the labor market, where they are likely to be permanently unemployed. Thus, the aging of industrial sectors and the aging of individuals reinforce a pattern of stagnation and decline.

Coalitions for Renewal

Olson is careful to point out that there is nothing *inevitable* about the decline and fall based on stability, time, and aging. Societal aging may entail tendencies toward stagnation. But one can equally recognize instances of renewal and rejuvenation. The effects of stability, time, and aging on social institutions come about, not from biological determinism, but from political forces acting through coalitions of interest groups.

Distributional coalitions naturally seek collective advantage for their members. But interest groups need not sabotage economic growth. The outcome finally depends on whether unions and companies have a stake in the larger economic well-being of society as a whole. On this point, industrialized countries differ considerably. In America and Britain, for example, there is little sense of concern on the part of organized labor for the economy as a whole. Antagonism between labor and management is widespread; cooperative planning is rare. But labor organizations in other countries, such as Sweden, Norway, or Japan, are more encompassing: almost everyone belongs to some such organization.

The power of such encompassing organizations means that the narrow self-interest of the organization tends to give way to a wider perspective. For example, younger workers and older workers may no longer be pitted against one another to divide up dwindling opportunities. Divided interests still exist, but the response can be bargaining, not paralysis. In Japan, for example, bargaining exists across entire industrial sectors or the entire nation. In Sweden, unions have acknowledged the need to allow the demise of plants while negotiating liberal allowances for retraining to aid mobility of workers displaced in the process.[2]

In countries with encompassing coalitions there has been more attention to economic policies to promote mobility of labor and retraining of workers in contrast to protectionist policies that simply shore up an existing pattern of labor and industry.[3] By contrast, in the 1980s in America we see repeated attempts at trade protectionism—in automobiles, shoes, textiles, electronics and other industries—combined with dwindling membership and declining influence for the American labor movement. The contrast is especially important in light of the critical strategic role of older workers, seniority rules, and labor unions in certain industries in the United States. In mature industries with an aging work force, it may be vital to promote policies for growth and retraining in order to counter the effect of distributional coalitions tied to age and seniority.

Protectionism vs. Growth

The productivity of an aging postindustrial society will depend on political adaptation to new economic circumstances. In the end, workers, industries, and regional economies are faced with a choice between protectionism or growth. A cycle of economic growth and decline, operating unchecked, hits older workers hardest, so unions seek to protect them. But today structural unemployment has taken on a new form, one that goes beyond the business cycle and affects the life cycle. Without policies to ease the impact of worker obsolescence, we are likely to find that older workers will oppose changes that threaten their interests, even if the final result is economic stagnation and decline: an outcome ultimately against their interest.

Both liberals and conservatives, for different reasons, fear for the future of an aging society. Their fears are rooted in a picture of how distributional coalitions will determine social policy in the welfare state. But again a pessimistic image of the future is not inevitable. There are significant national differences in political culture surrounding the welfare state. These differences are essential in understanding how different societies cope with the concurrence of postindustrial change with the aging of the population.[4] Whether we are concerned with equity between labor and management or intergenerational equity in aging policies, the issues are parallel: how to overcome a narrow definition of interest-group advocacy in order to arrive at policies framed in terms of the common good?

Later chapters of this book will spell out an alternative approach for aging policy based on retraining older workers, self-help groups, and fashioning programs of late-life learning. For the present it is enough to recognize that the specter of decline is not merely a phantom based on misleading biological metaphors. The threat of age-linked societal decline is real, but the outcome is not inevitable. It is not the aging of individual workers that causes economic decline. The deadening effect of seniority rules dampens innovation because a total institutional pattern is protected, as it is in all forms of protectionism whether they are based on age or not. The cause of decline, then, lies in the logic of *collective* action, not in the life course of *individuals*. In that respect, it is wrong to blame individuals and wrong to propagate stereotypes of decline based on age. In that respect, too, the biological metaphor fails. Age-related decline is not an organic inevitability. Rather, it is the *collective* aging of industries, regions, and whole economies that now challenges us to develop new policies to tap sources of growth in an aging population.

Challenge and Response

If there is a single, overriding theme in Olson's analysis it is simply this. Societies that become exclusively preoccupied with *distribution* of resources—for example, through selfish actions of distributional coalitions—end by weakening themselves and fighting over slices of a dwindling pie. This is the "war of all against all" of interest-group politics. We need a more encompassing approach. Along with redistribution, we must equally attend to the task of increasing the resources available. In addressing this problem, the elderly are not be thought of in a stereotyped role as passive recipients of the largess of the welfare state but must rather be seen as new resources of productivity in a postindustrial society.

Another part of the problem with conventional policy analysis has been a narrowing of the terms of the debate, the measures of cost and benefit, the definition of the choices we actually face. Responding to the challenge of an aging society means more than addressing issues of economic growth. In combating the specter of decline it would be a mistake to look simply for economic growth: for a "rising tide that lifts all boats" and breaks up the logjam created by vested interests and distributional coalitions. This economism takes conventional measures of productivity for granted but fails to challenge conventional assumptions.

For example, consider the problem of work and retirement. Advocates for older people too often have fallen into a trap of simply urging more job opportunities for older people as the means for contributive roles in later life. But we may well ask: Is a society of jobholders really an adequate vision of an aging society or of the good society? In this book I argue for a far broader version of productivity, growth, and enlargement of resources and human capabilities. This vision means attending to nonmonetized forms of social contribution and to quality-of-life issues that go beyond economic performance. The economic transition to a postindustrial society may actually make possible this vision of nonmonetized productivity.

POSTINDUSTRIAL SOCIETY

There is a growing consensus that the structure of the American economy is undergoing rapid and far-reaching change. Daniel Bell speaks of a "post-industrial" society, Marc Porat describes an "information economy,"[5] and Peter Drucker points to the centrality of "knowledge workers" in the economy of today and tomorrow. How is this transition to postindustrial society to be understood?[6]

The Industrial Revolution was marked by a rising standard of living as defined by material goods. The coming of postindustrial society, in Bell's view, will be marked by enhancement in quality of life through nonmaterial services and amenities, with health, education, recreation, and the arts promising a new quality of life in the future. The focus of society will shift from material to quality-of-life concerns made possible by the abundance of the postindustrial economic order.

One way to think of postindustrial society is to see it as a "long wave of innovation" spurred by the introduction of new technologies that are mutually reinforcing[7]: in Toffler's metaphor, an entire "Third Wave" of innovation affecting all aspects of social life.[8] Examples of the impact of such a new wave of innovation include:

- *domestic services:* the "automated household," involving the use of microprocessors for everything from household security to prosthetic devices for the homebound;

- *entertainment:* a trend toward demassification of mass media and, in its place, vastly expanded choices: multichannel cable, videocassette recorders, low-power TV, and other and new forms of social networking through computers and telecommunications;

- *transportation/communications:* electronic banking and shopping, for example, using teletext and videotext and new multiuser telephone services spurred by deregulation of telephone industry;

- *education:* interactive television, enlarged access to information utilities and data bases, as well as on-line cultural resources of through access to libraries and museums;

- *health care:* electronic monitoring of chronic diseases through biofeedback devices, development of new prosthetic devices and low-cost instruments for medical self-care.[9]

All these examples of Third Wave technology tend to reinforce one another as part of an emerging Information Society.[10] Some features, such as decentralized access to information, are likely to be beneficial to older people, while others could initially have the opposite effect. We can begin to anticipate the impact of Third Wave technologies in an aging society by looking at one specific technology—telecommunications—and its potential benefits for one group, the old-old (those over age 75). New information technology offers an abundance of possibilities for enhancing the life world for the frail or homebound elderly: for facilitating communication, monitoring chronic diseases, promoting greater control over the environment, and widening individual choices.

The coming of postindustrial society shifts our attention to nonmaterial resources. In a postindustrial information economy, material resources are no longer the driving force of economic growth. The information economy sidesteps those constraints because it depends on a different resource base. The industrial economy was dependent on finite supplies of energy, materials, and natural resources. By contrast, the next industrial revolution—the transition to an information economy—will be based on an unlimited natural resource: namely, the production and distribution of knowledge.[11] We are now seeing the substitution of information-intensive capital for energy-intensive capital: telecommunications instead of travel, automated control devices in transportation systems, fuel efficiency in the heating and cooling of buildings, automated factories to reduce costs and improve productivity.

At the same time, the information economy opens up new paths for including more and more segments of the population. Outside the monetized economy, the long wave of innovation could lead to positive opportunities for lifespan development. New technology enables more elderly people to participate in activities even when physical mobility is restricted. And because productive tasks can now be performed with less stress and physical labor, there are, in principle, many more ways in which an aging population could become productive. But here precisely is the contradiction. Participation and productivity are made technologically possible yet the system of politics and culture—the obsolescence of old age—prevents older people from making effective use of the new tools for life enrichment. This contradiction stands at the center of policy dilemmas faced by an aging population in the information economy of postindustrial society.

Productivity and Job Displacement

This introduction of information technology will be the key to future productivity gains: computers, telecommunications, robotics, automated manufacturing. But productivity gains have already meant a displacement of the work force. Indeed, job displacement *must* occur to achieve productivity gains in the service sector. The optimistic scenario—higher productivity—is simply the other side of a pessimistic scenario—rising unemployment. Many low-level service jobs—in supermarkets, gas stations, retail banking, car washes, and toll booths—will be altered, perhaps toward a deskilling of the work force along the lines that Marxist critics have contended.

The Future of Work

Deep pessimism prevails about future job growth in advanced industrialized economies. Among all the advanced economies of Europe and the United States, the question is being raised, Is a full employment service economy possible, given our present trends? There is doubt whether service employment will offset declines in other sectors. In government-funded, nonmarketed services, we see continued low rates of productivity, monopoly control by professionals, and limited incentives for social innovations.[12]

The present trends are clearly visible on many fronts. First, there is a drastic shrinkage in the old-line manufacturing sector. It is estimated that by 1990 as many as 10 to 15 million manufacturing workers will no longer be needed in their current jobs. Second, jobs in manufacturing and in the growing service sector depend increasingly on the use of new information technology. Third, the new technology in the information economy is accompanied by waste of human resources and disruption of lives. The gains of enhanced productivity are being distributed in highly unequal ways.

All of these trends are likely to be exacerbated by the coming of an aging society. There will be problems of resistance to innovation, high and inelastic salary levels, spreading demands for protectionism, job rationing by age and seniority, and reluctance to take risks. At the same time, with population aging and the growing proportion of the old-old, dependency costs can be expected to rise. Finally, proposals for worklife extension or retraining of older workers—discussed in a later chapter—are overshadowed by the pessimistic prospect of declining employment opportunities in the postindustrial society.

Implications for the Aging Society

Several implications for the future of an aging society are evident from the trends cited above. First, workers are being displaced from their jobs in ways that are linked to age. On the one hand, seniority rules or civil service protection helps older workers and hurts younger ones. On the other hand, older workers displaced by plant closings face formidable barriers to retraining and relocation to find new jobs. In sum, the impact of job change varies significantly over the life cycle and has different effects according to the age, cohort, and also the historical period when economic change occurs.

Second, the new information technology in the workplace puts a premium on innovation and speed of information transfer, not on the value of accumulated life experience. In an information economy, the experience of older workers falls in value. What rises in value is speed, response time, and short-term memory: all mental functions where older workers are at a disadvantage. Perhaps for this reason, older workers tend to be far more threatened and fearful of computers in the workplace than younger workers are. This fact means that programs to retrain older workers will face a major challenge if older workers are to remain productive in a competitive economic environment.

Third, a serious problem exists in regard to the distribution of unemployment over the life cycle. Will there be enough jobs for the young, the middle-aged, and the old? It is not clear that the introduction of new technology will, in itself, generate additional new jobs to replace old jobs that are eliminated. When routine functions are performed by robots and word-processing systems, what happens to workers who have spent decades performing those tasks? How will purchasing power be distributed, how will time be filled up, when a smaller proportion of the population is required for routine economic tasks that occupied more people in the past? We are at the threshold of an abundance of time, but that abundance is disguised as a surplus of unemployed, redundant workers. As Andre Gorz has insisted, it is not work, but *time*, free time, that will become the crucial center of debate.[13] The new politics of time is at the heart of the choices ahead.

Distributing the Abundance of Life

If this current, so-called "second industrial revolution" succeeds in releasing human energy from routine labor, it opens up a fundamental question. How do we distribute the gains of increased time made available for us? Over the last generation, that increase in time has increasingly been concentrated at the beginning and the end of the life cycle: in youth, with prolonged education, and in old age, with earlier retirement. In these years, there is more time available, but others have less and less time. In short, the abundance of time is distributed unevenly over the life cycle. Must the increase in time be channeled by the three boxes of life in the future? How will the monetized economy take account of the new "economy of discretionary time" in the years ahead?

The point to remember is that we are experiencing the *simultaneous* convergence of two separate trends of world-historical importance: first, the advent of an aging society with an ever larger proportion of the population surviving into old age and, second, the development of new information technology that frees time and energy. *Both* the demographic and the technological revolutions are occurring at the same historical moment. Both make possible an extraordinary upward surge in the availability of discretionary time. This abundance of time and abundance of life present a challenge to our economic system and to its customary ways of using human resources.

DESKILLING OR RETRAINING?

The problem of an aging work force in a postindustrial economy is not just the threat of unemployment. There is also the fear of the degradation of work as a result of new technologies adopted. One ominous scenario would argue that in advanced capitalist societies the introduction of information technology will lead to the deskilling of jobs.[14] Such gloomy predictions are not the monopoly of left-wing critics. The establishment business press, including such organs as *Fortune, Business Week,* and the *Wall Street Journal,* have all acknowledged a trend toward a bimodal job distribution.[15] According to the Bureau of Labor Statistics, the fastest growing jobs of the 1980s are in low-paying fields such as nurses aides, janitors, clerical help, and the fast-food industry. In essence, the postindustrial economy is creating high-paid and low-paid jobs but little in between.[16]

But this scenario for deskilling the workforce is not the whole story. The postindustrial society also creates jobs that demand training and are experience-rich: for example, jobs such as geriatric social worker, paramedic, real estate or travel agent, and so on. The information economy by no means makes these jobs obsolete. These jobs, too, are expected to grow in the future. Middle-aged and older workers can certainly by retrained for such jobs. More to the point, life experience is not a limit but instead is an asset in such jobs. Certainly it may be unrealistic to expect large numbers of older workers to be retrained for exotic high-tech jobs in robotics, lasers, or genetic engineering. But it is not unrealistic to imagine retraining older workers for jobs that draw on past experience while helping them cope with the demands of a new postindustrial environment. In short, there is no need to adopt a view of technological determinism that sees deskilling and job degradation as the inevitable fate of an information society.

THE NEW ROLE OF HOUSEHOLD PRODUCTION

Many writers have offered an optimistic forecast that in a postindustrial society quality-of-life needs, such as recreation, education, culture, will be at the center of life. The problem with this forecast is that it runs up against the stubborn fact that the cost of services is rising faster than other economic factors of production. The cost of services rises disproportionately because of lower productivity gains in the labor-intensive service industries. The result is that more and more of these activities are being displaced out of the monetized service economy and into the nonmonetized sphere of self-production and household production. What is happening is that final services are increasingly being produced by the aid of ever cheaper household capital goods. Final services become part of an unmeasured self-service economy.

This shift is accelerated by the rising cost for all paid services in the monetized economy, especially where the services are supported by government. Part of the shift shows up in the form of tax revolts and demands to cut government expenditures. The result is to further dampen prospects for increased service employment in the government sector. This is one reason to be skeptical of growth in service employment. It seems unlikely that in the future we will see the same increases in employment in health care or education on the scale seen in the last generation.

The critical new factor of production today is the direct labor of consumers who produce final products in a self-service economy. These consumers in turn depend on capital goods furnished by the manufacturing sector: goods like washing machines, videotape recorders, and automobiles. Final products or services, such as cleaning, entertainment, or transportation, depend on the skilled labor of consumers. Advances in automation in the manufacturing sector keep bringing down the price for these manufactured goods, while the price of personal services keeps rising. The result? A continuing shift toward self-service production. This can be seen in high-priced professional services: interest in home health care, in home repair, and in do-it-yourself activities.

Since there is more and more capital investment in the household, an ever growing proportion of final consumption is produced at home, and direct labor input there becomes an increasingly important factor in the total real product of the society.[17] What is happening represents a historical change in the configuration of economic activity. Investment in household capital may well offer a higher real rate of return on investment than other available alternatives in the monetized economy.[18] Instead of capital investment's occurring in centralized form, in industry, it is now taking place in decentralized form, in households.[19] Instead of large institutions providing services to individuals, we see a trend toward the do-it-yourself economy.

This economic transition has profound implications for an aging society. The combination of a high rate of return on household capital, plus opportunities for labor-intensive self-service production of use values, points to an economic scenario in which many groups in society could assume a broader range of productive roles outside the monetized labor force. With an expanded sphere of household production, activities such as home health care, lifelong learning, production outside the market, and all forms of self-help offer new options for contributive roles in old age.

The Self-Service Economy

The economic shift toward a self-service economy coincides with a new postindustrial ethic of self-sufficiency.[20] The hope is that through small-scale, user-friendly household technology, more and more activities, both in work and leisure, can be carried out in the home. This shift, at first glance, seems to offer promising possibilities for those groups in society who are homebound, such as the frail elderly. But for the elderly, this drift toward self-service, self-sufficiency, and household isolation may prove a mixed blessing. On the one hand, enhanced household production enables the elderly to assume productive roles outside the monetized economy. But on the other hand, isolation and loneliness remain serious problems for older people who live in smaller households to begin with. Thus the social policy goal should be to build on the trend toward a self-service economy while promoting patterns that emphasize mutual self-service and mutual self-help. Some examples might be communal or neighborhood vegetable gardening, groups promoting preventive health care and rehabilitation, arrangements to share expensive household capital goods, and group training in the use of new telecommunications technologies.

STRATEGIES FOR CHANGE

The postindustrial economy will involve a shift to services rather than manufacturing, but this shift may not generate enough service jobs to absorb those displaced from employment in declining industries. Instead of expanded service employment, what we are more likely to see is the growth of a self-service economy based on household production outside the monetized marketplace.

This forecast for the future of postindustrial society presents both a challenge and an opportunity to devise new policies for contributive roles for an aging population. Older worker retraining, self-help and production for use, and new uses of telecommunications technology for lifelong learning are only a few of the areas where policy interventions could make a difference. Following Gershuny, we can distinguish three major strategies to address to problems of "jobless growth" in a self-service economy:

1. *Industrial Policy.* One strategy is to encourage private industry to expand job opportunities for everyone who can work, including older people. This strategy comes down to some form of industrial policy, whether the name is used or not. Some proposals for retraining or expanding jobs for displaced older workers take this approach. Still other proposals not yet tried include tax-subsidized employment of older workers and various means of encouraging work-life extension: for example, modifying the Social Security earnings test. The basic idea in all these approaches is to get private enterprise to maintain jobs for everyone who can be productive, including the aging population.

2. *Public Sector Employment.* A second strategy is direct job creation in the service sector. This basically comes down to some form of public-service employment. The Comprehensive Employment and Training Act (CETA) was one version of this policy, which unfortunately acquired a very bad image in the United States. A promising model here might be the Title V of the Older Americans Act, which provides community-service employment to older persons on a part-time basis. This second strategy assumes that there are groups of people, such as the elderly, who want to work and contribute but who cannot find jobs in the private labor market as it presently exists. The answer is job creation by public policy.

Both strategies—industrial policy and public service employment—are attractive but face serious difficulties. Policy proposals
under either strategy find it hard to escape from the bane of old-
time liberalism: namely, the feeling that these are disguised protectionist schemes designed to shore up employment among favored
groups, whether industrial workers, minorities, or municipal employees. Applied to the elderly, the strategy might be more politically acceptable, but difficulties remain. Both strategies seem like
rear-guard responses to a threatening postindustrial future. As applied in the past, both strategies have done little to prepare workers
for the postindustrial economy of the future.

3. *Service Innovations.* Gershuny suggests a third strategy: to take
account of the economic forces leading to a decline in aggregate
employment but instead of working against these trends, to work
with them: that is, to acknowledge the informal economy as an
economic reality. Gershuny would encourage a new kind of dual
economy: one based on self-service, the other on monetized employment. Instead of trying to counter the drift toward a self-service
economy, the third strategy would try to build on its beneficent features.[21]

For the aging, this third strategy would favor enhanced investment in
household capital goods that can be integrated into the informal economy. Instead of a policy based on a "single vision" of monetized production, the third strategy would recognize the intermixture of quality-of-life
values (recreation, education) along with values of material productivity
(self-sufficiency, household production).

The third strategy requires explicit policy preference in favor of service
innovations rather than perpetuate the status quo of service delivery.
Gershuny and Miles argue that, between now and the year 2000, "the
new telecommunications, computing, and information storage technologies present the technical inputs for a new wave of social innovations in
the way of service provision in entertainment, information, education,
and possibly medical services. . . ."[22] What is proposed, then, is that a
new "long wave" of economic growth can be based on such service innovations when tied to new forces of production in the information
economy. What is called for is a sizable investment in the infrastructure
required by these innovations[23] to make possible new service innovations. Service innovations along these lines could make it possible for a

burgeoning older population to participate in productive, contributive social roles.

The new information technologies contain an extraordinary potential for social innovation. Yet in the delivery of human service today they are generally not yet being used for social innovation.[24] In the field of aging, for example, telecommunications and information technology have not been used to enhance client self-determination or empowerment. Instead, technology has been used to reinforce and mechanize the status quo. For example, staff from Area Agencies on Aging take training workshops on the use of spread sheet software to make planning and data processing more efficient. In essence, the new technologies are simply integrated into the existing production process of health, education, and social service provision. The conventional pattern of services remains the same, but older people themselves do not become more productive at all.

Social innovations are more far-reaching than the application of existing technologies to enhance efficiency within an existing production process. Social innovation, potentially at least, involves a transformation of the relations of production and not only the forces of production. The unanswered policy question is whether the advent of an information economy, coinciding with an aging society, will produce social innovations—changes in the relations of production—to unleash the potential of those new forces of production represented by information technology.

CONCLUSION: SCENARIOS FOR THE FUTURE

In this chapter, I have examined some of the forces creating the postindustrial society and the aging society of the future. But it is important to stress that the actual future we will face is not predetermined by the forces and trends discussed here. On the contrary, we confront different alternative scenarios for the future of an aging society.

One scenario involves a spreading crisis of the welfare state in which the elderly occupy the central role: the specter of decline prospect outlined in the preceding chapter. In this scenario a rising proportion of old people in the population means a "graying of the federal budget" with increasing amounts going for income transfers and health care for the aged.[25] Pressure on nonmarketed consumer services, such as education, health, or social services, results in a demand for privatization: i.e., shifting demand away from the public sector and into the private sphere. Reprivatization, in turn, reinforces delegitimation of public provision altogether.

Another scenario would be an extension of the interest-group or political bargaining model built on continued patterns of the liberal welfare state. In this model, key interest groups, such as labor, management, and consumers, renegotiate the social contract for age-based entitlements. In aging policy, this corporatist bargaining model is now familiar enough. Something of this kind in fact occurred in the Social Security crisis of 1983 when the Reagan Administration appointed a bipartisan commission that drew up a compromise plan to cut benefit levels modestly while raising payroll taxes.

But the political bargaining model has its problems. One difficulty is that it perpetuates the crisis tendencies of the welfare state: bargaining seeks to protect benefits of established groups and thus preserve the status quo. In fact, closely tied to the second scenario is the spread of interest-group liberalism in response to postindustrial change: a creeping protectionism, that again perpetuates the claims of major interest groups. In international trade, for example, this protectionist scenario is strictly a rear-guard action on behalf of declining sectors of manufacturing and heavy industry. In the United States, this means the smokestack industries of the North and Midwest with their aging work force. The political bargaining scenario might involve some version of industrial policy, but both industrial policy and national or local planning run serious risks of degenerating into crude protectionism. In essence, the second scenario is based on the management of decline and the politics of triage: hardly a cheerful prescription for the future.

As against both these scenarios, there is a third, or what we may term the best case scenario. Claus Offe describes this scenario as a positive view in which scarcity stimulates a resurgence of values of self-help, cooperation, and social justice.[26] In the best case scenario, pressure on nonmarketed consumption services, such as education and health, would bring about service innovations: essentially a shift toward enhanced production through the self-service economy. Effective use of the self-service strategy means, not deskilling but rather continuous *reskilling* and lifespan development into old age: for example, the expansion of self-help groups and opportunities for consumer education in health care to complement the formal service system. Instead of interest-group competition among age-groups, the old would be engaged in more intergenerational, community-based activities. At the same time, a new style of lifelong learning, made feasible by telecommunications technology, would lead to expectations of continued human development over the lifespan, including old age. None of this will happen on its own, as if by inevitable evolution toward a predetermined future. Instead, affirmative public policies are called for. Gershuny and Miles envisage "a process whereby the state, rather than producing final non-marketed services, moves towards providing facilities to enable people to produce more of their own services."[27] A concrete example can be found in long-term care for the frail elderly. Instead of putting capital investment overwhelmingly into nursing homes, we would provide more support to individuals and families for self-care, health promotion, and home health care. Another example would be the British Open University, which relies on central production of software and programming, while individuals produce their own learning and make use of household capital such as TV sets, tape recorders, etc. Similar initiatives could expand learning opportunities for older persons in the future. But social innovation and public investment, as well as technology, are required.

The entire argument of this book is based on the premise that the third, or best case scenario, is a tangible historical possibility: not inevitable, but possible. The second half of this book is devoted to spelling out how social innovations could help promote a best case scenario for the transition to an aging society. Postindustrial society offers a possibility of enhanced quality of life, but it is by no means a guarantee of any such historical outcome. The best case scenario would be to promote contributive roles in the informal, nonmonetized economy. Instead of an industrial economy or an information economy, we could look forward to what Lewis Mumford once called "an economy of life," an abundance of life.[28]

lier retirement thus disguise the actual level of unemployment in society. At the same time the more intensive use of labor involves smaller numbers of people during the middle period of life. This overarching structure of the life course is itself the source of the problem. Making individual work schedules more flexible, while certainly attractive, in no way responds to this underlying, structural problem.

A second solution—collective bargaining or broader legislative action to reduce the workweek—depends largely on the action of employers, unions, and public policymakers. On the American scene, there has been little interest in this second type of solution. In Western Europe, in recent years, there have been some successful efforts through collective bargaining to reduce the standard workweek—in effect, a structural version of work sharing. But on the American scene, the weakness of the labor movement, combined with the pressures for international economic competition, are likely to inhibit any moves in this direction.

A third solution envisages a far broader change in the relations among education, work, and leisure, and this change will be the most difficult of all to achieve. It would mean breaking up the three boxes of life and radically reshaping the sequence of education, work, and leisure.[4] It would require wholesale changes in our thinking about productivity, human capital formation, and the meaning of leisure. Any such change would be threatening to a variety of groups. Educational credentials, retirement benefits, and job security rights would all be up for reexamination.

THE POLITICAL ECONOMY OF DISCRETIONARY TIME

This problem of the balance among education, work, and leisure is not new. During the first half of the twentieth century, reduced working hours set the pattern adopted in industry and in public policy. Between 1909 and 1947 the average workweek in manufacturing industries in America fell from 51 hours to about 40. But in the post-World War II period a dramatic change took place. Average weekly working hours of those in full-time jobs did *not* decline at all. Average weekly working hours in the economy as a whole continued to drop from 40 to 35 hours, but that decline is largely accounted for by the increased proportions of part-time workers. And much of that part-time employment is not a voluntary choice about discretionary time at all but simply a result of adverse labor market conditions. Employers could hire part-timers more cheaply, without permanent commitments or fringe benefits.

OF TIME, WORK, AND CULTURE

Will these patterns persist or is fundamental change likely as we move toward a postindustrial economy? To answer this question we need to look in even broader terms at the historical origins of the modernized life course in the Industrial Revolution itself. In the new industrial world, labor itself became a commodity, but, more important, time became a commodity, too. "Time is money," went the maxim of Benjamin Franklin and other early proponents of the new capitalist order. These attitudes toward time became generalized: habits of haste and efficiency became ever more prevalent. The new order also imposed its dominant ideology on culture and leisure. These attitudes endure and pose serious problems for the future of a postindustrial society. E. P. Thompson puts it as follows:

> If we are to have enlarged leisure in an automated future, the problem is not "how are we going to consume all these additional time units of leisure?" but "what will be the capacity for experience of the men who have this undirected time to live?" If we maintain a puritan time valuation, a commodity valuation, then it is a question of how this time is put to use, or how it is exploited by the leisure industries. But if the purposive notion of time-use becomes less compulsive, then men might have to re-learn the arts of living lost in the Industrial Revolution. . . .[5]

Thompson has analyzed the change in the concept of discretionary time that came about with the advent of industrial capitalism. The implications of the new system for time in old age were profound. Unloosed from the prison of industrial regimentation, workers saw unbounded time as release from a life of drudgery. For those whose life experience deprived them of an active, constructive relationship to the cultural world, the advent of leisure may mean a form of culture that is largely passive: spectator sports, watching television, or being the audience for some new merchandising campaign.

In neither Europe nor America was the spread of institutionalized retirement accompanied by any other institutions to guide retired persons in how they might make use of their time. For working class culture, this proved to be a persistent problem.[6] In studies of British pensioners, for example, it was found that, upon retirement, the upper class groups reduce time spent in passive leisure—such as watching television—since they have other social skills and outlets for their interests. Unskilled workers, by contrast, tend to increase their passive leisure activities—television above all—until nearly half their day is taken up with such activities.[7]

Here again we face a peculiar contradiction in the advanced industrial societies. On the one hand, there is an increasing fragmentation of the workplace, leading to both specialization and deskilling: old craft skills atrophy or become useless in the new industrial environment. The result is an impoverishment of work and of general culture. At the same time, there is a growing abundance of free time, with the bulk of that time distributed either as forced unemployment or as voluntary retirement among the elderly. The experience of the workplace leads to progressive diminishing of human capacities for lifespan development, while the growth of free time calls for cultural and educational activities that could give meaning to this expanding proportion of nonwork time.

The contradiction springs from a deeper structural division between the demands of the economic order and the imperatives of the cultural order: what Bell describes as the contrast between the demands for efficiency in the economic technosphere versus enlargement of the self in the cultural sphere.[8] According to Bell, the postindustrial society exhibits a characteristic contradiction between these two spheres of life. The normative imperatives of efficiency and self-realization remain in conflict, and that conflict is reflected in the barren quality of life of retirement. Any solution must lie in efforts to overcome that contradiction between the cultural and the economic order.

But such solutions become more difficult to imagine today. The rapidly growing elderly population is often seen as surplus population: an unproductive group illegitimately drawing resources from the economy. The leisure of retirement living is financed, after all, largely by public provision through the welfare state. What will happen to this provision in a period of fiscal crisis? The "citizens' wage" of retirement comes to look more like an intolerable benefit of a new leisure class,[9] and the leisure-time benefits of old age become an obvious candidate for cutbacks. Why shouldn't Social Security be trimmed to encourage labor force participation by the old?

THE NEW IDEOLOGY OF WORK AND LEISURE

The new ideology of work and leisure has already had very tangible consequences for the debate on aging policy. In the 1983 Social Security crisis, Congress approved raising the age of entitlement for benefits from 65 to 68 over a period of several decades—in effect, endorsing a policy of enforced work-life extension. There is support among elite circles for enforcing a more vigorous work ethic among the young-old. That support frequently wears the mask of expanded opportunities, even when the consequences for vulnerable groups are likely to be very harsh, as in the case of older black men, who would be harmed by any weakening of norms favoring a fixed retirement age.

Liberals supporting expanded opportunity and conservatives in favor of the work ethic are apt to find common ground on behalf of work-life extension for the aged. Interest in work-life extension and moves to further raise retirement age are examples of the new prowork attitude, although such moves are strongly resisted by the labor unions, by minority groups, by the working classes, and others with poor working conditions.

But the problem goes deeper than the politics of age and employment. New appeals to the work ethic run up against the longstanding progressive erosion of all norms, restraints, or inhibitions throughout the normative-cultural sphere. The great irony here is that the enforced leisure of retirement is itself required by an economic system that cannot produce enough jobs for all who want to work. Thus, some form of enforced leisure time—as unemployment, lengthened education, or early retirement—turns out to be unavoidable whatever the normative-cultural imperatives dictate. The economic sphere is continually creating a surplus population of prematurely retired or unemployed workers who cannot be absorbed by the new postindustrial economy.

These contradictions leave the use of time in late life prey to conflicting normative imperatives: to be productive but to enjoy oneself, to live for the present but also to remember that one can easily outlive one's savings, to "act one's age" but to suffer a loss in status associated with old age in modern societies. What Bell called "the cultural contradictions of capitalism" are reflected in the conflicting expectations for the last stage of life. As growing numbers of people become part of this surplus population of old age, modern societies are less and less able to imagine what the use of time in old age might be.

THE RISE OF THE LINEAR LIFE PLAN

De Grazia, in *Of Time, Work, and Leisure,* provides a comprehensive treatment of the origins of modern attitudes toward the use of time.[10] In the eighteenth century, the 70-hour week was common. But after the early phase of industrialization, working hours declined while time for leisure increased. In 1860, Americans were still working, on average, 68 hours a week, a figure that dropped only slightly to 65 hours by 1900. The major reductions in the work week have taken place in the twentieth century: down to 40 hours a week by the beginning of World War II.

Not only was the workweek longer in the past, but also work itself was spread out over a larger portion of the normal life course. Around 1900, for example, one-quarter of boys between ages 10 and 15 were already in the labor force and it was unusual for men beyond age 65 to retire.[11] But after the inception of Social Security, labor market participation for persons over 65 began to fall dramatically. In 1900, two thirds of men over 65 were employed; as recently as 1950, nearly half were still in the labor force. Today the number is under 20%.[12]

With the spread of retirement, free time in late life was becoming available, for the first time, to large segments of the population. Reduction of unemployment rate was achieved through ever spreading educational credentialism and provision for retirement pensions. People stay in school longer or retire earlier, but in either case, the result is a drop in unemployment. These trends have improved employment prospects for people in the middle years—the same compression of work life into the midportion of the lifespan discussed earlier.

The Road to Consumerism

By the beginning of the post World War II period, the fundamental outlines of the linear life plan were in place. Social policy would displace leisure into late life, while enlarging the period of education in early life, allegedly as preparation for work. Aggregate economic demand would be maintained by transfer payments—such as Social Security—disbursed in such a fashion as to keep older people out of the labor market but with purchasing power in their hands. The distribution of employment during the middle years took the form of a dual economy with an increasingly bimodal division of jobs. The result was to keep the nominal unemployment rate down, while consumer spending and economic growth increased. Over the life course, leisure was displaced into the last stage of life on the model of consumerism.

But before the linear life plan attained its triumph, there had been voices of protest. In the 1920s, social critics and reformers had rejected the new economic gospel of consumption. The shorter hours movement of the 1920s was followed by the share-the-work plan during the Depression. Instead of a consumer society, the critics favored shorter working hours and more leisure for self-development. The goal of self-development urged by reformers had much in common with ideas that would later be advocated by writers such as Fred Best, Willard Wirtz, Gosta Rehn, Max Kaplan, and many others. Work sharing, flex-time, phased retirement, workers' sabbaticals, recurrent education, lifelong learning, and life cycle planning: these became familiar items on the liberal, humanistic agenda for human resource development.

But these ideals are not in the interests of everyone. During the 1920s, leaders of American business saw a threat to economic prosperity from overproduction and spreading leisure time. Business leaders were pessimistic. They feared that consumer markets were becoming oversaturated and that workers would take rising productivity in the form of free time rather than continuing to work. Declining working hours, along with declining production, spelled declining profits and economic growth. Responding to this threat were those who argued that consumption demands could be driven higher, primarily through advertising and marketing techniques to stimulate new purchasing power.[13]

In fact, it was the consumer view that triumphed. The consumer society of rising demand and stable working hours was supported by actions of the government itself. With the New Deal and World War II, the American government took on new responsibility for managing the economy in order to moderate the business cycle and insure aggregate demand in the economy. With the passage of the Social Security Act, and later with the spread of private pensions, public policy ratified the institution of a fixed retirement age.

Was this outcome inevitable? The problem was that shorter working hours might have compelled business to increase wages in a more competitive labor market. It was preferable for the working class to be divided on a bimodal pattern: no reduction in the workweek for a favored group (i.e., those with secure jobs), while part-time jobs, unemployment, and low wages became the fate of others. Here we have the origins of the dual economy that characterizes the U.S. labor market today.

The unions, fearing unemployment, had incentives of their own to ratify the linear life plan. Earlier, during the Depression, a shorter working week had been supported vigorously by organized labor: the AFL several times seriously proposed to call a national strike in behalf of the 30-hour week.[14] But after organized labor achieved legitimacy, it dropped this demand, preferring instead to reduce work time by negotiating earlier retirement and better pension benefits. Organized labor also sought to raise the age of leaving school and eliminate work options for teenagers. In both early and later life, labor sought to expand compulsory free time instead of enlarging work opportunities.

On the public policy side similar developments took place. Policy makers, accepting a "lump of labor theory," held that there were only a fixed number of jobs available in a society. Therefore, they endorsed mandatory retirement because it seemed to offer a fairer way to distribute the work available. It was precisely this assumption that shaped the Social Security Act of 1935[15] and discouraged older workers from entering the labor market. We should not assume, of course, that the free time of retirement is forced on people and therefore is not really leisure at all. In fact, just the opposite seems true. People are eager to leave most jobs, and for good reason: their jobs are boring and unpleasant. Except for elite groups who leave their jobs reluctantly, retirement is forced on people only to the extent that people prefer to retire rather than continue working at jobs that are unsatisfying.

The Ideological Rationale

The ideological consensus on behalf of the linear life plan has also played a role. For youth, the ideological rationale for extended schooling took the form of the human capital theory of education. Education was "an investment in the future." Young people were told to stay in school longer to insure getting a good job. The educational establishment, for obvious reasons, has promoted this view eagerly. As credential requirements for jobs rose higher and higher, this rationale in favor of more education became a self-fulfilling prophecy.[16]

For the elderly, the ideological rationale for retirement came through the Golden Age image of retirement living. Retirement was to be time of deferred gratification, on the model of consumerism. Social Security benefits for the old were justified by an image of old people as dependent and incapable of productive roles in the economy. The positive Golden Age image and the negative dependent elderly image coexisted uneasily as public policy came to support enforced leisure for old age.

DISCRETIONARY TIME

In the earlier chapter "The Specter of Decline," we saw that a dismal image of old age has been based on the spread of empty time in the last stage of life. If the empty time of late life were simply a burden and a source of strain, then prospects might seem hopeless. But the historical evolution of the postindustrial economy is forcing changes in culture and the economy that open up unexpected historical possibilities. In the previous chapter "Aging in the Postindustrial Society," we examined the emergence of the self-service economy and the problems presented by this new concept for traditional ideology and economic policy. We need to see the new role of discretionary time in later life in this perspective: not only as a period of empty time or consumerism but also as a potential phase of productivity. To recognize the discretionary time of old age as an economic resource opens up new possibilities for contributive roles for older people in the future.

A historical shift toward valuing the discretionary time in old age may come about from the economic development of postindustrial society itself. As automation takes over more and more production at the material level, the exchange value of time itself rises. Unlike capital, energy, or other factors of production, time is an inelastic resource: it is fixed and limited. Thus, as the speed of other productive forces increases, the marginal value of time increases. What is happening now is that time, the inelastic resource, is moving into a central position in the economy, even while it remains invisible in our policy debates.

Time and Public Policy

If discretionary time is now a fundamental, if nonmonetized, resource, what are the implications for public policy? In the first place, free time is not equally distributed among different groups in society. There are groups in the population with large amounts of discretionary time, such as the unemployed or retired persons. But these groups often lack the opportunities or skills to convert that resource into productive activities. The time owners—for example, retired persons—are like Arab real estate owners in the era before oil drilling equipment was available. They command a valuable resource, but they lack the means to convert their position into an opportunity for productivity. Thus, the time owners, like the Arabs before petroleum exploration, are both rich and poor at the same time.

It is precisely in old age that the use of the time becomes problematic while the exploding demand for monetized services of all kinds is a problem for all age-groups. The lack of time felt by so many in the contemporary world is sharply contrasted with the unstructured time of retirement. Indeed, this accelerating demand contributes to overload, leading to the fiscal crisis of the welfare state itself. The elderly, who of all groups consume the largest share of the federal domestic budget, bring out the contours of this crisis in its sharpest form.

Distributing the New Abundance of Life

If the current, so-called "second industrial revolution" succeeds in releasing human energy from routine labor, it opens up a fundamental question. How do we distribute the gains of increased *time* that the new technology makes possible for us? Today we are at the threshold of an abundance of time, but that abundance is disguised as a surplus of unemployed, redundant workers. As Andre Gorz has insisted, it is not work, but *time*, free time, that will become the crucial center of debate. The politics of time is at the heart of the choices ahead.

Over a generation or more, this dramatic increase in free time has been increasingly concentrated at the beginning and the end of the life cycle: in youth, with ever prolonged adolescence and education, and then in old age, with earlier retirement. The result is that the revolutionary expansion of time has been rendered invisible. Toward the beginning and the end of the life course, there is more time available, but others have less and less time. Must the increase in time be channeled by the three boxes of life in the future? How will our monetized economy take account of the new "economy of discretionary time" that is becoming central in the years ahead?

Beyond the Linear Life Plan

The three boxes of life have remained as rigid as ever, but discontent and criticism have grown too. The discontent responds to an unresolved contradiction in the social order itself. The problem is that the cultural ideal of the open-ended self is clearly in conflict with the specialization demanded by the economic order. Our cultural ideas urge us to keep our options open—whether in careers, human relationships, beliefs, or whatever. On the other side, the competitive pressures of the market-place urge us to specialize, to narrow our skills in order to gain a competitive edge. As we grow older and time gets short, it becomes more and more unrealistic to expect to start over, to embark on second careers, to explore unlived possibilities of the self.

This is the syndrome explored by Sarason, which he called the "one life-one career" problem of specialization.[17] This syndrome reinforces the three boxes of life and makes it difficult to upset the distribution of work, learning, and leisure over the life cycle. Sociologists have pointed out how the enforced unemployment and dependency of youth have contributed to pathologies of delinquency and mental illness. Similarly, it is now better understood how the exclusion of the elderly from employment or other social institutions contributes to the sense of isolation and depression. In short, there is now a better understanding that this structured dependency of old age has enormous social and economic costs for us all, young and old alike.[18]

In the new, postindustrial environment, it has become more plausible to imagine that we may be on the verge of breaking up the three boxes of life. Willard Wirtz, among others, has argued against the linear life plan with its rigid separation of learning, work, and leisure.[19] He decries this linear life plan as a "human convention," as mere "custom." Indeed, survey data suggest that Americans would prefer alternative work schedules: not merely those that make working time more flexible but also those that radically break up the three boxes of life. In one survey 80% of respondents favored some version of a cyclic life plan: reduced schooling during youth, more flexible retirement, and more options for education and leisure throughout adult life.

Individual preference aside, there are policy-based arguments for a more flexible life plan: namely, as a way to reduce the rising cost of student aid support, to avert threats to Social Security, and to engage people in productive work during more years of the lifespan. Why is this not done? It appears that the economy is not structured to create enough jobs for youth and the aged who want to work. The terms on which the young and the old could be contributive include features such as low productivity levels (e.g., teenagers who must be hired at the minimum wage) or a preference for part-time work by the elderly. These features are in contradiction to pressures for ever higher productivity, productivity that is best enhanced by intensive use of skilled human resources during the middle period of life.

If this analysis is sound, then the linear life plan, far from being based on mere human convention, is sustained by the most deeply rooted drives of the advanced industrial economies: i.e., the impetus toward maximizing profits and promoting efficiency. These long-term trends suggest that there may be limits to how far the linear life plan can be modified. On the one hand, we want old people out of the labor market in order to reduce unemployment and spread around available jobs; on the other hand, we want old people to keep working in order not to drain the Social Security system.

None of the proposals for breaking up the lock-step structure of life confronts these contradictions generated by the political economy itself. None of the solutions upsets the basic logic of specialization, the economic constraints that pull us in a direction utterly opposed to what the culture of modernity tell us ought to be our pattern of self-realization. Even as the economy tightens the bondage of specialization, a cultural image of freedom persuades us that we can remake our lives at any age.

The analysis offered in this chapter so far can be taken in several different ways. The most basic conclusion is that the linear life plan is rooted in the political economy of advanced industrial societies. It is not a mere convention, but constitutes the long-term historical pattern of industrial development, labor market dynamics, social welfare policy, and class structure. The phenomena of excess credentialization, structural unemployment, and early retirement are all related. The powerful interest groups who benefit from the present linear life plan will continue to favor rigidity—not flexibility—in the boundaries between education, work, and leisure. Breaking up the three boxes of life is a desirable objective that would necessitate, and in turn promote, a challenge to the ideological images of life stages from youth to old age.

There is nothing inevitable about the shape of the human life course in either its traditional or its modernized form. The emergence of the modernized life cycle was undoubtedly associated with the broader advance of modernization and industrialization. Today the new information technology of postindustrial society makes possible a reduction in the demand for human labor that may prove to be a blessing or a curse. Thus, the question about the uses of time in old age may actually prefigure a far-reaching question of social policy for *all* age-groups in the postindustrial society of the future. The implications of this condition for an aging society are explored in more detail when we examine new forms of education, work, and leisure in the future.

WORK, LEISURE, OR EDUCATION?

The power and persistence of the linear life plan could lead to several different scenarios for the future. Andre Gorz's forecast of the "abolition of work," for example, could be taken in two quite different ways: either as a step toward breaking up the three boxes of life in favor of flexibility or, alternatively, as a still greater displacement of free time into later life. Depending on which scenario comes to pass, the consequences for an aging society will be dramatically different. For example, if free time continues to be displaced into later life, then the social institution of retirement, far from disappearing or becoming more flexible, will remain a permanent and ever more important feature of the linear life plan in the future.

The problem is, how will this expanded free time be paid for and who will benefit from such subsidized leisure time? Are we to understand retirement as a kind of enforced unemployment? Or is it rather to be seen as a version of subsized leisure? And, if subsidized, how will it be financed and legitimated in an era when the fiscal crisis of the state has also become a permanent feature of the political scene? How does the declining need for work coexist with widespread scarcity in meeting human needs, of old and young alike? This set of questions—all interrelated—will be the focus for the remainder of this chapter: namely, an appraisal of work, leisure, and education as concrete alternatives in later life.

Two fundamental flaws—class bias and utopianism—severely limit the scope of social criticism on issues such as life-long learning, the use of leisure, or the feasibility of alternative work patterns for older people. The so-called freedom of flexible life planning fails to appreciate the way choices are structured in advance by patterns of socialization that restrict the imaginable alternatives people can consider. So it turns out that the flexible choices seem always to reinforce conventional values of individual opportunity, materialistic productivity, cultural pluralism, and self-esteem through careerism.

When these same values are extended into old age, then the ideals of flexibility and life planning eliminate retirement in favor of extended middle-age. The utopian ideal of life planning turns out to be a new way of integrating older people, along with everyone else, into the ethos of modern bourgeois culture. Like the age-irrelevant society, this new utopia turns out to be only a more easily accessible version of the status quo, where conventional assumptions are left unchallenged. Yet it is precisely these conventional assumptions—including the very definition or meaning of "work," "education," and "leisure"—that must be put under scrutiny. We can begin by looking at work roles.

EMPLOYMENT OPPORTUNITIES FOR OLDER PEOPLE

A notable trend in the last few years has been the spreading opinion that social policy has been mistaken in promoting retirement instead of employment for older people. Both liberals and conservatives, strangely, seem to agree on this: that the best solution to many of the problems of aging is to be found "in putting the old folks back to work." Conservatives endorse the idea because it means letting people take care of themselves instead of relying on transfer payments. Hence the attack on the earnings test in Social Security, an attack often joined by aging interest groups, who here find themselves in agreement with Ronald Reagan. But liberals, too, are in favor of work in old age. They endorse work-life extension as a means of promoting economic opportunity while combating age discrimination or denial of equality for older people. All sides agree that changes in the current pattern of work and retirement would significantly help the financial condition of the Social Security system.

In short, we begin to see the formation of a policy consensus to promote greater labor force participation by older people and to reverse a decades-old trend toward earlier retirement. Advocates for the elderly sometimes speak as if continued gainful employment is the only way to achieve a valued role in society. Disengagement from work—an idea discredited by gerontologists as a desirable goal—becomes a convenient target. Retirement, it is urged, is tantamount to loss of personal identity. This argument against retirement and in favor of participation appeals to those with high intrinsic job satisfaction—college professors, journalists, executives, and professionals—people who proudly proclaim that they never intend to retire, or, if they leave formal employment, plan to embark on still greater heights of activity and achievement. This change in attitude toward work and retirement takes shape initially among elite circles and the media, but eventually it begins to trickle down to influence public opinion.

The emerging policy consensus favoring continued employment by older people has two sources: first, a continuing drive to shore up public financing of retirement income and, second, the dominance of cultural ideals held by upper middle-class opinion leaders who themselves enjoy good jobs. The new consensus holds out the promise of preestablished harmony between public benefit and private satisfaction: keep working and you will feel better while contributing to the good of society. The problems with the new policy consensus arise from contradictions both in the economic system and in the cultural order.

Limitations on Work Options

Promoting work-life extension in place of retirement in later life will be a difficult task because it runs up against more than convention or attitudes. In fact, what Townsend has called "the structured dependency of the elderly" is the consequence of deeply rooted institutional interests. Barriers to employment of older workers historically did not arise from "ageism" on the part of individual employers but were a result of labor market conditions in advanced industrial society. Legislating against mandatory retirement or setting up job placement services will not have much effect if the jobs are not jobs for older people in the first place.

Since World War II, the policy of major unions in capital-intensive industries in the United States has been to trade away union resistance to labor-saving technological changes for annual wage increases, cost-of-living clauses, and job security for union members. Productivity gains flowing from new technologies were shared by workers in those favored industries but at the price of overall structural unemployment in the economy at large. The resulting pattern was one of full-time work during a normal work career, followed by abrupt termination—mandatory retirement—at the end of that career. Such a labor policy enhances the ability of capital-intensive industries to train new, preferably younger workers in new technologies while maintaining high utilization of plant and equipment through maximum working hours per week.

The outcome was to skew job security and income toward more senior workers. But security was purchased at the price of an overall decline in jobs in particular industries. In some cases—among railway workers, the printing or longshoreman's unions, for example—this practice has resulted in a dwindling number of older workers who hold on to an ever shrinking number of jobs while enjoying seniority and rising wage levels. By the mid-1980s, this pattern became extended through collective bargaining agreements in the automobile industry, airlines, and the postal unions. In these industries new union contracts ratified a two-tier wage policy in which new, younger workers would have lower compensation, while older workers with more seniority kept benefits intact.

For a generation or more, the labor movement and allies in industry have acquiesced in a policy of easing older workers out of the labor market through negotiated retirement benefits. Thus, a measure of job security for current workers was matched by pension security for retirees. In broad terms, these were the terms of the social contract for labor during the postwar period. This social contract presupposes and reinforces, of course, a rigid version of the linear life plan.[20]

During the 1970s, major elements of this social contract were undermined by inflation and then by the weakening of the power of organized labor. With crises in Social Security financing and with continuing high rates of unemployment, economic security for workers and retirees alike was under attack. The result has been a growing pressure to reassess the linear life plan and even to challenge the assumption that old people should be out of the labor market.

Among gerontologists, interest in work-life extension has sparked interest in older worker demonstration programs designed to show the feasibility of alternative work patterns: for example, flex-time, phased retirement, hiring of retirees, or other arrangements to make use of the labor pool of retired persons. Major companies, such as Atlantic Richfield and Travelers Insurance, have taken a lead in these demonstration programs. But, as subsequent experience shows, these older worker programs are largely window dressing to enhance corporate image. Only small numbers have been involved and the programs are generally not replicated elsewhere. The fact is that current older worker programs represent only a meager response by corporate management, and incentives to enhance hiring of older workers are unlikely to increase significantly the degree of older worker participation in the labor force.

Yet despite these repeated failures, the prowork ideology gains ever wider support. We might wonder, why is it that work for old people is so persistently attractive to gerontologists? It seems unlikely that any generalized appeal to the work ethic can explain why we persist in trying to find

ways to "put the old folks back to work." The real reasons may have more
to do with a deep-seated modern image of what human fulfillment ought
to be. The celebration of work constitutes a potent symbol of the ethos
of modernity.

Productivity: The Flight from Old Age

These prowork attitudes are widespread among an elite class of older
people, particularly opinion leaders such as executives, intellectuals, and
professionals. The favorable view toward productivity extends beyond the
economic sphere itself; it affects how older people see themselves. Forced
to retire, many old people will feel useless because they are now unproductive. The celebration of the work role for older people, at bottom, has
more than an ideological or economic motive. It expresses a wish to see
old age as a period of productive life.

Remaining in the work force takes on a distinct psychological function: gainful employment becomes a way of denying old age. By remaining in the work force, older people can act and feel middle-aged. Their
time orientation is toward the future and toward modernity: toward the
youthful values of change, progress, innovation, novelty. The work role
then becomes a way of opting for activity instead of passivity and thus
escaping the socially disapproved features of the elderly role.

For such people—and there are many among the young old—time in
late life is not empty but is fully structured by the economic workplace.
The great attraction of putting older people back to work, then, is that
lifelong employment resolves the troubling split between the progressive
values of modernity and the existential finitude of old age. The secret
hope is that somehow those great engines of the modern technosphere—
the corporation and the bureaucracy—can finally make a place for old
age. This is why the work role takes on such importance for aging advocates who struggle against the negative image of old age. In that struggle
they find eager allies among the professional elites who tell and retell
anecdotes about people who died six months after retirement. "Retirement is bad for your health," we are solemnly informed.

Aging advocates want to find new roles for older people that are valued, that are socially productive, and that are flexible enough to accom-
modate both the strengths and vulnerabilities of age. But these qualities
are precisely what the modern workplace, with its rhythms of bureaucracy and technological change, does not possess. It is not surprising that as

pension income has permitted it, more and more older people have opted for retirement leisure instead of the world of work.

THE USES OF LEISURE TIME IN LATE LIFE

Leisure Time: The Path of Self-Fulfillment

Over the last generation, we have seen the emergence of retirement as a public entitlement and a universal expectation. Retirement is portrayed as a golden age where individual desires are to be fulfilled as the reward for a lifetime of toil. Adequate pension income has, for the first time, allowed a majority of American workers to leave their jobs before ill health forced them to leave—an enormous social achievement. Americans have retired to leisure because they could afford to.

The new life-style of universal retirement was based on the axial value of self-satisfaction: not productivity—living for the sake of others—but, finally, living for myself. This set of values is not limited to any single age-group. Recent opinion surveys suggest that both young and old no longer see themselves as bound by obligations to sacrifice for the sake of other generations: all age-groups are increasingly on their own.[21] Self-fulfillment now becomes a right, and leisure in retirement becomes an entitlement. Living for myself sounds like the fulfillment of the dream of modernity: to be released from social bonds, to satisfy long-postponed desires, free at last. In the retirement ideology, this vision inspires a golden image of old age.

Leisure as Empty Time

In describing the specter of an aging society, I referred earlier to an image of old age as a period when time becomes empty and perhaps drained of meaning.[22] The fear of an aging society is, in part, a fear that masses of people, suddenly endowed with leisure, will not know how to use it. The fear of an aging society then becomes allied to a more familiar general critique of mass society and mass culture.[23] But this longstanding fear of leisure is also based on a traditional work ethic that is increasingly at odds with social reality. Increasingly, it seems we will be living in a society with high unemployment where some groups, at least, must enjoy, or endure, large amounts of nonwork time over the course of their lives.

The meaning and purpose of such nonwork time is precisely what is at stake in policies concerned with human development from a lifespan point of view.

Many critics of contemporary American leisure have been understandably dismayed by mass culture and by the uses to which late-life leisure time is now put: for example, watching television, which is by far the most prevalent leisure acitivity among retired persons. What Ortega Y Gasset denounced as "mass culture" fifty years ago is precisely what dismayed De Grazia twenty years ago and what troubles Christopher Lasch today.[24] The terms of the debate have changed—from mass culture to "culture of narcissism"—but the target remains much the same. To the critics, an abundance of life means only empty time enjoyed by uneducated masses. The coming of an aging society replays old arguments over mass culture and popular culture, but now the struggle is taken up into questions about the meaning and quality of the last stage of life.

The Classical Concept of Leisure

If leisure time in old age is more than simply discretionary or empty time, then what could its content be? A complete answer requires some appreciation of the classical concept of leisure. On this view, leisure has a qualitative content and demands of its own.[25] That is, leisure is not to be understood as simply the absence of work or the activity that fills time outside of work. Instead, leisure is understood to fulfill specific functions. Dumazedier identifies three such functions of leisure: *relaxation* (recovery and restoration); *entertainment* (escape from boredom); and personal *development*.

The first two of these concepts, relaxation and entertainment, have a negative connotation; they are defined in terms of what they are not: not work, not boredom. Leisure as relaxation is free time that revivifies us and prepares us again for work: for example, time spent on vacation. A second function of leisure—stimulation or entertainment—has had the clearer implications for the use of time in retirement. Indeed, gerontologists and policymakers commonly associate leisure in old age with activities for recreation and entertainment: ways of filling time to avoid emptiness.

Yet, at bottom, this second definition too has a negative connotation. Leisure as entertainment implies a need for external stimulus to prevent the organism from sinking back into lethargy or boredom. It is through mass media, principally television, that older people find cheap entertainment and a structure for leisure time. But the stimulation proves illusory. Vicarious participation in leisure offers no sense of cumulative development but simply the dispersal of attention in order to fill time with ever new stimuli. Like mass media, each day is different, yet every week is the same as the week before.

It is only the last of Dumazedier's functions of leisure—personal development—that has a fully positive meaning. It is this last concept —leisure as personal development—that is linked to the classical ideal of leisure. The word "leisure" derives from the Greek word *schole*. It signifies quietness and peace but also the pursuit of an activity for its own sake, an ideal of self-development. Instead of relaxation or distraction, leisure ought to be a period of self-development. True leisure cannot be equated simply with free time and should not be identified with consumerism.

This analysis demonstrates what is deficient about the use of leisure time in old age. Our culture lacks any positive image of the second half of life. We are tempted to see the abundance of time in old age as abundance of leisure. But the absence of a genuine concept of leisure becomes apparent when we realize that, in the modernized life cycle, leisure time is only time displaced from the middle into the last stage of life. What is missing is any concept of cumulative human development.

Even when leisure is properly understood as a mode of self-development over time, it is difficult to abruptly take up such an attitude at the threshold of retirement. Instead, free time becomes a privatized release from social obligations or even contact with other generations. The leisure-time ideology of retirement cuts the ties that bind generations together. The old-age ideology of leisure as entertainment finally reinforces the culture of narcissism: a world without children, without a future. The life course has been cut up into segments dominated by alternatives of production and consumption, engagement and release. Leisure time then becomes a commodity in the marketplace: no longer a path to self-development, but a new form of self-absorption and separation from other generations.

The Commodification of Leisure Time

The ideology of leisure in retirement is inseparable from the influence of media, advertising, and the machinery of the consumer society. Belief in the golden age of retirement serves a legitimation function, just as it was once important to believe in the Horatio Alger myth of economic advancement. Each myth points to a goal to strive for. The rainbow at the end of life held out to elders is a cult of leisure commodities—tours, games, hobbies, sports—fueled by merchandising in the mass media and by industries that cater to new desires. Business has discovered the gray market of mature Americans and now eagerly begins to exploit that new market.[26]

By 1984, the number of people in the sixty-five-plus bracket for the first time exceeded the number of teenagers, and businesses began to take notice. *Modern Maturity*, published by the American Association of Retired Persons (AARP), one of the most widely circulated magazines in America (10 million subscribers) reflects the new gray market today. The magazine refuses to accept the usual ads for laxatives, dentures, or wheelchairs. Instead the magazine favors a positive, upbeat image of well-groomed, smiling elders heading off for vacation enjoyment. In other mass circulation magazines, we begin to see the appearance of what one gerontologist dubbed "the sensuous grandmother": attratice gray-haired models offering furs, cosmetics, and luxury products designed for an upscale market and upbeat image of mature adults.[27]

Old age is being increasingly absorbed into the consumer world, just as children and teenagers have long been successfully targeted by advertisers on television. The uses of time for leisure are progressively being dominated by market forces: retirement villages, packaged vacation tours, commercialized sports, and above all, television. Until recently, the image of old age presented in mass media has been overwhelmingly negative. Now we are being treated to a new, positive image of old age as the engines of advertising appeal to the motivation for self-fulfillment in a restless search for consumer satisfaction. As Gorz puts it:

> . . . it will not help to enlarge the sphere of individual autonomy if the resulting free time remains empty "leisure time," filled for better or worse by the programmed distractions of the mass media and the oblivion merchants, and if everyone is thereby driven back into the solitude of the private sphere.[28]

Gorz's dismay over the distractions of commercial mass media applies with special force to the elderly, who are prime candidates for "programmed distraction." Old people spend more of their hours watching television than any other age-group. Leisure time in old age recedes into the darkness of privatism illuminated by a flickering screen: an internal exile, the solitude of the private sphere invaded by never-ending stimuli of commodities and imaginary gratification. In fact, deferred gratification and the solace of private self-fulfillment sustain both the retirement ideology and compliance with norms of the work ethic. But neither the public demands of work nor the private consolations of leisure develop or enlarge our human capacities.

EDUCATION IN LATE LIFE

This enlargement of human capacities is ultimately the task of education, including education for the last stage of life. This ideal involves much more than flexibility or access to options of work, leisure, or learning at different stages of life. It demands a new understanding of the lifelong task of human development and of the role of lifelong learning in building skills and knowledge.

In the linear life plan, education was concentrated in the first stage of life, in childhood and youth. But the postindustrial society and the information economy demands a far broader view of education. The current trend toward lifelong learning needs a deeper philosophical rationale and political justification. Exciting possibilities do exist. For example, older adult education programs for self-help, for adult literarcy, and for life skills such as nutrition, consumer education, or financial planning have shown the feasibility of late-life development. The key point is that education in many forms constitutes a strategic activity. That is to say, learning is not merely an end in itself—just one activity among others. Education also offers access to a wider range of activities, to new roles of work, leisure, and further self-development. By opening access to new possibilities, late-life learning empowers older adults to take charge of their own development.

Aging in the Information Society

Can such a vision of lifelong learning become a reality in the years to come? Some observers have argued that lifelong learning will become increasingly common as we move toward an information economy. The assumption seems to be that, throughout the lifespan, individuals will be challenged by the information economy to update skills and knowledge. In this scenario, we would look back at the present obsolescence of old age and regard it as merely a transitional problem of the older, declining industrial economy. The new technology and economy of the information society would make growth and change available to all age-groups over the entire life course.[29]

But will this vision of lifespan development actually come to pass? There are reasons for doubt. The instantaneous availability of information does bring all age-groups together in a common present. In that sense, it abolishes the historical separation of old age in favor of a juxtaposition of all age-groups. The advent of the information society accomplishes this just because it seems to abolish time in the same way that mass communications over the globe seems to abolish space. But domination by instantaneous data has its negative side.

In the information society, everyone has a duty to keep on learning in a continual battle against premature aging: to avoid being caught uninformed, with outdated ideas. This is the familiar picture of a population of "news junkies," of home computers and portable radios, a world where changing fashions and technology make information more and more into a commodity. In the new commodity market of information, the penalty for being too slow is to fall behind, to be uninformed. Maximizing the speed and flow of information becomes a criterion of youth and an antidote to age. But the dizzying speed of electronic technology makes old age itself obsolete. As the speed and proliferation of information accelerates, we are simultaneously witnessing the disappearance of institutions that might help people make sense of information.

The advent of an information society has radically changed the structure of the human life course: the relations among youth, adulthood, and old age. The institutions of the school and of mandatory retirement were both results of the modernization of the life cycle to conform to the industrial order. But the postindustrial society operates on a different logic, and the information society may demand new patterns for the life course. Here the volatility of information shifts the power balance between youth and age in unpredictable ways. If power now depends on instantaneous access to information systems, then age loses many advantages over youth. In this sense, the gap between age-groups shrinks. An age-irrelevant society becomes a natural consequence of telecommunications technology.

In contrast to age-based barriers, the cultural ideal of an age-irrelevant society sounds appealing indeed. Like the vogue for flexible life planning, it promises us a society where chronological age will be no barrier. But is this image really an adequate guide for human development in an aging society? In contrast to the illusion of endless change and growth, old age involves an acknowledgment of finitude. Late-life learning must be based on this reality. It cannot be a pathetic attempt to keep up with the youth culture of an information society. On the contrary, for older adults, the great project and task of late life involves building on the knowledge gained from life experience. The task of late-life development is the integration of the self, including the transmission of experience of future generations.

Viewed in this way, education in the last stage of life has an enormous contribution to make in overcoming intergenerational barriers. Education, whether for young or old, should not be viewed merely as an instrumental activity tied to productivity in the monetized marketplace. The educational arena is a sphere where young and old can meet, where the gap between generations can, in part, be bridged. Education can also have important effects in reducing dependency and promoting capacity for autonomy and self-help: in health care, in nonmonetized production, in mutual aid and community services. Here the educational system has a natural relationship to the sphere of voluntary action. Finally in leisure-time use, education involves activities of continuing self-development in the last stage of life.

This concept of education as self-development, as a cultural ideal, is more than filling time. It embodies the hope that the abundance of life will result in a deeper quality of life. Understood in this way, late life education would no longer appear as a frill or a luxury. It would be seen as a vehicle for social productivity and personal fulfillment, or even as the highest goal of life in an aging society.

5

Aging and Quality of Life

"A human being would certainly not grow to be 70 or 80 years old
if this longevity had no meaning for the species. The afternoon of
human life must also have a significance of its own and cannot be
merely a pitiful appendage to life's morning."
—Carl Jung, "Youth and Age"
Psychological Reflections

QUALITY-OF-LIFE ISSUES

The fundamental question of this book is a simple one: how can America's growing population of older people be mobilized as a growing national resource rather than be seen as a burgeoning problem? To ask that question is to demand a new approach to public policy for an aging society, an approach based on quality of life in old age.

Specifically, that approach requires attention to questions often overlooked in policy analysis in the field of aging; for example, education of older adults, voluntary action, leisure, and cultural activities. When these areas are considered at all, it is usually as an afterthought: as elements of life enrichment to be dealt with when "serious" questions of income, health care, or job opportunities are resolved. The assumption is that education, leisure, or continuing opportunities in late life are luxuries that come after the necessities are provided. In any case, when public policy is involved, quality-of-life issues inevitably involve value judgments. But judgments of value or quality are often difficult to make in democratic societies. How can public policy take a stand on such questions? Isn't quality of life ultimately a matter of individual values and subjective interpretation?[1] Whether luxury or not, quality-of-life questions are perhaps best left to private choice, not resolved in the public arena.

This view is strongly rooted in American political tradition: in the demarcation between public and private life, the separation of church and state, the weak support for public subsidy of culture and the arts, and, in general, in an insistence on the autonomy of local initiative, the voluntary sector, and pluralism in values and beliefs. There is something to be said in favor of protecting private values from the public world, but that separation has never been as absolute in the past as some would have us believe. Moreover, that very relationship between the public and private sphere—so problematic for the modern world—now turns out to have major consequences for public policy in an aging society.[2]

In any case, it would be a mistake to assume that the American past is a guide to policy debates in the future. It was only in this century that public policy in America assigned to government the prime responsibility for managing overall performance of the economy. Today, it is fair to say that economic models dominate policy analysis and policy debate. Indeed, this is an important reason why it is so difficult to bring policy analysis to bear on quality-of-life issues at all. Yet there are now signs of a major shift in American political culture. There are indications that we are moving away from an era when economic issues determine political decisions and toward an era when social issues—for example, conflicts between "traditional" and "progressive" values—are decisive in political choices. A new era dominated by cultural politics coincides with the shift of America to an aging society, with all the changes implied by that demographic transformation.

Transition to a Quality-of-Life Society

Throughout advanced industrialized societies, there is a growing recognition that arrival of an aging society constitutes a major historical watershed in how societies have understood themselves. It is a qualitative change, a shift in values, not just a slowing of population growth or a change in the age composition of society. It is a shift away from growth and movement of population size in favor of stability and maturation of the population as a whole.

This transition, instead of evoking fears of a specter of decline, might better be viewed as a welcome development. Instead of a gloomy future, a slower growing population could well promise more attention to measures that improve the quality of life. For one thing, a stationary population means higher per capita economic output: a rise in real wealth for individuals. It also means less population pressure on the environment through pollution and use of depletable resources. Above all, it means an opportunity to invest in quality-of-life concerns: education, government services, better use of leisure time. In short, an aging society, in this view, could mean the transition to a greater quality of life for all.

The transition to an aging society has consequences for the local, as well as the global, scale. With slower population growth and declining geographic mobility, people may be more willing to make long-range investments in quality-of-life improvements in their local community. A society where neighborhoods are aging in place could mean greater concern for long-range needs at the local level: an ecological ethic of caring for the local environment in place of the feverish mobility of the recent American past. This resurgence of a "new localism," according to John Naisbitt, is already well underway.[3]

Postmaterialist Values

Population aging in a postindustrial economy is accompanied by other shifts in values. The movement to a postindustrial society means a shift in public concern away from sheer quantity of services and basic economic sufficiency toward *quality* of services, especially those that define quality of life. What we are seeing is a movement away from deficit needs toward self-actualization concerns. For aging policy, this means troublesome questions about how to finance the demand for expanding public services; about the role of cultural activities, media and entertainment; and about new uses of time during an ever lengthening period of retirement. As more and more people live to enjoy the leisure of the retirement years, the quality of those years becomes a critical question.

This societal shift toward postmaterialist values parallels a movement along Abraham Maslow's psychological hierarchy of needs. According to Maslow's theory of needs, as lower order desires such as food, shelter, and clothing are satisfied, higher order desires come into play. A shift along these lines takes place as people enjoy more and more disposable income and therefore spend less on necessities and more on luxuries and quality-of-life items. At a societal level, this transition means a shift to comparable values: namely, concern for self-fulfillment and quality of life in work and leisure. Survey data analyzed by Inglehart[4] have documented the spread of these so-called postmaterialist values in Europe, as well as in the United States.

The shift by no means signifies that materialist motivation is dead; it simply indicates that other desires now take on prominence. Postmaterialist attitudes, for example, are visible in the movement for environmental protection, in demands for more leisure time, and in occupational preferences in the workplace. For example, across advanced industrial societies generally, a good job is widely felt to be something more than salary or economic security. This same trend has had major implications for business management and industrial productivity. In private life, too, quality-of-life concerns and self-actualization needs are felt as increasingly important.[5]

Viewed uncritically, Maslow's hierarchy might imply some such inevitable evolution toward higher concerns and a bright future. But a little reflection shows that this need not be the case. For example, the shift to quality-of-life concerns may show up as a decline in risk-taking, rising worker discontent, comparative status-seeking, and self-absorption, not to mention deepening gloom about the future of postindustrial society as a whole. A postmaterialist attitude is consistent with a strong ideology of privatism noted in recent years among college students.

These negative features of postmaterialist society are just as possible as a shift to so-called humanistic or spiritual values. The new prominence of quality-of-life values is by no means a guarantee of a future society where these values serve as guideposts to public policy. In an aging society, declining risk-taking and a culture of narcissism could have distinctly negative consequences for the old, as well as for the young. The critical question is whether new management styles, more imaginative social policies, and a positive image of the future will offer a genuine abundance of life in the future.

Self-Fulfillment and Late Life

In his work on the coming of postindustrial society, Daniel Bell originally predicted a shift away from the "economizing" mode of industrial capitalism toward the "sociologizing" mode of postindustrial society: that is, away from economic constraint and toward modes of collective fulfillment of social aspirations.[6] The postindustrial society, then, would be one where "immaterial needs" such as "health, education, culture, environmental protection, travel, security, leisure . . . are given highest priority."[7] Indeed, the most optimistic prophets of postindustrial society see in it "signs of an irresistible evolution of our society toward (a) golden age of services."

In such a world the leisure and abundance of life in old age would offer unparalleled opportunities for access to new information sources and would, through this vast upsurge of cultural and intellectual opportunities, enhance the quality of life in retirement. Postindustrial society and the in-formation economy would seem to create the conditions for achieving quality of life through lifelong learning, meaningful use of leisure time, and work-life enrichment.

But other commentators are more skeptical about whether the coming of a postindustrial society will actually lead to this rosy future of postma-terialist fulfillment. The new information economy that serves as the economic foundation for postindustrial abundance has its ominous side. Dupuy, for example, argues that "Rather than delivering us from material constraints, the information society intensifies the struggle for survival and strengthens the radical monopoly of economic activity over the so-cial and political dimensions of our life . . . ."[8] While enlarging the scope of information, the new order of an information economy simul-taneously destroys traditional sources of meaning. The crisis of meaning common in old age now coincides with a crisis of meaning in the larger culture.

This collapse of meaning and the erosion of quality of life in old age reflect a deeper failure unacknowledged by the optimistic prophets of postmaterialist abundance: namely, a failure of communication and legi-timation in the social order as a whole. The loss of meaning and purpose reflects a broader legitimation crisis in advanced industrialized societies. Jurgen Habermas sees the political tensions and conflicts of postmateri-alist society as rooted in the disruption of "communicatively structured forms of life." As material constraints are removed, traditional forms of life simply decay, to be replaced by new forms of domination in the in-formation economy. Overcoming material scarcity need not mean any advance toward self-fulfillment or quality of life at all. In short, we may have surpassed material limits only to be confined by new limits to self-fulfillment. A postmaterialistic abundance of life remains elusive as long as the political economy is organized in ways to prevent this abundance from actually becoming available to all. In our own overdeveloped soci-ety a familiar pattern of competitive materialism still dominates social re-lationships and imposes social limits to growth even where material scarcity is no longer the issue.[9]

It is these social limits that prevent the new abundance of life from becoming a basis for quality of life in old age. Still worse, we are blinded from seeing what is happening by the very categories used to analyze the problem. This blindness is nowhere more apparent than in the failure of scientific gerontology, and aging policy analysis in particular, to address quality-of-life issues in the public sphere. Quality of life, whatever it may mean, must certainly be different from the scales of life satisfaction by which social scientists measure the morale of old people.

This trend is not unique to gerontology. Habermas, for example, calls attention to what he sees as the "devastation of the communicative capacities of the life-world."[10] Old age appears as simply one more social problem to be dealt with by technical means of social control, chiefly the instruments of the health and welfare complex. We come to see aging as a social problem to be mastered by the devices of technical rationality. But more refined technical means are not really an answer to the disturbing question that served as the title for Robert Butler's book on old age —*Why Survive?*

Drawing on Habermas' analysis, one could cite specific and disquieting trends in aging policy. These include, for example, the growing instrumental orientation of professional life, the extension of concepts of accountability and systems management, the monetizing and privatization of the human services, the segmentation of life stages, and the dominance of bureaucratic rationality over the life world in old age. Beginning with midlife counseling and life planning, new specialities are extended ever further, even including death counseling. Habermas is particularly concerned over what he terms the "colonization of the life-world" where techniques of professional and administrative rationality invade these domains of meaning. It is just on this point where recent trends in gerontology and the human service professions offer ominous signs. As academic gerontology acquires an ever more technical and instrumentalized orientation, it contributes to a further colonization of the life world of old age. The problems of later life are treated with scientific and managerial efficiency but with no grasp of their larger political or existential significance. The life world of the last stage of life itself is progressively drained of meaning.

This analysis also has implications for the status of the aging in the welfare state. The elderly are the greatest beneficiaries of policies of the American welfare state. Yet, even where such social policies succeed, old age still retains its negative image and is deprived of meaning. Professional advocates for the elderly, in keeping with their own ideological framework, have a vested interest in presenting the elderly as victims: of crime, inflation, bad health, loneliness, and so on. An analyst like Laura Olson, writing from a left-wing point of view, falls into this pattern.[11] For Olson, as for Simone de Beauvoir, the aged are cast in the role of victims of the capitalist system.

But the problematic status of old age is more complex and contradictory than this. Habermas' analysis and the framework of Critical Theory allow us to view the condition of aging policy with greater subtlety. The devastation of the communicative capacity of the life world of old age is taking place at the same time when the material or political condition of old age has been improving, as it has markedly in the United States in recent years, even during the Reagan Administration. Casting the aged as victims will not help us make sense of the contradictory status of old age. How can the aged, as a group, be making economic gains, while at the same time old age, as a category of experience, becomes ever more marginal and deprived of status or meaning? Failing to grasp this contradiction means that quality-of-life concerns remain invisible for public policy.

Policy Analysis and Quality of Life

In order to assess the significance of quality-of-life concerns for the policy domain, we must recognize that historical and generational change has profoundly shaped the meaning of quality of life for different age groups. At present, for example, quality-of-life aspirations are expressed most intensely by the younger generation, who were brought up under conditions of economic affluence. The older generation, influenced by the Depression, the Second World War, and postwar economic conditions, has shown less affinity for postmaterialist values. But we can expect that succeeding generations of elderly will exhibit greater concern for quality-of-life issues. Even for today's generation of elderly, a major possibility for social productivity and the use of personal time is not being captured by conventional measures of cost or output: namely, conventional measures of paid employment or consumer buying. This failure distorts our appraisal of costs and benefits for alternative policy options. Neglect of quality-of-life issues by policy analysis restricts consideration of policies for an aging society in the future.

A major problem for policymakers today is the fact that claims on material resources are rising at the same time that new demands are being made for quality-of-life values. We want economic growth and capital investment, but at the same time we want a clean environment, fulfilling jobs, more leisure time: in short, higher quality of life. The same contradiction affects aging policy. We want adequate health care under Medicare, but at the same time we do not want simply to keep elderly people alive if prolonged life loses its quality and meaning. The policy dilemma is that both material and quality-of-life demands arise simultaneously, and public policy finds it difficult to address these concerns.[12]

Another problem is that quality-of-life goals are intangible and not easily measured: they are personal states of fulfillment (e.g., good health, self-esteem, etc.) or else they lie in domains that were previously not assessed at all (e.g., clean air and water). But the *cost* of safety or environmental protection is measurable, and therefore, measures promoting quality of life become vulnerable to attack, as they have been in recent years. Further, the shift toward quality-of-life concerns has macroeconomic implications. The cost of production for these intangible elements of quality of life is often buried and only indirectly acknowledged: in higher costs of production, in the rate of inflation, and so on. The benefits, and sometimes costs as well, are typically *invisible*. For public policy formulation what is visible is debated; what is invisible can be ignored, regardless of its importance.

But the shift toward quality-of-life issues demands an appropriate response from public policy. Policymaking in postindustrial society is dominated, and legitimated, by science and technology. But this framework of technological rationality creates problems in approaching quality-of-life issues. Policy analysis is too often dominated exclusively by quantitative economic models in assessing alternative options. The result is that quality of life is ignored. When we ignore nonmonetized factors of human productivity, the distortion is made worse. Thus, policies to increase the GNP will not be an adequate response to a shift of attitudes toward postmaterialist values if the GNP itself measures only monetized goods and services.

More to the point, our view of the aging of the American population will be seriously distorted if we ignore nonmonetized productivity and the quality-of-life concerns of an aging population. Since the elderly are largely outside the paid labor force, we will need to look to different measures for productivity. And because cost-benefit models give little help in appraising quality of life in old age, we will have to look at quality-of-life issues in more imaginative ways.

POLITICAL CHOICES

Discussion of aging policy today is still dominated by the unfinished agenda of the liberal ideology now under retreat. In broad terms, that liberal ideology has been linked to what has been dubbed the "failure model" of old age. This is the model that portrays the elderly as the deserving poor whose frailty entitles them to help. In opposition to this view, conservatives generally acknowledge some minimal obligation to help the truly needy but basically favor more incentives for people to help themselves. In debates over welfare policy for the poor, this pattern of opposing views has become tiresomely familiar.

In contrast to the failure model, the conservative view insists on latent strengths and personal responsibility, even if expressed in the language of punitive rhetoric. The difficulty with this conservative view is that the two elements in its perspective—latent strength, on the one hand, and genuine need, on the other—point to very different policy prescriptions. An appeal to latent strength would urge us to help people build on their own capacities while we are also urged to limit public expenditures to the truly needy. The two elements evidently can be in contradiction, and resulting policies may work at cross-purposes. The contradictions of welfare reform are a case in point. In social policy generally the result of these ideological contradictions has been paralysis in policymaking punctuated by periodic crises that legitimate drastic action, such as cutbacks in social spending. For example, the 1983 Social Security debate followed that crisis scenario; current debates over Medicare show all signs of following the same script.

Continuing along this crisis path poses a gloomy prospect for the future. A brighter future may depend precisely on those initiatives that offer hope of getting outside a debate that paralyzes action. The terms of the debate must be shifted, and it is just on this point that quality-of-life concerns can open up a new path. In citizenship, in cultural activities, in local voluntary action, there are unexpected "spaces for action" in the public world today.[13] Adult education, self-help, and other programs may well have importance in solving problems of an aging society in the areas such as income, health care, and work and retirement. An optimistic alternative may be possible.

A Paradigm Shift

This more optimistic view of the importance of quality-of-life issues for aging policy will be rejected by many. Are not quality-of-life questions about education, volunteerism, self-help, culture, and so on, after all just fringe or luxury issues? How can they be taken seriously alongside the terrible dilemmas we face in income, health care, or employment policy?

This apparently tough-minded objection assumes that the status quo in the macropolicy arenas will remain unchanged: for example, that Social Security, Medicare, and employment and retirement trends will continue along the lines of the recent past. But should we really expect that the policy environment of the remainder of this century will simply perpetuate the pattern of the past? During the decades of the 1960s and 1970s we have grown accustomed to a policy environment characterized by the following:

- *Earlier retirement.* Over a period of decades, we have seen an increasing incidence of early retirement, coupled with widespread mandatory retirement at age 65. The result was a continuing drop in labor-force participation by men over the last three decades.

- *Increases in entitlement spending.* Entitlement spending under Social Security and Medicare has become a nearly uncontrollable element in federal spending. Spending for old people now consumes more than a quarter of the federal budget.

- *Negative image of old age.* There has been wide public acceptance of stereotypes of old people as impoverished, sick, lonely, and needy. The result was a plummeting of public view of the status of the elderly during the 1970s at precisely the time when their condition was decisively *improving* relative to other age-groups.

It is striking that by the late-1980s all of these earlier trends were under challenge or in retreat. What is happening today is a dramatic rethinking of what it means to grow old in America: a fundamental paradigm shift in thinking about aging. Instead of the conventional assumptions about aging policy, we need a whole new set of assumptions that challenge past ways of thinking. In fact, this new paradigm turns the old assumptions upside down.

- *Work Incentives.* Mandatory retirement has already been pushed back to age 70 and completely eliminated for federal employees; more than liberalization is likely in the future. The long-term trend toward early retirement for men may have peaked, as higher numbers of women are in the labor force and as Social Security changes prompt more and more older people to seek employment.

- *Health Care Costs.* Serious efforts at health care cost-containment are now being put into effect. Since 1983 Congress has mandated a prospective payment reimbursement system for hospitals; similar cost containment measures for physicians and nursing homes have followed. A new environment of cost-containment is here to stay.

• *Changing Public Opinion.* Influential voices have challenged the failure model of aging and reopened a debate about age-versus-need as a basis of entitlement. Other critics are raising issues of "inter-generational equity" and calling for a radical assessment of aging policies.

The domestic policy environment—on taxes, the federal deficit, and aging policy—is in rapid flux. No one can be sure what the final impact of current changes will be or how the Reagan initiatives in domestic policy will permanently affect the larger society.[14] Yet some trends seem clear enough already. We may venture to predict that by the end of the 1990s we shall witness an aging policy environment very different from what we have been accustomed to seeing in the last two decades. The macro-policy areas of income, health, and work and retirement will still be the primary focus of attention. But macro-policy goals will be framed increasingly by a need for older worker productivity, budget pressures prompting cuts in services and entitlements, and continuing reassessment of the status of the aged as the "deserving poor" in public policy.

The End of Quality of Life Concerns?

Where do quality-of-life concerns and aging fit into this new policy environment? The most powerful imperative for domestic policymaking today is the drive to enhance the productive capacity of the American economy in an environment of international competition. For this reason quality-of-life issues in aging will seem to some people an anachronism. Amitai Etzioni for example, argues that the postmaterialist or "quality-of-life" society reached its maximum appeal during the sixties and seventies.[15] At that time demands for equality, environmental protection, and greater leisure and harmonious interpersonal relationships were part of a broader shift in public opinion favoring nonmaterial, quality-of-life goals over traditional values of economic productivity and growth.[16]

But the chilling winds of economic hard times have changed that mood. The imperative to "reindustrialize" American means that economic concerns today must receive top priority. Quality of life takes second place. In this view, quality-of-life goals are incompatible with economic imperatives. Thus, Etzioni argues that the new policy environment of the 1980s requires a shift away from the high-consumption, affluent values of the past.

Quality of Life and Lifespan Development

This call for sacrificing quality of life and deferring gratification in favor of productivity sounds plausible enough. Yet the choice may be a false one. A number of analysts have pointed out that the separation of productivity goals from quality-of-life goals has been a fatal flaw in the style of American business management—one that in fact may have even contributed to declining productivity in recent years. Peters and Waterman, in *In Search of Excellence*, make a strong argument that attention to quality—both in production and in worker morale—must be at the center of efforts to improve management of the American economy.[17] In the same vein Paul Hawken and Robert Reich argue that what is needed now is a transition to industrial techniques based less on standardized mass production (quantity) and more on product value-added (quality), where the essential value to be added is information and intelligence.[18]

This transition to an "informative economy" (Hawken) will mean not simply more widespread use of information technology, but also higher levels of skill by industrial workers who turn out the products and services. The economy of the future will be characterized by a high degree of uncertainty and by rapid change: hence, even more need for worker flexibility and lifespan education and retraining. The cybernetic workplace, far from deskilling employees, could be designed to promote worker participation and control, again giving work a developmental character just as it had in the era of craftsmanship. An aging population in the postindustrial economy need not inevitably mean obsolescence of older workers or devaluation of age and experience. The new economic environment could equally support lifespan development policies favoring productivity in new ways.

The information economy will demand continuing growth in intelligence and skill. Under such conditions, lifelong learning is no longer a luxury but an economic necessity. But equally, under such conditions, older workers could become productive in ways unimagined today. As Peters and Waterman argue, the excellent companies are precisely those that make best use of knowledge drawn from experience among both management and workers. This experiential knowledge can grow with age and experience, provided we create forms that nurture it. As we move away from a mass-volume production economy to systems using flexible production methods, the "value-added" component of a skilled workforce will prove indispensable for both quality control and quality of life. We cannot have one without the other.

Do we face, then, a forced choice between quality-of-life goals and material productivity? There are short-run tradeoffs, but in light of the long-run transformation of the postindustrial economy, the answer is no. The pattern for policy innovation does not lie in separating quality-of-life goals from productivity goals but rather in pursuing policies that strengthen both at the same time. The key lies in what Etzioni himself calls the power of "cross-commitment"—the ability to simultaneously fulfill goals associated with quality of life and with productivity, self-restraint, and social obligation.[19]

Etzioni's own examples of "cross-commitment" include industrial productivity as well as social welfare policies: enhancing worker morale and quality control in factories and greater reliance on home health care for the aged. Simultaneous growth in productivity and quality of life is possible both in the industrial economy and in nonmonetized activities such as home care services. In one case workers, in the other case older people and their families, achieve better quality of life while fulfilling goals of economic efficiency. Instead of conflicting values, we could have cooperation and mutual support, if policies supported those options instead of demanding a "forced choice" between quality and quantity, economics and equity.[20]

Quality of life, in short, should not become a codeword for affluent consumerism in a culture of narcissism. Self-fulfillment in old age, as in other periods of life, need not come at the price of social contribution. On the contrary, a more realistic approach would recognize that lifelong learning, self-help, and the productive use of free time are precisely the key to developing the capacity of an aging population to contribute to the wider community. Indeed, there is good reason to think that gains in longevity itself can be traced to such quality-of-life factors as diet, physical and mental activity, coping with stress, and maintaining productive social roles. Yet our health care system pays little attention to those modifiable lifestyle factors, concentrating instead on expensive disease-based interventions that often result in doubtful quality of life for the chronically impaired elderly. Yet the danger is that, in our present fiscal crisis and policy paralysis, we will fail to make the institutional changes necessary to take advantage of the abundance of life represented by new generations of older people.

THE TWO WORLDS OF AGING

A Hierarchy of Needs?

There is a deep-seated reluctance on the part of policy makers to consider quality-of-life issues in aging policy. Ironically, that neglect has been reinforced by advocates for the aging themselves. In the first place, advocates have tended to assume that quality-of-life questions are issues only for the affluent or the well-elderly. When advocates for the aging think about such questions at all, they define them in terms of recreation, leisure, education, or culture, assuming that these are matters of concern only to those whose basic needs are already satisfied.

But this view falls into the error of reifying Maslow's hierarchy of needs and separating basic needs from so-called higher needs. That error leads to a dualistic image of old people separated into what Crystal called the "two worlds of aging—the "ill-derly" who are dependent and the "well-derly" who are healthy and happy.[21] The proper concern of public policy, it is thought, is only with helping people meet minimal basic (i.e., material) needs. As they move up the hierarchy of needs, private decisions determine satisfaction of higher order, quality-of-life needs. According to this model, public and private decisionmaking are rigidly comparmentalized. The fatal flaw lies in separating quality-of-life concerns from basic needs in the first place. Quality-of-life and autonomy are needs for both the frail elderly and those who have greater resources. Even among the frail elderly, self-esteem may be absolutely crucial to their suvival.

> **Locus of Control.** Ellen Langer and her associates have found that even the most frail patients institutionalized in a nursing home have some margin of initiative or "locus of control" that they can exercise in their environment,[22] provided institutional policies permit such activities.
>
> In a dramatic experiment residents in a nursing home were divided into two groups. One group was given a plant to take care of and offered the opportunity to make basic choices about how to spend

recreation time. The other group was told that the staff would care for a plant placed in their rooms and were also directed to a prearranged recreation program. By the end of six months, the group exercising greater control over the environment—even in the minimal way of taking care of a plant—showed a dramatic difference in mortality and morbidity compared to a group who passively received services and direction.

There is abundant evidence that self-esteem is a critical element of quality of life in old age.[23] Aging involves predictable losses and stresses that threaten self-esteem, and this poses a challenge for those providing human services. For example, Bloom has noted how social welfare interventions, even when they provide assistance to needy clients, can at the same time weaken the client's self-esteem.[24] Professionals working with the aged commonly take a paternalistic attitude toward clients as people "in need of protection." Thus, a condition for receiving services may involve acknowledgement that the clients are "dependent" or "unable to take care of themselves." With the elderly, labels reinforce the widespread negative stereotype of old people as helpless victims: again, the "failure model" of old age.

The problem is that service intervention can lead to a self-fulfilling prophecy. It brings on a spiral or vicious circle where declining autonomy simply confirms the negative self-image. If quality of life is tied to self-esteem, it may turn out that providing more and more services will undermine quality of life in old age.[25] Here is exactly the point where policy confirms the worst features of practice: the failure model of aging policy reinforces paternalism and dependency in practice. The heart of the problem is that American social welfare policies have generally been legitimated on the basis of an image of the "deserving" dependency—or helplessness—of the target clientele.

But this definition of the problem presents us with a dilemma. Simply making opportunities or entitlements available may actually fail to improve the well-being of the least advantaged. For example, the participation in the age-based Medicare program has been twice as great for the middle-income elderly than for the poor elderly. Less than half of the elderly poor eligible for SSI are enrolled in that program. Self-esteem and stigma—important elements in quality of life—prevent many elderly poor from receiving benefits. When quality of life and personal motivation are ignored by aging policy, the results may be both inequitable and efficient.

It follows from this analysis that attention to motivation, autonomy, and quality of life are not "luxury" issues confined to the well-to-do elderly whose basic needs are already satisfied. Separating these issues from material resource questions is the fundamental strategic error. Moreover, that separation may not even be beneficial to the least advantaged elderly. The operative principle should be to consider both quality of life and the structure of opportunity, not to separate them.

Finally, there are policy implications here for the "age versus need" debate.[26] Those who favor an "age-irrelevant society" advocate maximum opportunities for everyone regardless of age: an appealing idea. But failing to take account of age differences will result in programs "that further advantage those already advantaged, and disadvantage the most disadvantaged." This means that age-neutral programs may have a serious drawback. While younger adults can utilize time to personal advantage, older people may turn inward in a pattern of self-denial and diminishing motivation. Under these circumstances arms-length "autonomy" for the frail elderly is not a sufficient principle for action.[27]

AGING POLICY: EXPANDING THE LIMITS OF VISION

In a poem William Blake once prayed "God save us from single vision and from Newton's sleep." These lines express Blake's rejection of the Newtonian mechanistic worldview that offered no place for values or judgments of quality and meaning.[28] Blake's charge of "single vision"— of narrowness and mechanistic thinking—is equally apt to describe aging policy in America. Public policy in the field of aging, as in other fields, has had its own single vision. It tends to be preoccupied with what is visible, what is measurable, and, above all, what presents itself as a problem or a need to be fulfilled. As in other policy domains, three major sectors predominate:

Government: whose single vision in domestic policy is limited by today's problems, not tomorrow's opportunities.

Business: whose single vision is limited to the economic marketplace of monetized production and consumption.

Human Service Sector: whose single vision is limited by needs and deficits in a client population to be served.

Within this tripartite division, public policy falls into the habit of limiting its scope to whatever falls within the single vision of one of these three sectors. A "solution" for one sector becomes a "problem" for another sector. For example, when a corporation eliminates redundant workers through massive early retirement, it may create a problem government must deal with. Under this view of policy, problematic issues can enter the policy system to the extent only that they are "constituencies" for government, or "dollars" for the marketplace, or "needs" for human service providers. Every problem and solution must somehow "fit" into the tripartite policy system.

Another way to describe the policy system is given by Richard Titmuss in his discussion of social policy.[29] Titmuss distinguishes two dominant models within the welfare state:

1. The *Industrial Achievement Model:* where public policy facilitates the efficiency of the private economy.

2. The *Redistributive Welfare Model:* where public policy responds to residual human service needs left unfilled by the private economy.

The two models need not be mutually exclusive. In fact, in the historical evolution of the welfare state, expansion of government has been justified both on grounds of meeting residual needs and also of promoting economic productivity. Training programs for unemployed youth would be an example of meeting both needs at the same time. But in recent years the goals of industrial achievement and redistributive welfare have become increasingly separated from one another. We have been led to think of social spending as "welfare," as something entirely opposed to making people productive.

As a result of the prevailing public philosophy, welfare needs are viewed as a kind of public sector charity, while economic development activities such as education or job training have been unconnected with programs such as unemployment insurance or benefit programs designed to meet residual needs of health care and social welfare. The industrial achievement model and the redistributive welfare model have drifted farther and farther apart. In the process, both models have lost public legitimacy. Robert Reich has argued that this separation of the two models has contributed to America's failure to develop its human resources to meet the challenge of international economic competition in the years ahead.[30]

This disastrous separation between industrial achievement and residual welfare programs has left American public policy ill-equipped to deal with the massive changes needed to cope with new economic challenges. In the face of automation, industrial decline, technological change, and high unemployment, policy options still neglect the dimension of human development.

> America's work force is stymied. . . . Indeed, the stagnation of America's work force has driven many workers to join in political coalition with managers who seek protection from imports. At the same time the lack of adequate job training and basic education among America's workers has made it difficult for firms to find and keep the skilled labor they need for flexible-system production.[31]

Reich is enthusiastic about creating a system where economic development and social welfare programs would be closely coordinated, rather than fragmented or working at cross purposes as they do now. He concludes, "rather than two separate systems that interact only incidentally —one geared to production and the other to passive dependency—we will have one system, serving both economic and human development."[32]

The need for both economic and human development in an aging society will be more pressing in the future. But the separation between economic and social welfare goals has been sharply exaggerated in policies for the aging. The elderly are seen as a dependent population. Aging policies tied to industrial achievement have been based on encouraging ever earlier retirement to make way for younger workers. Aging policies have also responded to the dependency of the old, but have almost never addressed contributive roles that might use the accumulated skills and experience of older people. Taking care of residual needs has meant that human development measures have been almost uniformly neglected. The assumption is that old people's capacities for productivity are not worth developing.

Legitimating Old Age Policies

These definitions of "need" and "productivity" are limited by the single vision of the human service sector and the business sector. Needs are defined by constituencies or voting blocs. Politicians and policymakers become fearful of antagonizing powerful groups or their advocates. By contrast, "productivity" is measured exclusively through monetized exchanges of work and consumption. The business sector controls the definition of productivity through the marketplace while the human service sector controls the definition of needs to be met by expansion of state-supported services. Meeting the needs of the elderly population is made legitimate both by ideology—the "failure model" of old age—and by the existence of powerful voting blocs who resist cuts or changes in benefit programs.

Here, in essence, is the logic of welfare capitalism over the last generation. Old age policies have followed this logic, so that "productivity" means putting old people into the labor market, while the needs of the elderly are met through expanding the number of human service professionals. Advocates for the aging, who are part of the human service system, develop an old age ideology linked to this service strategy.

The survival of this system of welfare capitalism has been tied to its legitimacy. Acceptance of the policy system as legitimate depends on how these "problems" are "solved" by each of the three sectors: marketplace, human services, and government itself. The legitimation process—the definition of what is a problem and what is a solution—thus becomes crucial. But government's control of the legitimation process in turn is limited by the behavior of all the competing interest groups, so that public policy itself never breaks out of the single vision imposed by each of the sectors in the policy system. And what is not perceived by single vision, it is assumed, does not exist.

Aging and Policy Analysis

Questions about quality of life involve value elements that cannot be reduced to the categories of single vision nor treated by conventional policy analysis.[33] In the pluralistic framework of competing interest groups, the groups themselves become definers of value preferences.[34] Beyond the sheer fact of intergroup conflict there is no court of appeal. Policy analysis then serves only an honest broker among these different values. In all cases, questions about quality of life do not "fit in" to a policy system that is intent on "solving problems."

When we think seriously about aging it becomes evident that all the conventional "problem solving" models of policy analysis must rapidly reach their limits. At the boundary of old age—for example, in ethical dilemmas of life prolongation—quality-of-life issues can no longer be avoided, yet our policy system cannot adequately deal with them. In our present historical position, what is demanded is for a deeper, more critical approach to the policy analysis of quality of life in an aging society. Following Habermas' framework, the task of policy analysis must become

> communicative action within structures of systematically (that is, nonaccidentally) and unnecessarily distorted communications [and] the apparent responsibility would seem to be to work toward the correction of those unnecessary, disabling distortions and to work toward the opening of communications. Examples are the prevention and correction of false promises, the correction of misleading expectations, the elimination of clients' unnecessary dependency, the honest creation of nurturance of hope.[35]

To overcome the legacy of single vision would be to break through the systematically distorted communications and to achieve an alternative vision of human services for an aging society.

SOCIAL INDICATORS AND NONMONETIZED ACTIVITY

"Single vision" has been responsible for the hegemony of professionalized services in the welfare state. We need to ask the question, "Could it be otherwise?" In its original inspiration the Older Americans Act (1965) had a different vision—an aspiration toward drawing multiple community resources to improve the lives of older people. But in the course of time, Older Americans Act agencies gradually adopted a "service strategy" and became professionalized service delivery channels in their own right. Indeed, the prevailing movement in all the human services has led to a magnification of the role of professionals in providing services, with consequent "monetizing" of activities in nutrition, child care, home health care, and so on.

"Monetizing" means cash payments to employees who provide the services. In the monetized world of service delivery, it is only monetized activities that count. The overriding policy issue becomes *who* makes the cash payments—the public or private sector—and where the money will come from. But regardless of what answer we give, the assumption still remains within the restricted circle of monetized expenditures. Transactions not paid for are ignored.

Defined in this way, the problems of aging policy are bounded in a highly artificial fashion. Only certain transactions—monetized expenditures—

are registered. The problem is that nonmonetized activities, whether women working in the home or old people growing vegetables in the garden, simply fall outside the scope of public policy. Whole categories of productive activity are simply not even registered in the GNP. The reality is that there are two basic modes of production: autonomous and heteronomous, but it is only the second kind that public policy recognizes. Autonomous production is what we create for ourselves; heteronomous production is what is generated for monetized exchange.

> We can render a service to someone asking for help, or we can refer him to people who provide those services. In contrast to the heteronomous mode, what is produced by the autonomous mode cannot in general be measured, estimated, compared with, or added to other values. The use values produced autonomously thereby escape the control of economists or national accountants.[36]

Because the use values of autonomous production are not measured, they are not visible and are easily ignored. But ignoring the phenomenon is another error of single vision which results in a complete misstatement of what goes on in the real world. Clearly, groups such as housewives or retired people spend most of their time outside the monetized labor force. Ignoring their nonmonetized productivity severely distorts public policy planning. The same issues arise when we attempt to examine the "unofficial" individual uses of time: learning activities unrelated to credentials or degrees; volunteer roles, and so on. There is no question that such uses of time are important. But all of these "nonmonetized" uses of time appear nowhere on the agenda of public policy.[37]

Recognition of this problem is what led originally to the movement for "social indicators."[38] It was understood that conventional economic indicators, even complemented by cost calculations, did not measure the full impact of social activities. Instead, it was hoped that quantitative social indicators would use techniques of public opinion suvey research to identify those elements of the good life not captured by the conventional economic statistics. In this way, social indicators would be tied to a new measure for quality of life. In a variety of methods, such as technology assessment, environmental impact statements, corporate social accounting, life satisfaction, and indices of urban quality of life we can see the influence of this approach.[39]

It is precisely this kind of methodology that is needed to give support to quality-of-life goals in aging policy. Despite abundant raw data, we lack clear social indicators for measuring culture, leisure, and time use. Although we do not have reliable statistical measures for these activities, we know that their contribution to individual and collective quality of life is enormous.[40] But the limited vision of the policy system becomes a form of systematic blindness to many of our most cherished values of life and the very activities that make life worth living in old age.

There are serious problems presented by any effort to focus policy analysis on nonmonetized contributive roles and personal uses of time by the elderly. Unpaid voluntary action or late-life learning pursuits do not have the same status as such measurable human needs as employment, health care, or housing. The elderly are also involved in private subsistence production and exchange relationships, among them family labor reciprocity, in-kind barter networks, and subsistence production. In the emerging postindustrial economy, this self-service economy is likely to become more important. Yet because the policy debate is monopolized by measurable, monetized transactions, these other contributions tend to remain invisible. Like the growing underground economy in America, these exchanges become part of a vast system of reciprocity providing services outside the cash nexus.

For some groups, such as the rural elderly, these skills and latent strengths are an indispensable part of their economic well-being. For example subsistence vegetable gardening serves to supplement government programs such as welfare or food stamps for the rural elderly poor. For the welfare of the frail elderly, family care-giving has comparable economic value, amounting to perhaps 80% of the total value of home care services in the United States. Other nonmonetized activities extend beyond the economic sphere to include contributive roles in citizenship, political action, religion, volunteerism, child-care, and the arts. But under the single vision of prevailing policy analysis, all these elements are relegated to the invisible domain of private life choices.

An aging policy that ignores invisible, nonmonetized contributions not only ignores latent strengths but also may, from ignorance or neglect, actually worsen the condition of older people: first, by expanding professionalized human services in ways that foster dependency rather than promoting latent strengths; and, second, by shifting costs to create the illusion of efficiency while damaging real quality of life in the process.

What is called for is a policy analysis of the "invisible economy" of old age. Current discussions of aging policy do give some recognition to these issues: for example, in the customary call for more attention to volunteerism or family care-giving. But a much broader perspective is needed here. We need to look beyond conventional volunteerism and natural support systems and consider an entire range of nonmonetized exchanges: bartering of goods and services, such as home repair; mutual-aid and self-help groups, such as widow-to-widow groups; subsistence production and production-for-use, such as home vegetable gardening.

What I have called the invisible economy has an impact on major policy issues. In geriatric health care, the major issue is long-term care and family care giving. Here a critical question is preventive health maintenance and the need for low-technology, low-cost care for chronic illness. The major policy issue for income maintenance is the role of cash income, assets, and in-kind income. Some components are readily monetized, others not. The major policy issue for social supports is coping with loneliness, isolation, and depression. The mental health problems of old age often arise from the lack of social support systems in time of crisis. In all these cases, nonmonetized transactions are of overriding importance in promoting autonomy and well-being. Yet such transactions are likely to be ignored by the prevailing policy framework. They are consigned to an invisible private world inhabited by old age.

VALUE ISSUES IN POSTINDUSTRIAL SOCIETY

With the rise of industrialization, the course of human life became more rigidly segmented into separate stages: youth, adulthood, and old age.[41] In the last stage of life, withdrawal from the public world would be marked by retirement from work. In later life, instead of work and activity in the public world, people were to seek self-realization through hobbies and projects, as well as leisure-time and consumer activities in the private sphere of life.

This segmentation of the stages of life has been ratified by aging policy in the welfare state. The result of this historical expansion of the welfare state has been to channel the activities of later life increasingly into the private sphere. Such "privatizing" of values and meanings has had negative consequences for our collective political life. It has signified a progressive erosion in the quality of life in the public world. The consequences are most visible precisely in areas such as education, culture, communications, and mental health—all fields where values and quality of life play an irreducible role.

Decisions about values or quality of life present great difficulties for policy making. These issues are not amenable to the tools of technological rationality prized by the modern world. The prevailing attitude on value issues tends in the direction of pluralism and laissez-faire: defending the right of private choice on fundamental questions of values, which remain beyond the proper reach of social welfare concerns. Finally, the liberal mind concludes, in Walzer's words, that "with the provision of material needs the state reaches or ought to reach its limits. That is the end of its history, the culmination of its legitimacy. There is no state beyond the welfare state."[42] But this final pessimism and exhaustion of possibilities, Walzer will argue, is itself what must be rejected. Quality-of-life issues somehow must find their place in the public world and in our public policies.

THE PUBLIC WORLD ON A HUMAN SCALE

What is clear enough is that the conventional liberal concept of the welfare state—in particular, the separation of the public and private sphere —has now reached its limit. In Peter Berger's words,

> There is good reason to think that an increasing number of people have become dissatisfied with the classical "solution" of dichotomizing their social experience between the public and private spheres. There are strenuous efforts afoot to modify the institutions of the public sphere so as to make it more responsive to the needs and aspirations that were originally located and, to a point, satisfied in private life.[43]

Berger's own answer to the problem is a revival of an "intermediate" dimension of the public world on a human scale. Walzer too, writing from a democratic socialist perspective, calls for a revival of "secondary associations," such labor unions, professional groups, and other voluntary associations, which exist in tension with the centralized administration of the welfare state. These relatively autonomous groups would in turn have the power to challenge the utilitarian ideology of welfare state policy in the name of values overlooked by the conventional policy process. Walzer, citing Simone Weil, describes these local associations and neighborhood groups as "life-giving nuclei" of work and culture, serving as a bulwark against the dehumanizing tendencies of mass society. This, in essence, is the same problem addressed by Berger in his analysis of "privatism" as a problem of modern life:

One way of describing [the problem] is to say that the private sphere is "underinstitutionalized." This means that the private sphere has a shortage of institutions that firmly and reliably structure human activity. There are, of course, institutions within the private sphere. The most important of these is the family, which still derives legitimation and legal sanction from the state. There are also religious institutions, in whatever stage of privatization. There are voluntary associations, ranging from neighborhood improvement groups to hobby clubs. But none of these is in a position to organize the private sphere as a whole.[44]

What Berger and Neuhaus were later to call "mediating structures" are precisely those secondary associations called for by Walzer. Thus conceived, such "life-giving nuclei" would have a very different function from either competing interest groups in pluralistic democratic theory or centers of countervailing power. Both interest groups and centers of countervailing power serve to channel existing resources according to accepted desires and preferences. They reinforce the assumptions of interest-group liberalism that have dominated aging policy in the welfare state. But this image of interest-group liberalism fails to address either quality-of-life issues or deeper needs for citizen participation beyond the formal patterns of voting behavior.

What is called for in this vision of political life is not simply a new vehicle of decentralization or returning power to the local level—a goal many conservative voices would urge. Decentralization without a qualitative change in the forms of citizen participation cannot change the quality of civic life. The implications for aging policy here would call into question the whole superstructure of the "aging network" created originally during the Nixon Administration as a vehicle for decentralization within the federal system. Decentralization of the status quo accompanied by token representation does nothing to challenge the prevailing order. The generally dismal experience of seeking representation by senior citizens on Area Agency advisory councils simply underscores the point. Tokenism and illusory participation mask continued domination of elites. Without a qualitative change in the forms of citizen participation all such vehicles quickly degenerate into familiar forms of symbolic politics.

What is needed is a new approach to older ideals. Walzer's analysis represents a repudiation of a narrow version of a socialist utopian dream: namely, to seek decentralization *after* the achievement of centralization at the national level. In contrast, Walzer is advocating: (1) promoting the growth of secondary associations as a policy goal; and (2) tangible experiences of self-government right now. Far from being utopian, this approach to social policy grows out of living experience of secondary associations and mediating structures. It represents a feasible alternative to incremental "tinkering" with the welfare state in general and with aging policies in particular.

Empowerment and Quality of Life

It is at this point that Walzer's analysis of the welfare state links up with the practical experience of neighborhood self-help movements. What Walzer called the "politics of insurgency" has shown its power on local issues such as housing, crime prevention, transportation, and other topics of immediate concern to the elderly. Yet left-wing theory has repeatedly failed to see the significance of such local initiatives. Harry Boyte writes:

> Like the market, the dominant left perspective has supposed that the sundering of traditional and historical identities is not only inevitable but essential to the production of "emancipated consciousness." In the mainstream left, to be free means to be uprooted, detached from particularity, the new man or woman of socialist mythology.[45]

Political struggle and the struggle for meaning and quality of life must go together. Movements for citizen empowerment can grow precisely from "life-giving nuclei" identified with traditional values and institutions. This is a point of crucial significance for political struggle and quality of life in old age. For old people, especially the poor and those in minority groups, citizen empowerment must draw upon those traditional values that have contributed to their historical identity and strengths. Those traditional and historical identities are the basis of a new politics of insurgency embodied in the recent fortunes of the "New Citizen Movement":

> The citizen movement largely grows out of those places in modern society which have not been destroyed by the force of contemporary life—families, religious groups, civic traditions, ethnic organizations, neighborhoods, and so forth. And the movement incubates an alternative vision, seeking to preserve people's heritage while it also changes society.

Clearly, such a perspective has vastly different implications for public policy than conventional slogans of "decentralization," "non-service approaches," or "interest-group liberalism." The conventional policy perspective sees old people as simply one more political interest group: as people with needs, rather than people with something to contribute. It fails to see how public policy might capitalize on the special strengths of old people. As a result, the old are cast as a "burden" or as a "favored constituency" or as a "social problem" to be dealt with by professionalized interventions. What is needed instead is a policy to build on strengths and achieve empowerment through traditional institutions that over generations have nurtured historical identities. In this way it is possible to define an alternative moral vision of the welfare state: one which brings together, instead of fragmenting, the public and private worlds of old age.

6

Old Age and the Welfare State

POPULATION AGING AND THE WELFARE STATE

When the American public hears the phrase "welfare state," the most common impression is of food stamps or ghetto mothers receiving family assistance payments. But this impression is wrong. In America, it is the aged who are the prime beneficiaries of the American welfare state.[1] Expenditures for the poor, under all means-tested programs, are dwarfed by the sheer magnitude of federal spending for the elderly: $225 billion for Social Security, $75 billion under Medicare, and federal civilian and military pension obligations, which total more billions extending into the future. All told, about half of all federal domestic spending goes to older Americans.

In the early years of the Reagan Administration, welfare programs for the poor were severely cut back. But middle-class entitlement programs for the elderly, principally Social Security and Medicare, continued to grow. Cuts in aging programs were modest. A comprehensive study by James Storey of the Urban Institute showed that the elderly did better than other groups in facing Reagan Administration cutbacks.[2] On reflection the reasons are not hard to understand. The political strength of older people prevented cuts aimed at them, while the other domestic policies of the Reagan era did not harm and sometimes even favored the elderly. For example, rising unemployment did not affect retired persons, while indexing of Social Security heavily protected beneficiaries from inflation, and high interest rates actually benefited those, such as older people, with greater savings and financial assets.

But the future is less likely to repeat that happy picture. The 1983 Social Security amendments brought the first real reduction in benefits in the history of the program. Medicare cost-containment measures, the Diagnostic Related Groups (DRGs), have curtailed health care benefits and may succeed in cutting costs.[4] The pressure for rising expenditures for an aging population is moving on a collision course with opposing forces that restrict government spending.

This problem is not unique to the United States in the Reagan era.[5] During the fifteen-year period from 1960 to 1975, among the seven OECD nations, expenditures for pensions rose nearly 40% (after inflation). From 1960 to 1981, pensions jumped from 31% to 38% of all nondefense spending, while health care costs increased from 18% to 23%. In the years after the turn of this century, the United States will witness a rapidly aging population. By that time the entire nation will have an aging population structure comparable to what Florida has today. Does this scenario of population aging in the welfare state mean the specter of decline scenario outlined in the opening chapter of this book?[6] Or are there alternative policies for aging in the welfare state?

Aging Policy: The Balance of Success and Problems

Any account of the American welfare state has to begin by acknowledging that, in policies for the aging, we are dealing with an unparalleled success story. To appreciate the point, we only need to compare the results of aging policies with other domains of social policy—for example, programs for the poor or minorities, public education, criminal justice, and so on. Results in these areas are controversial, sometimes discouraging.[7] Critics have argued that the problems have only gotten worse. But that argument cannot be made about aging programs. In the last two decades, spending public money on the elderly population has drastically reduced poverty, improved the health and life expectancy, and, generally, increased the well-being of America's older citizens.

Public opinion frequently gets this story wrong. Ironically, those with opposing ideological agendas find it useful to insist that social policy has failed for one reason or another. Not so with aging policy. On the contrary, programs for the aging can only be declared an astonishing success, and this is good news that needs to be heard more clearly.[8] Instead of destructive disillusionment with government or pessimism about social spending, we need to build on the solid successes of the past.[9]

The signs of success are everywhere. One of the clearest is in the falling poverty rate of the elderly population. In 1960 nearly a third of people over 65 were below the poverty line. By 1983, the number had dropped to under 14%, no different from the average. And the health status of the older population has also improved markedly. In large part because of Medicare, more older people are able to see a doctor on a regular basis. Medicaid has enabled those who need nursing home care to have access to it without bankrupting their children. The programs have worked.

At the same time, the limitations of present social policies have also become painfully clear. First and foremost is the cost of the programs and the inequities in how those burdens are distributed. Increases in health care expenditures are no longer likely to be sustained at the levels of growth in the past. As for aging entitlement programs, it is increasingly clear that the tax burden can no longer be ignored. The financing of Social Security is tied to a regressive payroll tax that hits low-wage earners hardest and transfers wealth across generations, not across social class lines.

A popular conservative view is that massive welfare programs for the poor were instituted by the Great Society, which almost bankrupted the country.[10] But many analysts have shown that this view is simply a mistake, a rewriting of history. Through the 1970s spending in the poverty programs of the Federal budget—AFDC, Food Stamps, Medicaid—did rise modestly. But since 1965—the high-water mark of the Great Society—there has been a *smaller* proportion of public monies going to the poor under need-tested programs than before. The impressive gains of recent years have been made by the aged *nonpoor*, who got the bulk of social spending since the 1960s.[11]

If the decline in aged poverty was a dramatic success, the cause was equally clear. In 1960 only 60% of the aged were covered by Social Security. By 1981, the figure had risen to 92%. Throughout the 1960s and 1970s, Social Security benefit levels were raised by Congress and then, in 1973, were indexed to the consumer price index. During the high inflation of the late 1970s, the elderly, at least under Social Security, were well protected against inflation.

No Developmental Perspective

If programs for the aging have been such an overwhelming success, why are they not perceived that way by the public? Part of the problem lies in

the exaggeration on the part of aging advocates who are reluctant to con-
cede too much success lest that concession be a basis for future budget
cuts. The advocates are not entirely mistaken on that point. The recent
debate over generational equity has introduced the idea that old people,
as a group, are now so affluent that perhaps we should freeze or cut spending for them. There is also a feeling that social spending is essentially
unproductive for society as a whole, that the elderly, as consumers rather
than producers, are a burden on society.

But to lump all social programs under a category called welfare is misleading. Some social spending helps people become more productive, while
other social spending is aimed at helping people in need without regard
for productivity. But the two purposes remain distinct. The broad question for American social policy in the future, and for aging policy in particular, can be phrased in these terms: Will the substantial social spending of the welfare state be used to make older people more productive or
will it remain bound to a view of transfer payments defended by competing interest groups in the name of a redistributive ethic?

The Reagan Administration had its own answer to this question. That
answer is based squarely on a specific view about how to promote productivity and development: namely, by dismantling government programs and
by turning back social problems to private responsibility. If social spending, for the aged or any other group, is unproductive, then to get more
productivity, we should curtail government spending to encourage more
investment. But this view, in its allocation of productivity and consumption to the private and public spheres, ignores the possibility that public
investment in people could have significant impact on their productivity.

For years advocates for the aging have been comfortable in the fact
that the elderly were a favored constituency for public spending. The only
question was how to insure that this constituency would get their share
of public spending. An example can be seen in the rise of a separate service system for the elderly, the so-called aging network, with services
funded under the Older Americans Act since 1973.

In many ways, the aging network has been an extraordinary success.
At the same time, this aging network, from the Administration on Aging
down to local area agencies in cities and counties, has itself become more
and more preoccupied with service delivery while at the same time it also
retains responsibility for coordination, planning, and advocacy—in short,
for broad social policy development. But the two goals do not easily coexist. The result has been a symbolic politics of the aging network where
aging advocates lack the time, the knowledge, or the power to influence

serious issues in work and retirement, health care, or income maintenance. It is not surprising that this system has failed to challenge the historical premises of aging in the welfare state.

THE FAILURE MODEL OF AGING IN THE WELFARE STATE

America was historically late in supporting a spectrum of welfare state
programs, and it was concern for the elderly that prompted the most significant measures in this area.[12] The elderly, like the blind, the disabled,
the orphaned, and the widowed, were regarded as a legitimate object of
public charity. That is, they were seen as a group whose condition of need
arose from causes beyond their control.

The fundamental contradiction of aging policy in the welfare state can
be summed up concisely: spending for the aged is regarded as legitimate
at the same time that government spending in general, indeed government itself, is losing its traditional sources of legitimation. This erosion
of confidence or support for government—the "legitimation crisis"—is a
broad trend across advanced industrialized societies.[13] The accelerating
legitimation crisis, combined with the fiscal crisis of the state, helped bring
about the election of Ronald Reagan in 1980:

> At the end of the 1970s, liberals, independents, and conservatives
> alike were overcome by a pervasive mood of discontent with the
> nation's government. . . . By the dawn of the 1980s, it was widely
> believed that the government had become dangerously oversized;
> that the government's programs had done little to rectify the na-
> tion's problems, particularly considering the programs' vast costs.
> . . .[14]

By 1980, 63 percent of the American public agreed that "government
is run by people who don't know what they're doing": a dramatic increase
from the comparable figure of 27 percent during the early 1960s.[15] Even
among liberals, it became fashionable to be cynical about the effectiveness of any initiative of public policy. In his presidency, Ronald Reagan
continued to picture himself as somehow separate from his own government—an almost monarchical figure who stressed the themes of legitimation crisis he articulated so well.

The Overload on the Welfare State

The legitimation crisis and the fiscal crisis of the state are now intertwined and are expressed in the widely heard feeling that the mature welfare state is becoming ungovernable. Conservative analysts see the decline of allegiance or legitimacy vested in the welfare state as the result of an overload of demands for an ever expanding range of entitlements exceeding the resources of the state.[16] Others see the legitimation crisis as rooted in a profound political transformation of the role of the state itself. Both neoconservative theories of the ungovernability of the state and socialist critiques of late-capitalist social formation diagnose the problem in a similar way.[17]

Crisis theorists see rising expectations linked to an overload of demands on the state. There is a growing burden of obligations that the state can neither fulfill nor repudiate. There lies the contradiction that paralyzes policymaking. As political parties compete for power, they make promises to powerful interest groups, but they cannot fulfill the promises from resources available, as the recent history of aging policy in America makes clear. Over several decades, political leaders responded to the needs of the aged with increasing Social Security and health care until, by the late 1970s, these systems were threatened with insolvency. Promises had outrun the capacity to deliver.

One response to this problem is the decoupling of politics and economic welfare, so that the state is no longer involved in redistribution. The idea is to rechannel claims and expectations away from the public sphere of the state and into the private sphere: either into family life or the private marketplace. But privatizing can mean different things. It may mean greater reliance on the marketplace and monetized solutions, or it may mean use of volunteers and mediating structures such as churches, families, neighborhood groups. A critical question is whether the marketplace element and the voluntarist element can effectively coexist, since they are based on diametrically opposite views of human nature: selfishness versus altruism.

The Vanishing of the Public World

This contradiction between various forms of privatization underscores a more fundamental point. The dilemmas of the welfare state should not be seen in purely economic terms, as if it were chiefly a matter of making the production and exchange of services more efficient. There is a deeper political issue at stake here. The triumph of the welfare state, argues Michael Walzer,[18] involves a demystification of state ideology in favor of selfishness as articulated through organized interest groups, whether called democratic pluralism or interest-group liberalism. What this amounts to is a legitimation of the welfare state just insofar as the state meets demands of key constituency groups in the population.

As the state becomes an instrument for human welfare, the role of the state, and of politics, increasingly becomes that of an administrative agency. This transformation of the state has in turn the consequence that the state no longer commands moral allegiance. The life of politics, of the public world in the broader sense, becomes a specialized occupation of no personal interest except to the political professional or to the media, who convert it into a spectator sport.[19] Redistribution along interest-group lines becomes justified by welfare economics since the welfare state increasingly becomes a vast "public household."

But in this evolution, something crucial has been lost. An older concept of citizenship appears almost nostalgic. The strange passivity engendered by the welfare state has definite consequences for older people and for our image of the quality of life in old age. Old people become, in the private sphere, consumers, or, in the public sphere, an interest group in the public household. Thus, the last stage of life becomes fully removed from the public sphere and remains a period of privatized leisure, lacking either political engagement or social contribution.

Old Age Dependency: The Evolution of a Policy

American public policy in aging, from the Social Security Act (1935) through Medicare (1965) and beyond, started from the premise that the elderly were a needy population. Need was the basis on which special attention to the elderly was legitimated. The policy goal for the aged was never understood as the development of the capacities of old people.

By contrast, human development programs were targeted at youth. Youth was seen as a time of development, old age as a time of decline. Old age was a period when the welfare state would meet residual needs. The separation between productivity and need was reinforced as the social service system provided segregated services to groups on the basis of age. Thus, we had vocational education for youth, senior centers for the aged. Income maintenance programs, such as unemployment insurance or public pensions, were strictly separated from economic development programs such as job training.

This separation between need and contribution, and between youth and age, has had far-reaching consequences. Increasingly, during the 1970s, age-based entitlements and age-segregated services became the basis for service delivery. A far-flung aging network grew up to provide such services, and in turn, that network supported an ideology of old age consistent with the service strategy that evolved. Discrete categorical programs —such as Medicare or Meals-on-Wheels—were based on meeting needs, not on developing capacities for self-sufficiency or self-help. And so the image of the elderly as incapable of development or productivity was further reinforced by aging advocates themselves. The result has been that today, at a time when budgets for social spending are threatened, a pro-development aging policy is not really taken seriously as a practical alternative. Instead, we can only debate how to reallocate scarcity.

Manpower Development Policies

Another policy alternative was, however, possible and still remains possible. Lessons for aging policy can be drawn from both the successes and frustrations of manpower development policies. The social programs of the 1960s spawned a variety of responses to the problem of poverty in America, including those that could genuinely be described as human development policies. These were policies designed not only to provide adequate income or benefits to needy groups but also to enhance skills in order to enable poor persons to achieve independence and self-sufficiency. These human development policies, such as Head Start or the Job Corps, could be properly seen, not as transfer programs, but as investments in human capital formation.

The latter type of human development programs included the Manpower Development and Training Act (MDTA) of 1962 and its successor the Comprehensive Employment and Training Act (CETA) of 1973.[14] But in order to sell the CETA program to legislators, it was necessary to show that a satisfactory proportion of participants would go on to become wage earners in the private sector and thus repay the public investment in human capital.

Whatever drawbacks this approach had for other unemployed groups, for older workers the criteria for evaluating success were seriously flawed. If older workers, because of disability, age discrimination, or other barriers, were unlikely to get jobs in the private sector, then it made no sense to train them in the first place. This mismatch between manpower training programs and the aged in fact originally led to Title V of the Older Americans Act, which provides for community service employment at a minimal wage. The vast majority of these older persons under Title V are employed in useful jobs in public service employment, as of course, were many of the old CETA participants. Yet during the 1970s manpower development policies progressively lost ground to income maintenance and in-kind benefit programs.

For the elderly, income transfer programs became the primary means of lifting old people out of poverty. The programs succeeded, but they brought with them a specter of uncontrollable entitlements targeted at a dependent, unproductive segment of the population. Unfortunately, in the public mind, other manpower development programs, such as CETA, were too quickly identified as failures, and thus any basis of support for human development policies that might be extended for an aging population was eroded. Under the Reagan cuts, entitlement programs and transfer programs for the aged remained, but manpower programs were tagged as failures and were severely cut. The criteria for success and failure remained narrowly tied to single vision and monetized productivity, measured by wages and salaries in the private marketplace. While Title V escaped the fate of CETA under Reagan and managed to survive, the rejection of the promising human development policies for all age-groups became enshrined in a new conventional wisdom that turned away from the ideals of the Great Society.

Need for a Prodevelopment Aging Policy

Policy debates today are dominated by a single vision that overlooks *both* human development and quality-of-life concerns. While liberals worry about fairness in allocating resources, conservatives worry about the cost of human services. It is redistribution, not productivity, that sets the agenda for both. The two sides of the political debate are mirror images of one another. Economic pressures for cost containment and the momentum of spending for entitlement programs clash directly in programs for the aging. One side wants to cut away at public provision; the other side doggedly protects the status quo. But a genuine policy alternative—a prodevelopment policy—is missing from the debate.

This contrast between a needs-based and a development-based policy perspective is not unique to old-age policy. One of the most difficult problems faced by social policy in the welfare state is how to provide social services for dependent groups while also preserving incentives for personal initiative. Opponents of the welfare state have always feared that, without the spur of marketplace incentives, government-supported social services simply promote dependency and fail to encourage development of capacities. Conservatives favor old-time virtues of personal responsibility and see development strictly in marketplace terms. If you want people to develop new job skills, keep unemployment benefits low. If you want them to be better educated, enforce tough competitive grading standards. These examples reflect a common assumption that marketplace incentives and competition are the most reliable key to motivation.

Motivation, Capacity, Opportunity

How does the prodevelopment position apply to policies for the elderly? Obviously, development will require a degree of motivation, a capacity for growth and opportunities to build skills and capacities in practice. To get results from a prodevelopment policy, we need to assume not just motivation on the part of a dependent group but also capacity and opportunity for that group.[15]

It is just at this point that a problem arises. Single vision measures incentives and results entirely in marketplace terms. The best example of the difficulty is to be seen in current discussions on how to avert a coming financial crisis in Medicare. Conservatives put forward proposals for higher co-payments under Medicare or full-scale health care voucher plans, on the assumption that marketplace incentives will reduce excess utilization of health care services. In the short term, incentives may do that. But they are likely to have other, longer term effects such as allowing diseases to go undetected and untreated. The net result of such alleged savings could be higher rates of illness and death. And, from one point of view, this result could be counted a success for cost containment. For example, failure to give prompt attention to an elderly person who suffers a stroke can lead to deterioration, loss of potential for rehabilitation, and death. How do we count premature death in the cost-benefit calculus?

Similar problems arise when we turn from the calculus of benefits to qualitative issues of autonomy. During the period of expansion of the welfare state in American—from the New Deal through the 1970s—liberal social thought gave little attention to concepts of autonomy or development in late life. The dominant image of old-age dependency bolstered the role of professionals who would protect the aged from the destructive forces of modern society. But this benevolent paternalism toward old people had a more sinister side to it. The structure of services for older people involved progressive dependency and loss of personal autonomy or responsibility. The health care system is a case in point. Services provided by professionals are reimbursed, but health education or preventive care are not. In long-term care, government subsidies encourage nursing home admissions but not home care or other interventions that would allow older people to develop capacities for self-care. In medical or social service settings, old people who needed help have been forced to accept conditions that contribute to loss of control and low self-esteem.

This design of services has been built upon the failure model of aging. But new research on cognitive development over the lifespan has challenged the failure model and poses major implications for social policy in an aging society.[16] First, it demonstrates the overwhelmingly destructive power of labels: for example, the labels of dependency required by the bureaucratic or scientific descriptions of aging as decline. The authority of these professional, bureaucratic, or scientific labels is often internalized, becoming a self-fulfilling prophecy.[17] Second, it establishes the continuing importance of personal responsibility and personal control over the environment as critical variables for motivation, self-esteem, and quality of life.[18]

The thrust of recent psychological research on aging and human development calls into question the social policies that were designed on different assumptions.[19] There is strong evidence that care-giving is more effective when individuals have a measure of control over their own environment and over their transactions with professionals. Failing to provide opportunities for self-efficacy is likely to result in excess dependency, which in turn will entail very tangible, and expensive, consequencies: for instance, atrophy of muscles and loss of mobility when an aged client is not quickly returned to a situation where walking is appropriate.[20] This new line of research suggests that we take more seriously the role of indigenous institutions such as self-help groups, institutions that strike a better balance between help from others and personal responsibility for one's own situation.

Empowerment and Self-help

In precisely the period when welfare state expenditures reached their peak in the United States, the 1970s, we also witnessed an explosive proliferation of self-help groups consisting of individuals spontaneously organized to help one another face common problems by mutual aid. What is interesting about the rise of self-help groups in recent years is that self-help offers a way out of the dilemma of conflicting values in the welfare state. Mutual self-help activities offer a way of potentially reducing costs associated with expansion of expensive and sometimes unnecessary professionalized services.

At the same time, self-help also offers a way to recapture some of the cherished values of liberty and self-determination that are threatened by the power of the welfare state. Instead of the specter of decline and dependency, the self-help alternative would promote autonomy. Whether such a self-help strategy in aging policy is actually feasible will be explored in more detail in a later chapter in this book. For the present it is enough to see how the value-laden ethos of the self-help movement—often cherished by both liberals and conservatives—offers an alternative to the erosion of values and meaning so often associated with the expansion of the welfare state.

Autonomous Production in the Welfare State

The need for a new and positive image of lifelong human development, including a productive old age, appears at a moment in history when several different crisis tendencies are occurring simultaneously throughout the advanced industrialized societies. During the late twentieth century the transition to an aging population coincides with a movement toward a postindustrial economy. In social welfare policy an ongoing fiscal crisis and legitimation crisis of the state means that the traditional liberal policies for social provision confront contradictions that demand resolution.

It is this convergence of all three trends—welfare state crisis, postindustrial economy, and population aging—that may prove to be the key to a solution. The crisis tendencies in the welfare state provide the negative stimulus, while the postindustrial economy offers new opportunities for lifespan productivity.

But an ideal of positive growth over the entire lifespan remains utopian unless it is linked to a policy agenda for concrete human services as well. Without that linkage, we are left with vague appeals to lifelong learning, more productive use of leisure time, or private sector initiatives. An equally fundamental task will be to tie social welfare policies to policies that promote productivity and economic growth in an aging population.

This central point—the concept of economic growth—in recent years has proven the weak spot in the liberal ideology of the welfare state. Liberals have put redistribution ahead of productivity or economic growth. It is just this liberal dogma of redistribution versus productivity that must be challenged. But alternative policy options must go beyond the economic plane itself. The challenge must also include an attack on the way that productivity has been measured in the past. What is called for is a more inclusive definition of productivity that goes beyond exclusive attention to monetized values of industrial production:

> Socialized distribution of production, according to need rather than effective demand, was for a long time one of the central demands of the Left. This is now becoming ever less the case. In itself, it can only lead to the state taking greater charge of individual lives. The right to a "social income" . . . replaces or complements, as the case may be, exploitation with welfare, while perpetuating the dependence, impotence and subordination of individuals to centralized authority. This subordination will be overcome only if the autonomous production of use-values becomes a real possibility for everyone.[21]

What Gorz describes as the "autonomous production of use-values" is not a utopian idea but is already being fulfilled in productive activities of the nonmonetized economy such as home vegetable gardening, home repair, barter, and exchange of services. Within the postindustrial society we can also find the autonomous production of use values—for example, in mutual-aid activities of the self-help movement.[22] Self-help represents autonomous production of use values in a tangible and practical fashion. For this reason, self-help activities exist in tension with the professional monopolies of the welfare state, whether those monopolies are controlled by commercial enterprises or human service professionals in the nonprofit sector. The autonomy represented by self-help is incompatible with the commodity values represented by the welfare state itself.

> The right to autonomous production presupposes the right of access to tools and their conviviality. It is incompatible with private or public industrial, commercial or professional monopolies. It implies a contraction of commodity production and sale of labour power, and a concomitant extension of autonomous production based on voluntary cooperation, the exchange of services or personal activity.[23]

Crisis tendencies within the advanced welfare states provide a negative stimulus for self-help and autonomous production. For example, in Northern Europe, state social spending is approaching 50% of the government budget, yet people remain dissatisfied with the quality of bureaucratized services. The welfare state is straining under the overload of demands by clients and interest groups competing for services. Foremost among these client groups are the aged, whose numbers, and expense, are growing. As long as conventional assumptions remain unchallenged, a burgeoning aged population must appear as a burden. The only question will be how to allocate the scarcities.

The entire argument of this book is based on challenging those convential assumptions and therefore breaking out of the pessimism about the future of an aging society. The allocation-of-scarcity scenario is not a solution to the problems we face.

POLITICAL CHOICES

It is one thing to call for new directions in public policy. It is quite another to assess the political conditions that determine whether any policy options are enacted. Dangers are associated with prodevelopment policies in the current political climate. Self-help and self-sufficiency easily become slogans justifying cost-cutting and planned shrinkage of social services. Since conservatives have adopted the language of personal responsibility and productivity, liberals are left defending redistribution and the historical achievements of the welfare state. When self-help or volunteerism become code words for cutting government benefits, then social welfare advocates begin to distrust these concepts altogether. We need to avoid the ideological trap of seeing aging servics as caught between false alternatives.

Liberal Dilemmas

Historically, twentieth-century liberal ideology has been allied with values of secularism, individual rights, self-determination, and expanded job opportunities. The liberal sees progress as the enlargement of self-fulfillment through job opportunities, legal rights, and liberation from traditional community institutions. The engine of progress has been government, especially the federal government, through public entitlements.

The problem here is that, increasingly, liberalism itself is under attack from two directions. First, there is the fiscal crisis. Beginning with the economic crisis of the industrialized world in the 1970s, the traditional liberal agenda was stalled and, with the Reagan era, received a further setback. But traditional liberal goals, for older people as for other groups, remain legitimate and necessary at the same time that they seem less and less historically feasible. Expansion of public home health care, job opportunities for older workers, expansion of income support programs for the poor—all these goals seem to outpace government resources and public support.

In addition to means, there is also the qualitative problem of ends and purposes, the question of quality of life. Is it possible that the traditional liberal agenda—work, secularism, individualism—is itself inadequate as a definition for a good age? Problems of meaning and autonomy are not simply resolved by public spending or government programs. There needs to be greater attention to competing values—of family, religion, leisure time, and self-development. And this in turn means that securing quality of life in old age will require different public policies from those that traditional liberalism has offered.

The crisis of old-age policies, then, is a crisis of both means and ends, resources and purposes. Liberals can no longer maintain the hope that more of the same in policy initiatives will do the job.

CONCLUSION:
A "SOFT PATH" FOR AGING POLICY

Before concluding this chapter on aging and the welfare state, it seems appropriate to offer a positive image of what the future may hold. The basis for this scenario is taken from geriatric health care policy. But similar scenarios could be constructed for areas such as work and retirement, education, and social services.

Lessons of the Energy Crisis

During the late, great energy crisis of the 1970s, Amory Lovins proposed a distinction between what he called the "hard path" and the "soft path" to energy policy.[24] The hard path was based on centralized, high technology, while the soft path was based on what Schumacher called "appropriate technology." The hard path meant reliance on large-scale, centralized methods of energy production that depended in turn on ever higher consumption of fossil fuels. But this dependence resulted in short-ages, rising costs, and threats of environmental pollution. Efforts to cope with fossil fuel limits by nuclear energy—a classic instance of govern-ment-subsidized, large-scale intervention—led to still higher, often in-visible costs, not to mention the more familiar problems of safety and environmental danger.

Looking back over the past generation, it was clear that the hard path on energy policy had become the conventional basis for economic growth for both government and private industry. Conventional wisdom took the continued existence of the hard path for granted. Then came the energy crisis and the conventional wisdom was turned upside down. When fore-casters extrapolated into the future, they saw a grim specter of decline scenario, depicted, for example, in books such as *The Limits of Growth* of Heilbroner's *Inquiry Concerning the Human Prospect.*

But another alternative was available: the so-called soft path. The soft path would avoid the energy addiction patterns of the past. Instead of centralized, heavily capitalized dependence on fossil fuels or nuclear en-ergy, the soft path would shift toward renewable energy resources: solar, wind, or geothermal power. Instead of focusing on producing more petro-leum or electric power, we would shift attention to conservation. The aim would be balanced economic growth—not halting growth altogether but also not lurching from crisis to crisis or searching for a high-tech quick fix to somehow save the day. The soft path was to be based on living within limits.

An economy built around the soft path would have lower costs, be more stable, and be more flexible because of appropriate technology used on a local scale. Instead of a risky, crisis-prone system (e.g., nuclear power plants, OPEC oil), we would increasingly rely on bottom-up decisions about trade-offs between quality of life and efficiency.

"Two Roads Diverged"

The energy crisis has come and gone. But important lessons can be learned from that crisis, and those lessons have direct relevance to aging policy in the welfare state. Virtually all the principles of the soft path can be applied to health policy for an aging society.

In table 6.1, I have summarized what I describe as the hard path and the soft path toward aging policy in the future.

The hard path in aging health policy concentrates on increasing the supply of scarce, expensive high-technology services that foster ever greater dependency. The soft path—hospice, home health care, self-care, mutual aid groups—would have lower costs, be more stable, and be more flexible in its use of biotechnology for chronic illnesses. Instead of large centralized institutions, whether nursing homes or hospitals, we would opt for a decentralized system: for example, using geriatric nurse practioners, promoting health education, or providing more support for informal care-giving. Instead of a crisis-prone Medicare system now threatened by rationing or triage, we would move toward decisions based on quality of life and autonomy. We need not abolish Medicare any more than the soft path in energy policy would do away with electrical generating plants. But a new system would grow up alongside the old and would offer hope for the future.

Just as the experience of limits required rethinking energy policy, so the same will be true for aging policy. We need to fashion new ways to think about growth in a world of limits. The hard path, whether in energy policy or aging policy, leads to crisis scenarios: boom or bust growth curves, profligate spending followed by imposition of cost controls.

TABLE 6.1 TWO PATHS TOWARD AGING POLICY

Hard Path	Soft Path
Aged as dependent (the failure model)	Autonomy/self-help
Disease-responsive	Health promotion
Acute care/heroic measures (curing)	Chronic care/preventive measures (caring and coping)
Life prolongation (intensive-care units)	Quality of life (self-determined death)
High technology (surgery, prosthetics)	Appropriate technology (diet, exercise)
Centralized-monetized services	Nonmonetized services (mutual aid)
Medical-industrial complex (reimbursement controlled)	Holistic/alternative care (individually controlled)
Crisis approach to policy issues (Medicare)	Incremental bottom-up approach to social policy (hospice programs, respite programs)

But an alternative is not impossible. Over the last decade demonstrable movement toward the soft path in U.S. energy behavior has taken place. There is no reason to believe that a soft path in aging policy could not come into place in the future.

I am not eager to present the soft path as one without problems of its own. One of the most serious is that, under the soft path, the scope for innovation lies exclusively in the hands of individuals. It is a model for self-reliance and privatism, for individual problem-solving rather than for social policy planning. Yet, along with individual responsibility, we will need a broader sense of social solidarity and public provision. To make the soft path actually feasible for large numbers of older people, we would have to make substantial social investment—for example, in health education and health promotion—which is not happening today.

Nonetheless, there are forces at work that are moving society gradually toward the soft path. These forces include pressures for cost containment in health care spending, the widespread appeal of self-help, popularity of holistic and alternative health approaches, and the continuing vitality of cultural values of autonomy and self-determination. Concrete policy initiatives to promote the soft path are explored in the second half of this book.

7

Ideology and the Politics of Aging

"Illusions that are afforded the power of common convictions are what we name *ideologies.*"

—Jurgen Habermas,
"On the Concept of Power"

I have argued that public policy on aging in America is dominated by a single vision that contributes to policy paralysis. It is now time to examine the ideology of old age in more detail. In using the term *ideology*, I am deliberately taking up a position quite different from how gerontology has viewed the wide acceptance of falsely held images about old age.[1] The prevalence of falsely held images about old age is beyond dispute. Americans in general, and old people themselves too, hold a dismal and inaccurate picture of what aging in America is like.[2] Why do these stereotypes and myths persist?[3] What motivates their persistence and whose interest do they serve?

I argue that these images are not lamentable mistakes or fears easily correctable by public education. Rather, such distortions express a dominant ideology of old age that itself contributes to the problem of aging in America. Further, those who work as advocates on behalf of the aging are themselves affected by distortions of perspective.[4] This ideological factor, in the framework of interest-group liberalism, compromises those who advocate for the aging in ways that maintain the distortions and perpetuate false consciousness.

Even the enterprise of academic gerontology is not free from distortions. What presents itself as an impartial academic inquiry is often very far from that. The academic discipline of gerontology is distorted by a failure to examine competing paradigms that might lead to very different directions for theory and practice.[5] Those distortions seriously compromise the effectiveness of advocacy, of scientific research, and of public policy.

The most insidious element of the current ideology of old age is that it is not recognized as such. Because the condition of old age is typically not a matter of ideological controversy in America, ideological distortions go unchallenged and unrecognized. When distortions are systemic and fundamental in this way, we fail to recognize their source and fail to understand the relation between ideology and interest, since the ideological dimension is disguised:

> Today our ideologies are disguised. Their language has changed. The utopian element has disappeared. One might say that our own society holds some vague beliefs in democratic progress through the application of science to human affairs and that in recent times this belief has come to include social science. . . . Not only does this application fall within our definition of ideology, but, as applied to collectivities, it is increasingly political.[6]

Social gerontology has always understood itself to be an application of science for the improvement of the condition of the aged. Few people have questioned or challenged the desirability of that commitment. After all, who could be against helping the elderly? Scientific research, like benevolent social action, includes elements of self-interest and ideology. Habermas has argued that, more generally, science and technology themselves embody structures of ideology that disguise human interests.[7] The relationships between science and values, between interest and ideology, have rarely been made explicit in gerontology.

A FRAMEWORK FOR IDEOLOGY AND SOCIAL CHANGE

A framework for the examination of ideology in social change can be derived from Marx.[8] In its classical form the Marxist critique of ideology explains changes in ideology as a means of containing those contradictions that threaten to overwhelm social stability.

The classical pattern is illustrated in the history of the Industrial Revolution. Factory owners and wage earners had contradictory interests. At times, ideological constructions of social reality might offer a pessimistic image: for example, the Malthusian doctrine on population or the ideology of Social Darwinism. Pessimism implied that efforts to change the situation were hopeless. These pessimistic images had the effect of reinforcing the power of existing institutions or legitimating new forms of control. At the same time, there could be optimistic constructions of social reality: for example, the belief in progress through technology. In short, *both* the positive and the negative ideological images served the purpose of restricting challenges to the dominant interest groups. The pessimistic Malthusian image discouraged efforts at improving the lives of poor people, while the positive technological image of progress gave reassurance that things would be better in the future.

The ideology of old age today also contains a dialectic with both positive and a negative images. One image of old age portrays the elderly as dependent and deserving of social services. Another image of old age portrays the elderly as healthier, living longer, and leading active, happy lives. There are groups of old people who match either set of descriptions, but the two descriptions together are evidently in opposition. Like nineteenth-century industrial society, we have a contradictory image of the social change we are undergoing. Both pessimism and optimism can serve an ideological function in suppressing contradictions in the social system.

THE OVERT IDEOLOGY

Overt Ideology: Theory

One face of the overt ideology of old age is the picture of aging in America produced by social science and social gerontology. This ideal of value-free social science is based on a systematic separation between facts and values, a view that denies the role of human interests except as those interests seek to *apply* knowledge already validated on its own internal criteria. Social science, presented in the guise of experts or scientific expertise, plays a central role in legitimating actions by policymakers and in setting the terms for public debate.

But the structure of value-free social science also contains a hidden ideological dimension that supports the status quo in aging policy. In the behavioral sciences, for example, prestige and rewards go to investigators who make the greatest use of quantitative methods: statistics, survey research, econometric data, and so on. But quantitative measurement favors investigation of only those activities already predefined by the larger policy system. For example, we have ample statistics on enrollment of older people in higher educational institutions but none on self-initiated learning activities. We have quantitative data on labor market participation and earnings by people over 65 but virtually nothing on self-help groups.

In other words, it quickly becomes clear that the preference for quantitative measurement in the behavioral sciences is not merely a methodologically neutral or value-free style of research. Dominant measurement approaches were developed for younger age-groups and overstate the deficits of old age, while ignoring latent strengths or gains. Quality of life in old age is ignored because single vision ignores what it does not see. What results is a style of empirical knowledge that overlooks value issues while it implicitly gives support to what is measurable in the status quo for health care, income maintenance, and social services.

This hegemony is exercised by mechanisms of ideological control that are all the more insidious because they are never made explicit. A brief survey of leading journals in gerontology leaves no doubt that the prevailing ideology is a brand of liberal interventionism that supports a professionalized service strategy within the welfare state. It is rare to find either politically radical or politically conservative styles in gerontological research or policy analysis. Neither style is acceptable since both appear to involve value commitments and both call into question the historical development of welfare state institutions. Hence, the prevailing ideology of old age continues unchallenged by the one intellectual group, that of academic gerontology, which has in its power the capacity to call assumptions into question.

Overt Ideology: Practice

A comparable overt ideology can be found among practitioners, including both professionals and policymakers. Practitioners are committed to action and pragmatic incremental changes that take for granted the legitimacy of the existing system. At the policy level, the practitioner has recourse to legitimation by means of data drawn from the social sciences, where the precision of instrumental reason gives credibility to decisions reached on other grounds.

At the level of professional action, the ideology takes different forms. On a day-to-day level, the ideology amounts to little more than working within the aging service system. At higher management levels, the aging network today spends effort on planning, analyzing, and reporting on the operation of the service delivery system. The very debased language of service delivery reflects a world of uncritical practice standing over against a world of abstract theory. In fact, practitioners of all kinds tend to feel unrespected by academicians and theorists. Yet, ironically, at professional meetings, the same practitioners end up aping a bloodless academic language that mystifies the political forces that dominate their practical lives. By speaking a language so remote from their own experience, they end up deprived of any voice to articulate the contradictions felt in practice.

The result is a depersonalization, and the experience of old age itself begins to vanish from sight. The forms of planning, policy analysis, and professional legitimation in aging services take on the same language as any other domain of human services. The language seems to have nothing to do with the process of growing old or with the situation of old people. On the contrary, in both theory and practice of the overt ideology, any personal relationship to the subject of aging is suppressed.

These two branches of the overt ideology—theory and practice—are constantly at war with each other. Both feel the other misunderstands them. In some national professional groups, such as the Gerontological Society of America, academicians gain the upper hand, while in others, such as the National Council on the Aging, practitioners prevail. Practitioners feel that academics do not give them the knowledge useful for action. On the other side, academics move at a level remote from the daily experience of old people. The contradiction between theory and practice remains unresolved and unacknowledged. The result is that the sources of contradiction within the overt ideology are never made explicit and never become the subject of rational reflection or criticism. Instead, the contradictions of the overt ideology prevent the emergence of any intelligible concept of praxis and equally block any socially meaningful concept of development over the lifespan.

THE COVERT IDEOLOGY

The covert ideology of old age also contains contradictions of its own. Nelson summarizes the prevailing ideology during the historical period between the enactment of the Social Security Act (1935) to the establishment of Medicare and the Older Americans Act (1965). During this period, he writes:

We can clearly discern an overall impression that old age is a time of economic dependency, physical and intellectual decline, and personal isolation. These images, presented sympathetically and presumed to be rooted in the very nature of things, provided a generation of advocates for older citizens with the primary rationale for the programs and policies they championed.[9]

This failure model continued its hold on the public mind throughout the 1970s.[10] The Harris Polls of 1974 and 1981 confirm that the same negative image of old age was shared by the public at large, including persons over sixty-five.[11] While older people themselves shared the generally negative appraisal of the elderly, they regarded themselves as an exception to the rule, in the same way that families who care for their frail elderly relatives regard themselves as exceptions to what everyone assumes to be widespread abandonment of the elderly in American society.

At the same time that aging advocates have been promulgating a negative image of the weak and dependent elderly, at least one group of older people themselves—the Gray Panthers—have sought to promote a normalized view of "older people as energetic, capable, assertive, sexually active, and powerful."[12] The Gray Panthers' positive imagery, taken up by some aging advocates, embraces a wider cultural and societal critique. The Gray Panthers charge that it is ageism, not inevitable nature, that has brought about the negative facts of old age in America. Hence, along with the cultural critique goes a hopeful attitude toward old age: aging—like poverty, pollution, or mental illness—is produced by social conditions and those conditions can and should be altered.

We recognize here the outlines of a familiar vein of social criticism that identifies problems as socially caused and therefore curable. In its broad tradition, this view can be characterized as environmental meliorism: an optimistic doctrine of progress. Social action, even government intervention, is justified on the optimistic ground that social problems can after all be solved.

The Strategy of Normalization

A fatalistic view of old age, it is clear, is utterly opposed to any kind of environmental meliorism that optimistically sees the old as, potentially, normal, just like everyone else. The progressive stance of meliorism is committed both to normalization as a standard of justice and to a cultural critique that would make normalization possible. The covert ideology wants to remind us that old age is a terrible social problem. But it also wants to insist that aging one day might no longer be a social problem if only we committed resources to normalizing the condition of old age: an optimistic stance.

When asked once what was the purpose of life, Sigmund Freud answered "Lieben und Arbeit"—to love and to work. The normalization of old age means, above all, that this formula must apply to the elderly as well. From that prescription follows a set of normative proposals, such as an end to mandatory retirement or the promotion of an age-irrelevant society, which in turn have become part of the platform for the new liberation of old age. The positive strand of this covert ideology culminates in a middle-class ethic of lifelong activism: lifelong learning, second careers, sex after sixty, and other upbeat slogans. This ethic of activism involves a deep denial of that biological fatalism so central to an earlier image of old age.

The Contradictions of the Covert Ideology

The covert ideology of old age includes two images of old age—a positive one and a negative one—that contradict each other. The aging advocacy movement, in Nelson's terms,

> encompasses a range of programs and policies, which . . . rest on fundamentally incompatible definitions of what being old means. These contradictory assertions simultaneously characterize old people as: dependent—independent; appropriately retired—inappropriately excluded from work; isolated—involved; frail—vital; impoverished—affluent; deserving of special status—subject to arbitrary discrimination; ill—well.[13]

The contradictions of the covert ideology of old age are visible in the mass media, in advertising, in the legal system, in social policy, and finally, almost everywhere in our culture.

The contradictions are never made conscious. For public policy, the consequence is that we have an aging policy that embraces the "two worlds of aging." Our aging policies are legitimated by appeals to a negative image of old people as victims. Yet the policies are constructed in such a way that the most needy elderly do not benefit as much as the well-off elderly. The most important point is that these contradictions are apparent in the public *uses* of the covert ideology by advocates on behalf of the elderly and, even more deeply, in the way that ideology acts to inhibit "impermissible" debate among those who advocate on behalf of the elderly. Perpetuating a false consciousness of old age perpetuates the status quo in the welfare state, in industrial policy, and in our approach to education, leisure, and the uses of time. In short, the covert ideology is of fundamental importance in restricting our vision of what old age is or might be.

Among advocates for the aging the contradictions of the covert ideology are embodied in a critique of "age-ism." The term was coined by Robert Butler[14] based on the analogy that discrimination against older people is comparable to injustice against a minority group. This ideological agenda provides solidarity and unity among interest groups who otherwise have divergent interests. Among all aging interest-group organizations the anti-ageist ideology has been adopted alongside the traditional liberal view of aging as a social problem. The aged, like minorities, women, etc., are to be seen as a vulnerable group, thus obscuring differences, particularly class differences, among the elderly themselves.

Leadership and Legitimacy

A deeper function of the campaign against ageism is to be found in internal ideological needs of aging interest groups: in the relation between leaders and the membership of those groups, such as AARP or NCOA. The professional leaders of the aging groups are all young or middle-aged. But they must legitimate that leadership role toward elderly constituents for whom they pretend to speak. The position is inherently contradictory. Could we imagine a Women's Liberation Movement led by men or a black movement led entirely by whites?

In the 1930s, old age movements—the Townsend Movement is the best example—were in fact initiated and led by elderly people themselves.[15] In these groups the legitimation of leadership was not an issue. But today old age politics and advocacy have moved toward "professionalization of reform." We find a professionalized leadership group, generally young or middle-aged, sometimes with old people playing symbolic roles on a board of directors.

There is a profound split in the psychology of advocates for the aging. Young or middle-aged leaders of aging advocacy organizations will always be on a precarious psychological footing in legitimating their leadership.

Just as a traditional Marxist was embarrassed to be "outflanked to the left," so aging advocates cannot afford to be outflanked in their opposition to ageism in all its forms. Aging advocates must be true believers at pain of questioning their own legitimacy as leaders of people old enough to be their own parents.

Clifford Geertz has emphasized the complex character of ideological systems, above all, their ability to incorporate contradictory motives.[16] Geertz observes that there are two main approaches to ideology: the interest theory and the strain theory. For interest theory, "ideology is a mask and a weapon," for the strain theory, "a symptom and a remedy." The interest theory explains the role of ideology in political tactics; the strain theory points to self-delusion and the dynamics of group solidarity in political movements. By "solidarity" here we mean the power of an ideology to knit a social group together, to give it a sense of morale.[17]

In the politics of old age, we can expect to find ideology serving both functions. Some ideological discourse acts as a weapon for gaining advantage in political struggle with competing interest groups. But other expressions of ideological thinking—such as the struggle by aging advocates against mandatory retirement—are best understood, not merely as tactics in a war of ideas, but also as expressions of deep longings, symbolic aspirations for group solidarity.

HISTORY OF THE AGING INTEREST GROUPS

The ideology of old age came into being in conjunction with a complex historical evolution of interest-group politics. By the middle of the twentieth century, the early outlines of a professional aging industry began to take shape in the United States. Like any industry, this "Aging Enterprise," as Carroll Estes would call it, developed an ideology that serves as a rational justification for interest-group concerns. Yet unlike most other groups contending for public support, the needs of the aging have been relatively uncontroversial.

For any group to achieve dramatic gains—as the elderly have—while still retaining a sympathetic image and rationale for public support is testimony to the power of a remarkable ideological achievement. How was this achievement made possible? A crucial role was played by media, by legislators, and by professionals—all of whom were pivotal in shaping a policy framework that became supported by the new ideology of old age. The three groups were joined in an "Iron Triangle" that reinforced public images of old age demanding public sympathy: the negative strand in the covert ideology. Each group—media, legislators, and human service professions—could see itself acting for beneficent motives. Each group also stood to gain by enlarged public attention to "the aging problem."

At the same time, professional, scientific, and academic researchers gave support to an overt ideology—the claim of value-free scientific knowledge—that would reinforce the failure model of aging and legitimate the intervention of professionals and experts. The dominance of the professional arose from the very definition of aging itself. The aging process was seen as a disease, and with the adoption of medical metaphors of senescence, the seeds of the "structured dependency of old age" were already laid down. At the same time, a rationale was at hand to remove the elderly as a group from the mainstream of society—for example, through pensions and mandatory retirement, thus creating objective social conditions that would parallel the ideological rationale that was taking shape.[18]

Origins of the Gray Lobby

Over time the aging interest groups achieved a measure of influence resulting in what Pratt has called the "Gray Lobby."[19] Predecessors of the Gray Lobby had been visible as early as the 1920s, and a few groups reached the proportions of a social movement during the Depression. From a historical point of view, the rise of a potent Gray Lobby was something of an anomaly. The only previous time when old age politics had actually reached the scale of mass political mobilization occurred during the 1930s with the Townsend Movement. But by 1940, the Movement was on the decline. Throughout the 1940s and 1950s, old age politics lacked either a mass base or an effective organizational structure. In the early 1950s the National Council on Aging (NCOA) had been established and the American Association of Retired Persons (AARP) began its process of growth.

By the 1960s the picture had changed. A new ideological climate encouraged claims of social justice on behalf of the aged. Groups like NCOA and AARP took up the cause. Meanwhile, for the first time since the 1930s, major federal policy initiatives in aging took place. The result would be a vast expansion in entitlements and services provided for this new constituency group, America's elderly. The pattern of successful advocacy was shown by other disadvantaged groups, above all by the civil rights movement. Using the same broad strategy, aging interest groups cast the elderly in the image of a minority group suffering from disadvantages. This strategy and rhetoric worked, as Achenbaum noted:

> The elderly 'fit' into the Great Society mold. The 'problem' of old age was perceived as a legitimate 'welfare' issue. . . . By presenting their case in politically astute terms, the elderly were able to capitalize on the politics of interest-group liberalism.[20]

The Aging Network

Along with the expansion of benefits and services came the rise of a "New Class" of professionals who identified themselves as specialists in providing human services for the elderly. This professionalization of reform in aging politics found its institutional expression in what came to be called the "Aging Network" of practitioners and advocates working on behalf of the elderly. In the mid-1960s, when the official "War on Poverty" became institutionally embodied in the old Office of Economic Opportunity, aging advocates proposed that the elderly too should have their special agency. The Older Americans Act (1965 and amended since) created the Administration on Aging and, over time, authorized a series of additional programs: Meals-on-Wheels, neighborhood Senior Citizens Centers, information and referral agencies, and a network of Area Agencies on Aging operating through state and local governments across the United States.

While never commanding vast resources, this aging network did insure that a cadre of advocates and allies of aging interest groups would remain in place to press for the concerns of older Americans.[21] In that sense, the liberal ideological view of old age acquired a permanent niche within the federal system and the policy process. By 1973 The Older Americans Act created what might be seen as an empty "policy space" for political action. During the 1970s new interest groups, such as the National Association of Area Agencies on Aging (N-4A) and the Association of State Units on Aging (NASUA) moved into the vacuum. By the 1980s, this policy space had become filled by a dense network of State and Area Agencies on Aging (AAAs), each serving to coordinate other agencies and local interest groups.[22]

The Triumph of Liberalism

Achenbaum, reviewing the history of federal policies in aging, takes note of the "central paradox" of Great Society legislation and its impact on aged: namely, that the programs of the 1960s eventually had greater benefit for the elderly than for the disadvantaged groups they were intended to address.[23] While the poverty programs have disappeared, the aging network has remained and flourished. It did so at the time when public benefit programs for the elderly reached their highest scale and broadest public acceptance.

Where aging interest groups could not claim exclusive credit for these achievements, the Gray Lobby still remained vocal and visible and would from now on be in a position to advance ideological claims about the situation of old age in American society. But the ideology of old age articulated by the aging interest groups was different in style and sophistication from the global ideological aspirations of old age movements of the 1930s. The ideological claims supported by aging interest groups in the 1960s and 1970s were closely integrated with the organizational structure of aging interest groups and their goals.

That organizational base was becoming more secure through the growth of interest groups themselves. NCOA began to grow in size and sophistication as it secured support through sizable federal grants and contracts. AARP, on the other hand, achieved its growth through services, such as publications and insurance, available to its membership. Membership in turn exploded in size until AARP reached more than twenty million members by 1985. Other Gray Lobby organizations drew their strength from traditional alliances with other interest groups: The National Council of Senior Citizens had strong ties with the labor movement, Green Thumb with agricultural interests. By the convening of the 1981 White House Conference on Aging, there were twenty-six major aging interest groups who banded together to constitute a "Leadership Council of Aging Organizations."

The organizational and political success of the aging interest groups came at a favorable period for the ideology of old age. In the "golden age" of aging policy, from 1965 to 1981, there was little need to be explicit about ideology. The elderly were a favored social welfare constituency; no politicians proposed to take away benefits from this group. The only question was what benefits would be added. And when the Reagan Administration succeeded in slashing benefit programs, middle-class entitlement programs for the aged were barely touched. Indeed, they were still regarded by politicians as untouchable in budget cuts.

AGING POLITICS:
THE LIMITS OF LIBERALISM

The dominant liberal ideological view of aging has been supported by the mass media, by academic gerontology, by aging interest groups, and by the public at large. Survey research seems to confirm that public opinion, including older people themselves, sees the aged with more problems than older people actually experience.[24] The script for this ritual is by now familiar. The old are cast in the role of the deserving poor. The problems of old age are recited and duly noted by organs of official opinion. Nursing home scandals or crime against the elderly make the headlines. Editorials are written; legislative hearings are scheduled; public officials are interviewed. Before long, there is general public consensus that "something must be done." Protective legislation and health or welfare appropriations follow in due course. The "plight of the aged" becomes a rallying point for resisting budget cuts.

But the price of this advocacy is that it perpetuates the failure model of old aging. Old people appear as helpless, even pathetic victims requiring our protection: "Grandma Found Beaten and Robbed," "Goldengrove Nursing Home Cited for Filthy Conditions." It is this image that sells newspapers, wins elections, and supports enlarged budgets for police departments, social service staff, and gerontological professionals whose livelihood comes to depend on this ideology. The success of this ideological construction of old age means the spread of false consciousness even among the elderly themselves. Those old people who are doing relatively well consider themselves exceptions to the general state of disaster of old age in America.

Knowledgeable people are, of course, aware of many facts inconsistent with the liberal ideological view. Crime statistics suggest that the old are *less* likely than the young to be crime victims. Only 5% of the elderly reside in nursing homes, whatever their quality. And as a result of indexing Social Security against inflation, the proportion of the old who are below the poverty line has dropped dramatically over the last two decades. By the mid-1980s, the old were less likely than the young to be below the poverty level.[25] Crime, nursing homes, and poverty are convenient public images that support the liberal ideological view of old age. But the image is further and further removed from reality.

The Structured Dependency of Old Age

The negative public ideology of old age is reinforced by the structure of professional services for the elderly: for example, not only in medicine or the health professions but in social work, too.[26] Phillipson charges that prevailing methods of social work "transform problems of class and gender into private experiences. Events which occur in aging and retirement are identified as exclusively individual dilemmas, to be resolved primarily by individual casework."[27]

Ideology, public policy, organizational interest, and professional practice are all mutually reinforcing. Mainstream liberal diagnosis of the problem of aging assumes that the problem can be addressed within the existing institutional framework. This ideological starting point affects not only professional practice but also the design of research in social gerontology. As Phillipson notes, "Research on the elderly inevitably comes to the conclusion that with more government aid, additional family support and voluntary help, adequate services will emerge."[28]

The Gray Panthers, among others, have repeatedly been critical of the major aging interest groups, first, because they are not politically radical enough; second, because they pursue advocacy along age-group lines; and, finally, because they fail to offer true mobilization of the elderly on their own behalf. The Gray Panther criticism amounts to a restatement of the familiar dilemma of the "professionalization of reform." From a left-wing view, the professionalization of reform eliminates any radical possibilities for participatory democracy. From a right-wing view, one could equally argue that it supports the interests of a "New Class" of professional gerontologists.

Yet even when we acknowledge the link between organizational interest and ideological formation, there is no simple explanation for the old age ideology and its persistence. An interest theory of ideology would explain it in terms of political tactics masking a dominant ideology. The strain theory would explain the same phenomenon in terms of group solidarity: legitimation of the leadership of age-based membership organizations. Both explanations are consistent with incremental bargaining and the professionalization of reform that we have seen since the 1960s.

The Strange Silence Toward the Liberal Consensus

It is a striking fact that until quite recently, it was difficult to find strongly expressed opposing views about old age policy. The situation is all the more strange since on all other matters of domestic policy, clear-cut ideological differences abound. On crime, for instance, or education, or race relations, one can find an articulate conservative viewpoint represented, for example, in the pages of *The Public Interest* or *Commentary* magazines. Not so for aging policy. The case here is sharply in contrast, say, to the vocal controversy surrounding abortion, prayer in schools, or capital punishment. The liberal consensus on aging policy has dominated public opinion.

But this strange silence and monolithic ideological agreement have not necessarily been beneficial. They deaden our thinking and make us confuse facts with values, the status quo with future possibilities. The silence is all too reminiscent of the late 1950s when sociologist Daniel Bell declared an end to fundamental ideological debate in the United States. This so-called "end of ideology" was a disguise and an evasion. Widespread silence was an ominous absence of critical thought concerning central matters of public policy. Something of the same development has occurred during the "golden age" of aging policies from the mid-1960s until the 1980s. Liberal ideology easily captured debate on old age policy because most political actors held an essentially benevolent and generous view of the elderly as a social welfare constituency. But with the rise of an intellectually articulate neoconservative ideology in recent years, major elements of the entire liberal consensus have come under attack.

Neoconservative View of Aging

The lines of a neoconservative view on old age policy were first proposed by Rabushka and Jacobs in *Old Folks at Home*.[29] They noted that 80 percent of older people own their own homes and thus are shielded from recent high interest rates, while at the same time amassing large assets in the form of real estate. Government housing programs for the elderly, argue Rabushka and Jacobs, are generally out of tune with the consumer preferences of the elderly themselves. The liberal housing programs for the aged are inefficient and unnecessary in terms of any demonstrated need or benefit.

The case of housing for the elderly is only one instance of a larger failing of the liberal approach to the problems of the aged. When multiple transfer payments and subsidies are taken into account, old people today are hardly to be seen as victims. Compared with other groups in the population, in fact, the elderly are doing remarkably well. A similar line has been taken by advocates of generational equity. The message is that old people are doing well and they are getting too much. While older people have gained from social spending, other age groups have not fared as well and there is fear that future generations of elderly will be further disadvantaged.

Are the Elderly No Longer Needy?

If these critics are right, then it is difficult to see why the elderly, as a group, should be entitled to more age-based benefit programs. Perhaps age-based entitlements should be replaced by programs based on need, for example, employing a means test to target services to the truly needy.[30] This reopening of questions about age-based entitlement was the political backdrop for the emergence of the age-versus-need debate among gerontologists. Aging advocates sense, correctly, that the need-versus-age debate or controversies over generational equity could open the door to means testing, budget cuts, and loss of power for older people as a group. These debates shatter the unity of the aged as a constituency group and reintroduce the contradictions of social class into aging policy.

It is precisely because the social class problem is so divisive that the liberal doctrine of equal opportunity seems appealing. The traditional liberal view has always stressed equal opportunity, and so the appeal of an age-irrelevant society springs from the historical liberal commitment to liberty and equality before the law. Why should not old people be treated just like everyone else? Why should not they be free from discrimination? In replying to this question, liberals are caught in a contradiction. The problem is that advocates want to keep *positive* discrimination for the elderly in the form of entitlements based on chronological age alone—such as Medicare—while at the same time they fight against *negative* discrimination for the elderly based on chronological age—such as compulsory retirement or age stereotyping. Adovcates want the benefits of age-based categories but not the burdens. While social welfare spending was expanding, this contradiction could be ignored, but now different historical conditions obtain.

The Social Security funding crisis of the early 1980s brought wider calls to cut back entitlements for the elderly. Critics, like former Commerce Secretary Peter Peterson, argued that the Social Security system is unfairly subsidizing older people at the expense of other groups in the population and at the cost of other pressing economic needs.[31] For the first time in memory, benefit programs for the aged were under attack. The liberal consensus on aging politics suddenly became vulnerable.

For the ideology of old age, the 1983 Social Security legislation was a turning point. Taxing the benefits of the well-to-do elderly introduced a needs-based criterion, even if not an outright means test, into the heart of the Social Security system. The final legislation amounted to an acknowledgment that, in fact, the elderly are not all needy and deserving of public subsidy, as the liberal consensus had long insisted. As a result, the old consensus, and the golden age of policy-based incrementalism, was shattered forever.[32] Not only have easy votes on Social Security come to an end, but also an entire set of public myths and beliefs about aging policy has been brought into the open.

The Liberal Consensus at Risk

Attempts to promote a wide-ranging debate about the future of aging policy in America have not been notably successful. Instead, public discussion has been dominated by appeals to sentiment and fear of antagonizing interest groups. Stereotypes have abounded, opinion has been polarized, and policy initiatives have been made only through crisis management.

Advocates for the aged continue to defend the liberal consensus, but contradictions in the ideology are becoming insupportable. The bulk of benefits go to the middle-class elderly, and the effect of spending for the aged has been to drastically cut the poverty rate among the elderly and to improve the health of all older people, rich and poor alike. Liberals resist means testing today's age-based entitlements because they fear, probably wisely, that such a move would drive a wedge between the middle-class and the poor elderly. Yet blind defense of this liberal consensus view puts liberals in the position of defending programs that are, from a targeting point of view, inefficient and inequitable.

Neoliberalism

In recent years one response to policy paralysis and ideological stagnation has been the rise of what has been labeled "Neoliberalism." Morton Kondracke, editor of the *New Republic,* once defined it as an attempt tot retain Democratic compassion for the least advantaged without being tied to political institutions such as categorical grants, government bureaucracy, quota systems, or entitlement spending.[33]

The neoliberal agenda is best understood in contrast to traditional New Deal liberalism. New Deal liberals sought to advance human welfare through centralized government responding to claims of interest groups such as labor, farmers, minority groups, and so on. Liberals such as John Kenneth Galbraith or Arthur Schlesinger, Jr., kept the faith of earlier exponents like Eleanor Roosevelt or Adlai Stevenson. Policymaking was characterized by a tendency to underwrite claims to need in the language of rights. When enacted into law, such rights became legal entitlements applying to whole groups on simple criteria: in the field of aging, Medicare is the best example. But once guarantees of entitlements are enacted into law, they take on a life of their own, and expenditures rise accordingly. Political bargaining no longer controls the process.

Traditional liberalism assumed that government intervention was benevolent; the marketplace, and the private sector generally, were suspect. Liberal policymaking was based on the idea that vast resources, available only to government, could be mobilized to solve social problems. The focus was on redistribution, not production of wealth or economic growth, which was taken for granted. Part of the problem was that policies such as quotas or age-based entitlements tended to allocate benefits to groups on a categorical basis, even to members of those groups who were no longer suffering hardships, like the affluent elderly.

The neoliberal agenda in some ways is a reverse image of traditional liberalism. Instead of emphasis on government, neoliberals emphasize investment and economic growth; instead of macroeconomics, they emphasize appropriate technology, microeconomics, and entrepreneurship; and instead of competitive interest-group politics, they emphasize cooperation between contending groups.[34] These are policies intended to go beyond the zero-sum society.[35]

A few neoliberal politicians, like former Arizona Governor Bruce Babbit, have been willing to address age-based entitlements or broader issues of aging policy. But in the 1984 presidential campaign Republicans were frightened by the Social Security issue, while Democrats were eager to win back a middle-class constituency for the future. For both Republicans and Democrats, after 1984 it proved impossible to debate aging programs in public. Ironically, even though neoliberalism came into being in response to the neglect of productivity by old-time liberals, neoliberals themselves have not paid any serious attention to prodevelopment of pro-ductivity options for social welfare policy in an aging society.

There are those, particularly on the left, who would see the problems of social welfare policy and population aging as yet another instance of inevitable contradictions in late capitalist societies.[36] According to this political economy analysis of the aging policy, inequities are structured into the system through labor markets and monopoly control of capital. Welfare policies are vehicles of social control that provide meager bene-fits and legitimate the system. The weakness with this political economy perspective is that the aged tend to be assimilated to the category of vic-tims of the capitalist state, the medical-industrial complex, or other agencies of oppression. But this perspective obscures the ways in which the aged are also a privileged group and a favored constituency of the welfare state. At the policy level, the political economy perspective ap-pears to deny the need for any hard choices at all. Instead, the left-wing critique favors a total systematic approach to economy, ideology, and po-litical change, but it fails to identify incremental opportunities or lever-age points for social action.

IDEOLOGICAL CRISIS AND THE FUTURE

Aging Interests and Hard Times

Unlike the 1970s, the 1980s have posed hard choices for aging interst groups. It is no longer enough to be on the side of the angels—that is, in favor of "helping the elderly." During the 1970s the position of the elderly improved markedly relative to other groups, and during the first years of the Reagan counterrevolution, the elderly did well compared with other groups. These successes could be claimed as victories by aging in-terest groups. "Gray Power" was working. But could the advocacy groups equally claim responsibility for the alternative of going along with cut-backs in entitlement programs? Now that the aging interest groups have become participants in the political bargaining process, it may prove harder to distance themselves from the outcome.

The problematic choice of insider or outsider strategy is a comment on how far aging interest groups have come in a very short period of time. During the 1950s and 1960s other groups—such as organized labor, churches, and traditional social welfare constituencies—represented old people's interests. But the professionalization of reform was already underway. By the end of the 1960s, as aging interest groups expanded their numbers, size, and visibility, the ideological agenda became defined and dominated by professionals.

The coming of hard times has brought the aging interests together, into the common front of the Leadership Council of Aging Organizations that was so active in the 1981 White House Conference on Aging. This interest-group coalition has continued to work together on many issues, with ideological contradictions remaining suppressed. Yet, for all the reasons offered earlier, it may prove impossible to suppress indefinitely the contradictions embodied in the ideology of old age. The most serious of these contradictions, of course, is economic or social class. The threat of divergent class interests was apparent at the time of the compromise solution on Social Security financing—e.g., taxing Social Security benefits of higher income beneficiaries. AARP, adamant among the aging-interest groups in 1983, remained opposed to the very end to any Social Security compromise plan that, for the first time, would tax beneficiaries. But the Social Security battle was not the end of controversy over aging policy. These contradictions are likely to reappear as aging interest groups seek to exercise their power in their legislative arena.

By virtue of their history, visibility, and presumptive legitimacy, the Gray Lobby will retain a degree of power to influence the definition of issues. Access to media, influence over public opinion, and possession of knowledge are valuable assets here. Aging interest groups retain a power of agenda setting even if they cannot "deliver the votes" of the elderly as a group.[37] But how will they regain ideological clarity in an environment where ideological consciousness is becoming mystified by government officials and advocates alike? Without such clarity, it is doubtful if we will see the emergence of a "radical gerontology" that would correspond to the political economy analysis. The defensive response of aging interest groups to the controversy over "generational equity" shows that the ideological problem is serious.[38]

Part of the problem lies in the collapse of the old liberal consensus. In many ways, the elderly represented the liberals' most attractive constituency group, and liberals are reluctant, at least in rhetoric, to let the elderly pass beyond their historical status as victims claiming special protection from the welfare state. Yet the conventional liberal ideology of old age no longer reflects the new reality of aging in America, and it is unprepared to confront the opportunities presented by an aging population that is increasingly better educated, healthier, and more affluent than in the past. The erosion of ideological coherence is combined with declining political strength among sectors who have historically defended liberal causes: unions, students, minority groups, the mainline liberal churches, and so on. All have lost power. The New Right is confident about its ideology, but liberals are not. Yet neither liberals nor conservatives are in full control of developments in aging policy, and neither can do much to break the policy paralysis. The system muddles through.

But the familiar contradictions remain. The result is that both thought and action, debate and policymaking, become driven by covert agendas. Political leaders are reluctant to be labeled as "against the elderly." The result is that, when cuts are made, it is the least advantaged, including the poorest of the elderly, who are most harmed. As long as the interest-group liberalism of aging politics retains its present form, it is hard to see how the logjam can be broken. In the current environment we seem destined to endure a permanent legitimation crisis of aging policy in the welfare state. With this legitimation crisis we face a fiscal crisis, symbolized by Federal budget deficits.[39] The problems do not disappear, but the familiar solutions no longer work. For the ideology of old age, the result is something of a paradox. We see a vanishing of ideological consciousness at precisely the moment when the crisis calls for clear analysis in terms that transcend both the false consciousness and the technical rationality promoted by public discourse about aging in America.

8

Mediating Structures

Political power must always be twice won—it must be won first with the help of the state, then it must be won again by new popular forces against the state.

—Michael Walzer

EVOKING THE WORLD WE HAVE LOST

From time immemorial old people and others have mourned the passing of "the good old days," the vanished traditions of the past. Since the influential work by Toennies, *Gemeinschaft und Gesellschaft* (1887), there has been an important sociological literature in praise of traditionalism —a theoretical evocation of the "world we have lost." Toennies' work is based on a fundamental distinction between natural, small-scale groups ("Community") and larger, more alien social structures ("Society"). The smaller domain of Community includes families, voluntary associations, friendship groups, and religious bodies: the whole network of intimate social bonds that Berger and Neuhaus were later to designate as "mediating structures."

Toennies' work is one of the earliest and most powerful statements in the sociological literature calling for a return to tradition. This literature sings the virtues of small-town life and its dominant institutions—church, family, neighborhood—the institutions that nurtured life from generation to generation. The nostalgic memory of small-town virtues has been an important element in the political program of conservative political movements. The 1980 Republican National Platform put heavy emphasis on an appeal to the small-town virtues of family solidarity and neighborhood pride—virtues, it was said, "that once made America great."

What the antimodernist and right-wing views have in common is a suspicion of the disruptive power of the modern welfare state. In this view, the evil of the state is set over against a nostalgic evocation of the world we have lost.[1] The world we have lost, it is said, was a world where filial responsibility, religious piety, and pride of neighborhood yielded a strength of character that made dependence on government unnecessary. And where the virtures of individual responsibility reached their limits, in the dependency of old age, then families would, as the saying goes, "take care of their own." Long before the modern welfare state was conceived, these mediating structures furnished the traditional support for old age.

Social policy proposals favoring a return to the world we have lost have special importance in the field of aging. It is impossible to get very far in thinking about public policies for an aging society without addressing the issues raised by the appeal to tradition. The ideas behind the world we have lost have such plausibility because of the great and enduring importance of mediating structures in the lives of the elderly today.

WHAT ARE MEDIATING STRUCTURES?

"Mediating structures" are those social institutions midway in size between the private individual, on the one hand, and large megastructures such as corporations or government agencies, on the other hand. The most important of these mediating structures are the family, neighborhood, organized religion, voluntary associations, and ethnic subcultures.[2] All represent powerful traditional social ties that retain their importance even today. An appeal to mediating structures in social policy calls for strengthening institutions that nurture a smaller, human scale of life.

The appeal of mediating structures in aging goes beyond care-giving alone. Mediating structures constitute a network that gives quality of life to old age quite apart from questions of dependency or service delivery. Indeed, mediating structures need to be seen according to a calculus of meaning, and not simply a calculus of efficiency[3] in the delivery of social services. Mediating structures represent the life world of shared values and human purposes that give life its meaning in old age. Within traditional mediating structures—family, neighborhood, and church—the elderly are more likely to have well-developed contributive roles in which their life experience becomes a basis of status and respect. Mediating structures incorporate traditional values—family solidarity, local neighborliness, and religious piety—that give dignity and meaning to the last stage of life.

Despite the rapid changes of modern life, these mediating institutions continue to play a vital role in the life world of old age. A growing literature in gerontology documents the continuing importance of the family life of older people.[4] What is true for family life holds in different ways for other mediating structures. Church and synogogue membership is heavily skewed toward upper age-groups. In many congregations today, the elderly make up the majority of parishioners. A similar age distribution can be seen in community associations such as the Elks, Kiwanis, veterans groups, and so on. In local neighborhoods older people act as custodians of culture, language, customs, and history, which they can pass on to future generations. Finally, ethnic identity, like religious identity, often assumes a distinct meaning and importance in old age. In the last stage of life, more and more people "return to their roots" and affirm enduring ties that bind together the whole cycle of life.

Mediating Structures and Aging: Some Policy Dilemmas

Once we have acknowledged the power and continued vitality of mediating structures for old age, we are left with questions about how public policy or formal services should take account of mediating structures in old age. The appeal of mediating structures for the aging poses policy dilemmas for consideration:

Family. Does relying on the family to provide services for the elderly—for example, in home care—actually strengthen or damage other aspects of family life for different generations? Further, how far should the resources of the family as a whole—of adult children or other kin, as well as spouse—be taken into account in allocating health care resources to the elderly? This question comes up in controversies over filial responsibility, spousal responsibility, and other issues.

Religion. Religious institutions have traditionally been the cultural framework through which individuals have interpreted the meaning old age, death, and dying. Today death and aging are more closely associated than ever before: more than two thirds of deaths occur among people over age sixty-five. How will life-and-death decisions be made concerning prolongation of life or termination of treatment for people at advanced ages? Traditional religious counsel tends to favor some ideal of "sanctity of life" or "natural death," but these ideals are difficult to interpret in the era of medical technology. In complex health care systems, these ethical dilemmas, these existential decisions can no longer be kept outside the public sphere.[5]

Neighborhood. With advancing age, geographic mobility tends to decline. Contrary to a common stereotype, most old people remain in their neighborhoods after retirement. But, often enough, retirement income no longer keeps pace with inflationary value of housing assets and local taxes. Neighborhood change and development is a fact of life. How far should public policy assist elderly homeowners in coping with neighborhood change—for example, in helping the elderly to remain in their own homes? What role could older people have in neighborhood revitalization or other efforts to improve local quality of life?

Voluntary Associations. The growing retired population offers some possibility that recruitment of older volunteers could meet needs for human services in a variety of sectors, such as education, child care, and health care. But is such a strategy of volunteerism today actually feasible? Should policy seek to strengthen existing community voluntary associations or promote new programs especially designed for older volunteers, such as Senior Companions, Foster Grandparents, and so on? What role should voluntary associations have in mobilizing the productivity of an older population in the future?[6]

Ethnicity. Modern liberal values of equality and universalism seem to forbid invidious discrimination on racial or ethnic grounds, and such discrimination raises serious civil rights questions. But the appeal of ethnic identity among older people is commonly felt to demand living arrangements that support ethnic solidarity and therefore exclude other ethnic groups. Should government permit ethnic groups to acknowledge ethnic distinctions in access to facilities such as nursing homes or senior centers run under voluntary auspice? What about when voluntary organizations receive public funding? Is ethnic separatism a matter of freedom of association or is it unlawful discrimination?

These are only a few of the policy questions raised by an effort to favor the idea of mediating structures in an aging society. While the importance of mediating structures concept for old age is clear enough, no attempt has been made to examine the implications of this concept for public policy in aging. There is an important body of work on natural support systems for the aged, focused primarily on care-giving for the frail elderly.[7] Much of this work has been preoccupied with policy issues in long-term care and, in particular, with the feasibility of community-based alternatives to nursing home care.

The large body of work on policy analysis of informal support systems is relevant to mediating structures and aging, but the two domains are by no means equivalent. Mediating structures and informal supports should be treated differently for several reasons. First, focus on support systems skews our attention entirely toward the needs and dependencies of the elderly and away from their positive productive or contributive capacities. Second, the stress on informal or individual ties to caregivers such as relatives, friends, and neighbors overlooks the role of *formal* institutions such as churches, clubs, voluntary groups, and other social organizations. The result is that aging is understood as an individual problem to be dealt with by private—largely individual or family—resources. But some of the most difficult policy questions revolve around actions by groups and organizations, not the informal ties of natural support systems. A distinct ethos of traditional values is embodied in mediating structures that is frequently in conflict with the dominant values embodied in megastructures of corporation or government or the professions. At bottom this points to a clash between modernity and the experience of old age.

Aging and Modernity

The relationship between modernization and aging is a subject of continuing controversy among historians and sociologists of old age.[8] Modernization has brought forth a view of the world in which institutions such as the family, church, or tribal groups are rejected in favor of values associated with the "modern" or "progressive" point of view, regardless of whether these values are promoted by the state or the marketplace.

Some on the left, such as Jurgen Habermas, for example, would regard mediating structures as ingredients of the life world: part of those shared human meanings that make up the qualitative fabric of experience.[9] In this view, mediating structures constitute a residue of the precapitalist heritage gradually being consumed and eroded by the exchange relationships of capitalist society. Indeed, Marx himself identified capitalism as the greatest force for modernization as it uproots local neighborhood ties or family bonds and substitutes the nexus of the cash economy.[10]

Today that process of dissolution is widely felt in the spread of extreme individualism and the erosion of values tied to traditional mediating structures. Claims of group solidarity that were once sustained by mediating structures are gradually displaced in favor of an ethic of autonomy and self-realization.[11] This ethic of autonomy is actually embraced, in different ways, both by liberals and by free-market conservatives in contemporary America:

> Both the Left and the Right have seen traditional mediating structures as supports for the dominant society and protections against social change. According to the conventional wisdom, movements for social change arise in opposition to mediating structures. But this conventional wisdom presupposes a sharp demarcation between life and politics, between the public and private sphere. In this stereotyped view, mediating structures embody everything that is traditional and fixed, while detachment from communal institutions is the precondition for social reform and progress.[12]

Misunderstanding Mediating Structures

This conventional opposition between tradition and modernity has become so commonplace that it shapes our thinking about social policy and, in particular, about those mediating structures critical in the lives of old people. For example, a widely read monograph by the World Future Society recently concluded that "Family solidarity appears on the verge of total collapse." The authors add that, by the year 2000, it is likely that "Belief in the spiritual realm will have declined (and) a greater proportion of people in the developed countries will be unchurched."[13] These sentiments express a common conventional wisdom: namely, an assumption that family and religion are dying or dead. Yet a recent study of Middletown confirmed the continuing importance of family and religious values in the lives of ordinary Americans.[14]

The future forecasters have repeatedly missed the persistent importance of family and religion in the modern world. Yet their views, including predictions of the demise of family and church, have been influential and widely propagated. On the other side of this debate are those conservatives who insist that mediating structures are strong enough to take up the slack of cutbacks in government programs. But should mediating structures in fact be expected to play such a role? And will the services provided under private auspice meet public standards of social justice and adequacy for those most in need?

The slogan of mediating structures is often taken to be a code word for what is an essentially neoconservative, antigovernment policy agenda. The modern welfare state, it is argued, is now facing an intolerable overload of demands leading to fiscal bankruptcy. It is time to turn responsibilities back to the voluntary sector. In an era of budget cutbacks, it is said, churches will take care of the homeless, adult children will pay for their aged parents, and local communities will take care of their own without meddling from big government. The appeal to mediating structures easily becomes the politics of nostalgia or worse: a perpetuation of discrimination and inequality, a way of making more demand on groups already overburdened while at the same time appealing to their deepest wish to preserve those values that give their lives dignity and meaning.

Mediating Structures and the Welfare State

There is a recurrent conflict between the values of mediating structures and the values of the welfare state. The growth of welfare state institutions—such an unemployment insurance, old age benefits, or state-supported health care—has owed little or nothing to the values or style of traditional mediating structures. On the contrary, the modern welfare state has reinforced modern values at the expense of traditional values. For example, instead of stressing personal responsibility, religious altruism, or taking care of one's own, the welfare state has emphasized values of universal entitlement, monetized services by professionals, and a democratic and secular ethic far removed from the ethos of traditional institutions.

Critics of the welfare state have been unhappy with the results. Conservatives have charged that expansion of state provision has eroded personal responsibility and weakened social ties—to family, church, or local groups. The claim is that personal responsibility and family ties in the past were the best response to old-age dependency: a recurrent motif in the "world we have lost" syndrome.

By contrast, liberals have often been hostile to government policies that give support to traditional mediating structures. Liberal doubts are based partly on a suspicion of disguised budget-cutting and cost-shifting. But the hostility goes deeper. Liberal values have often been framed directly in conflict with the values of mediating structures themselves. Traditional social institutions—traditional family roles, fundamentalist religion, and neighborhood ethnic solidarity—have often been seen as guilty of inequitable treatment for women and minorities. Strengthening mediating structures, it is feared, would only end up strengthening that in-equitable treatment. Any policy to support mediating structures for the aging runs into the same suspicions that liberals have held about the reactionary influence of mediating structures in other areas of social policy: for example, the role of the church schools as opposed to public education or the use of neighborhood zoning regulations to keep out minorities.

Blurred Ideological Lines

Yet a simple ideological opposition on the matter of mediating struc-tures would be a serious mistake. In the first place, mediating institutions such as voluntary associations or religious groups have themselves be-come major sponsors of service delivery in the American welfare state, and their activities in the private sector depend very heavily on public dollars.[15] In the field of aging, the blurring of public and private auspice has long been visible in long-term care with sponsorship of nursing homes by churches or fraternal groups. But voluntary homes are still in most cases dependent on public funding, regardless of auspice.

The role of mediating structures is not confined to long-term care. Un-der the Older Americans Act, Area Agencies on Aging subcontract with community groups—typically mediating structures—to administer sen-ior citizens centers and nutrition sites. For example, the Meals-on-Wheels program originated in such mediating structures and was only later brought under government funding.[16] The closer we look, in social welfare activ-ities, as in the economic sphere, the more difficult it is to set boundaries between the public and private sectors.

In short, the welfare state and the appeal to mediating structures are not necessarily *opposing* ideas after all. In the typical style of American pragmatism, mediating structures have become intertwined with the for-mal service system in complicated ways. Just because of this fact, cut-backs under the Reagan Administration had a serious effect on the vital-ity of those mediating structures involved with social service delivery. The strength of mediating structures is not a substitute for public spending but depends upon it, and the dependency runs both ways.

A Left Perspective on Mediating Structures

Another reason why ideological lines are blurred is that the *values* of mediating structures themselves are not by any means always conservative in their outlook or their impact. There has frequently been a liberal, even a radical undercurrent in the concept of mediating structures. In fact, both the left and the right can find common elements in the appeal of mediating structures. For example, family care-giving and home health care today are goals embraced across the political spectrum: from profamily advocates on the right to liberal advocates for the elderly such as the Gray Panthers. Similarly, neighborhood revitalization and resistance to commercial developers has long been a theme of liberal activists at the local level. Elderly homeowners, concerned to protect their equity and their way of life, have been at the forefront of efforts at neighborhood preservation. Finally, insistence on pride in ethnic heritage—e.g., among blacks, Hispanics, Native American, and other groups—has been a strong point on the cultural agenda of grassroots groups fighting for community control. Family, neighborhood, ethnicity—the values of mediating structures—are by no means the monopoly of conservatives.

Furthermore, liberals and radicals themselves have had their misgivings about the evolution of the welfare state. Critics on the left have been skeptical about the expansion of a more and more elaborate "delivery system" for human services. Radicals hostile to the capitalist welfare state have been suspicious of human service professionals as agents of social control. In short, the dominant themes of the mediating structures idea are by no means confined to the right.

There are other critics, generally on the left, who refuse to accept the global antigovernment animus that inspires conservative proponents of the mediating structures ideal. At the same time, these voices on the left share some suspicions of government intervention when that intervention works against democratic values. Harry Boyte, for example, has demonstrated the progressive role of grassroots/neighborhood movements in the tradition of Saul Alinsky.[17] It would be a great mistake to dismiss the potential of community institutions, as some on the left are inclined to do:

> Community institutions that embody historical traditions offer an opportunity for people to discover their own identity in ways that elude the definitions of elite institutions. In so discovering their identity, they can more to resist elite domination and even become a force for political change. So-called sophisticated observers are too easily inclined to see traditional forms of community life in stereotyped terms: to dismiss traditional cultures as "false consciousness" or worse. Yet that cosmopolitan perspective is severely defective and

overlooks the possibilities contained within the culture of mediating structures. [18]

The left has identified the progressive movement of history with the creation of even more powerful centralized structures of the state. But this vision of history may conflict with the imperatives of democracy today: The crisis of democracy in advanced industrialized societies today arises in large part because the centralized structure of modern bureaucracies, in both the state and the private sector, serves to erode citizen participation. At the same time, those structures of domination also weaken smaller forms of community life—mediating structures—which reinforced communal values and offered opportunities to acquire the skills of self-government. [19] Public policies to protect mediating structures from erosion could benefit both the elderly and the broader ideal of citizen participation.

This vision of American democracy is what Tocqueville recognized when he pointed to the prevalence of voluntary associations in America as mediating insitutions that offset the effects of competitive capitalism. The parallels between the backyard revolution and mediating structures are clear enough. Both are alternatives to the single vision of monetized productivity. [20]

We move now to consider in more detail some of the policy dilemmas raised by public support for mediating structures in an aging society. This discussion looks at three of the most crucial areas: the family, ethnicity, and neighborhood.

AGING AND THE FAMILY

For nearly a century social critics have portrayed the family as an institution under siege. The death of the family has become a stock motif of popular sociology. Yet more serious analysts have recently drawn a very different and much more positive picture of the survival power of the family. [21] Care for the elderly by the modern family is coming at a time of far-reaching changes in the family itself. Capacity by the family to care for its aged members has been weakened by structural changes such as lower birth rates, increased frequency of divorce, the influx of women into the labor force, and the general rising of women's expectations—an important fact, since women have traditionally served as caregivers for the aged in most families. To all these factors must be added again the fact that today the old-old population (75+)—those most likely to be impaired or need regular care-giving—has been increasing more rapidly than any other age-group.

In approaching the policy issues, certain myths can be easily laid to rest. First, there is the romance of the extended family. Historians of the family have shown that the prevalence of the nuclear family is at least two hundred years old and that, far from being a casualty resulting from modernization, the nuclear family *predated* modernization and industrialization. Second, attachment to family values is far from dead in contemporary America. Surveys show that the family remains of overriding importance in the lives of most Americans. Third, the abandonment of the elderly by the family is largely an invention of journalists and moralists whose gloomy view is so widely accepted that people who do visit or care for elderly relatives are likely to feel that they are exceptions in a tidal wave of abandonment of the elderly.

Repeatedly we come up against the persistence of what Ethel Shanas called a "hydra-headed monster," namely, the myth of the abandoned elderly, the loss of family support in old age.[22] Yet, as Brigitte and Peter Berger point out, ideological opinions are divided among those who accept this popular image of the family in decline. Those attracted to individualism and a liberal ethic of self-fulfillment are likely to insist on the inevitability of the erosion of the family; the big question for them is how to get government programs to replace the declining family. On the other side, those attached to profamily values are likely to demand action to shore up traditional values, to stop the decline of the family. So it happens that an issue like enforced filial responsibility by adult children to care for aged parents can act as a lightning rod to galvanize public opinion on issues of the family and aging.

The family is the single mediating structure most suited for caring for those who are dependent. It follows that public policy should do whatever possible to strengthen and preserve the family in this care-giving capacity.[23] But this move to single out the family as the primary care-giving vehicle immediately runs into problems: above all, the fiscal crisis of the welfare state. Assuming that it is desirable to support the family in its care-giving role, how can this be done, and done cost-effectively, in an aging society? As care-giving tasks are shifted back toward the private world of family life, can the family sustain the burden it is called upon to bear?

Cost-Shifting

Recent health policy changes have promoted cost containment, which actually amounts to covert cost-shifting: for example, denying home health care support in order to shift the cost of care of the elderly onto available family members. Cost-shifting means asking families to bear burdens in the care of elderly relatives that, in other circumstances, government would support. For example, under the current reimbursement regulations for Medicaid, keeping a frail elderly relative at home means that families are denied the support that would be available under Medicaid if the same relative were placed in a nursing home.

But this policy has perverse results. Shifting costs to family caregivers actually means imposing *negative* incentives for those families naturally inclined to try to care for their elderly family members at home. In the name of cost containment, we end up punishing families for the very virtues celebrated in the name of mediating structures. In the last five years, support for home care has become harder for families to get, costs have been shifted, and negative incentives have sharpened. Politicians across the spectrum are to be heard applauding family care-giving. Yet the same profamily rhetoric is paralleled by cost containment strategies that damage the integrity of mediating structures: in this case, the care-giving function of the family. The effect of cost-shifting policies is to strain and to weaken family care-giving rather than to strengthen it. Covert cost-shifting finally distorts and subverts the ideal of mediating structures in aging policy. It would be a quite different matter to adopt a policy providing positive incentives to help family members do what they may want to do in any case; in this instance, to extend care to their elderly relatives. Offering positive incentives—for example, chore services or free respite care for families overburdened with care-giving tasks—would be in keeping with the maximalist position of making use of mediating structures to provide needed services wherever possible.

A policy inspired by the mediating structures perspective should avoid, on the one hand, cost-shifting—as, for example, punitive filial responsibility proposals would involve—and, on the other hand, should also avoid crude schemes for paying family members to do what they would do anyhow, i.e., monetizing the family. Most observers agree that filial responsibility laws do not recoup revenues, but they do exert a chilling effect on families inclined to seek out nursing home care. Punitive filial responsibility legislation saves money by displacing costs onto families. But the savings vanish as soon as we get outside the framework of single vision and look at total cost and benefits. A mediating structures perspective would reject such narrow policy calculations.

A maximalist position of monetizing family care-giving presents problems of its own. What is in question here is not some version of family allowances or incentives for dependent care, whether for children or old people. What is involved is rather a proposal to convert family members into employees of an elderly relative, which, like parents' wages, extends the cash nexus into the heart of the family. Of course, a monetizing strategy could involve vouchers or cash grants or make use of other indirect incentives, such as tax incentives. But using the tax system to promote family care-giving suffers from problems: first, it would inevitably be used more extensively by the more informed and more affluent groups in society, and, second, the real costs (forgone revenues) would appear only as tax expenditures and thus be more difficult to recognize and control in public budgets. On all these grounds, direct grants, such as family allowances, would be preferable, especially in providing greater equity for the poor.

Even aside from equity dilemmas, a problem with schemes to monetize family care-giving is that, like other economic subsidies, it is never clear how far they actually increase total net resources available. We need to think about family policy for the aging in a larger context. Much of the popular rhetoric favoring home care is based on an assumption that such care would be cheaper than care in a nursing home. But comparison of costs is difficult: is room and board to be counted? What about nonmonetized services rendered by family members? Finally—and here is the real fear of government officials—if publicly funded home care programs were to vastly expand, would not the availability of such programs encourage more people to apply for benefits and drive up the total cost in any case?[24]

A seasoned observer of the social welfare scene, Bertram Beck, among others, has voiced concerns about the mediating structures approach to public policy:

> How can we support natural structures without making those structures unnatural? How can we pay relatives when collusion is always a problem in public funding and when relatives are supposed to volunteer in their role as family members? Since what may be good for individuals in the family may not be good for the family structure as a whole, how can we avoid broader issues of redistribution of income?[25]

One could make a case for home care strictly on grounds of quality of life and profamily orientation, quite apart form efficiency or cost-effectiveness, namely, that it is socailly desirable for elderly family members to remain at home as long as possible. But this moral argument—or rather, quality-of-life argument—is rarely advanced in those terms. The argument is clouded by claims that home care is not only better but cheaper as well, a claim that remains debatable, depending on what is measured or counted as part of costs or benefits. Unless quality of life and values are factored into the policy perspective we can never come to a consensus on the role of public policy in family care of the aged.[26]

ETHNICITY AND AGING

The Revival of Ethnicity

The last decade has witnessed a revival of ethnicity in America as more and more Americans are rediscovering their roots and celebrating their ethnic origins.[27] An earlier image of the American melting pot has given way to acknowledgment of the continuing importance of ethnic identification.[28]

A similar appreciation of ethnicity has been seen in the study of aging. An understanding of ethnic diversity in the aging allows us to grasp patterns in family care-giving, relationships across generations, and differences in how people grow older.[29] Appreciation of ethnicity is especially important in understanding the different ways ethnic groups make use of services provided by formal organizations such as social agencies, health care providers, and other components of the network of aging services.[30] Ethnicity opens up a deeper understanding of historical and cultural values that have given meaning to the last stage of life.[31]

Analysis of ethnicity in aging from the standpoint of mediating structures must take account of all three of these elements. Ethnicity designates an enduring set of relationships in which an older person's life history is anchored. In that sense, ethnicity overlaps with other mediating structures such as family, religion, and neighborhood.

Importance of Ethnic Identification for the Elderly

Ethnic identification of the aged is an important source of personal identity and continuity over the life cycle, often becoming even stronger in old age. Ethnic foods, words from the language of childhood, folk customs, and other cultural practices can be powerful symbols. They may have special importance for today's ethnic old-old, who in many cases immigrated to the United States before 1920. For such groups there may be a sharp contrast between position of respect and esteem traditionally accorded the elderly as opposed to the position of the aged in modern America.

The Politics of Ethnicity

Nostalgia for a vanishing cultural past underscores the political significance for mediating structures in aging. Appeals to ethnic identification are likely to emphasize cultural continuity—preserving family, neighborhood, and a traditional way of life. By contrast, liberal advocates of the modern welfare state have historically viewed ethnic identification with suspicion. Ethnic identification created barriers among oppressed groups who might have joined in a common struggle. According to proponents of the welfare state, reliance on neighborhood ethnic ties should be replaced by professionalized services open to all. Liberals have been committed to modern, universalisitic values associated with legal rights such as equal proteciton under law, due process, and other universalistic values very different from a traditional ethos based on taking care of one's own. Ethnic subcultures that preserved traditional life-styles were seen as a sort of tribalism inconsistent with cosmopolitan, universalist values.

The conflict of value assumptions comes to the surface in policy questions surrounding provision of services to the ethnic elderly. Policy choices here include location of service, auspice, and staffing patterns, while larger issues include access, equity, and future policies for aging services in light of demographic shifts. For example, locating a service—such as congregate meal site or a senior citizens center—outside the neighborhood may be unacceptable to some ethnic elderly.[32] But relatively small numbers of elderly from a specific ethnic group may make it unfeasible to duplicate services in each pocket of ethnicity in a large city. Some formal services —for example, the Title III nutrition program for the elderly—can have an aura of stigma if offered by government, but the stigma may be overcome if a legitimate local institution—a church or synogogue, or ethnic club, or a neighborhood group—sponsors the service. Black churches have long played this role among minority populations, as has the Catholic Church among Italian and Polish elders.[33]

One of the attractions of voluntary long-term care facilities sponsored by religious or ethnic groups lies in a feeling that lifelong affiliations to one's own tribe are more to be trusted than assurances from professionals or government agencies. Ethnic elderly who are first-generation immigrants are likely to be uncomfortable with professionals coming from a different ethnic background. There are differences of language, cultural style, or values that call for sensitivity. Gelfand cites the examples of the Chinese elder who expects status deference from a younger service provider or the Hispanic elder who may be accustomed to rigid demarcation between male and female roles.

Policies in behalf of mediating structures raise the question of how to draw boundaries between public and private spheres in modern life. Would mediating structures based along lines of religion, ethnicity, and so on encourage people toward taking care of their own? What about old people who lack families or ethnic support groups that can provide this help? There is a common presumption that all ethnic groups would support a tradition of caring for their own elderly rather than use government-provided services. But current research suggests this may not be true.[34] The reason for the oft-cited failure to use formal services may not lie in a cultural mystique of ethnic roots so much as in lack of effective service design.[35]

Future cohorts of elderly will probably exhibit diminishing identification with ethnic culture. From 1970 to the end of the 1980s the number of foreign-born elderly will decline from 14 percent to 5 percent of the elderly population.[36] As this second generation grows older, it will reach old age without a network of associations, informal supports, or traditional expectations that were reinforced by life in the old ethnic neighborhood. How will those informal supports be replaced, particularly in a period when budgets for formal service are under attack?

Policy Issues

For the future, we can expect that efforts by public policy to favor ethnicity among the aged will face the following unresolved dilemmas.

Informal Supports. We need to know more about the long-range viability of informal support systems among ethnic groups. This issue is especially important in long-term care since the bulk of informal services is provided in the home, generally by family members. But different groups of ethnic and minority aged have very different rates of poverty and capacities to bear the burdens of family support. How far should a fair public policy take account of these ethnic differences?

Service Providers. The particularism of ethnically tailored services clashes with the universalism of legal provision in the welfare state. There is a challenge to service providers to take account of ethnic life styles, whether in food preparation in nutrition programs or in admissions patterns to nursing homes. How far can this actually be done in a cost-effective yet equitable manner?

Culture and Meaning. There is a clear role for ethnic culture in sustaining a sense of meaning in old age. The "old country" and the "old neighborhood" embody quality-of-life dimensions that ethnic older Americans value, perhaps even more than formal services provided through the aging network. But public policy, for reasons discussed earlier, finds it very difficult to address issues of culture, meaning, and values explicitly.

Consitutional Issues. Questions are raised by public funding that reinforces segregation along lines of ethnicity: for example, nursing homes whose population is entirely Jewish, Irish, black, and so on. Patterns of preferential access have been challenged, particularly by groups claiming discrimination. Does a mediating structures strategy commit us to what amounts to racial segregation in old age? Can one make a case that such discrimination has a different meaning in a nursing home than it does in a school or a hospital? How do we reconcile competing demands of private association and public equity?

Conclusion

There is a danger today of sentimentalizing mediating structures. The warm extended family and the friendly old neighborhood express an "ideology of family solidarity and filial piety."[37] But sentimental images of the world we have lost can easily be a pretext for cutting budgets on grounds that ethnic groups take care of their own.

In the past, mediating structures flourished for reasons of necessity, as well as cultural preference. Three-generation families living under one roof was a living arrangement born out of poverty, not necessarily filial piety. The good old days were not always that good for people trapped in a ghetto. Some of the genuine virtues of living in the ethnic ghetto were the result of a way of life that few people would want to return to: economic hardship, discrimination, and the anguish of immigration.

At the same time, ethnic identity still offers vital ingredients of ego integrity in old age: a sense of meaning and generational continuity in the last stage of life. For the immediate future, there is no doubt that ethnic identity remains important for the elderly in modern America. Public policies concerned with quality of life and meaning in old age will have to confront the issues it raises.

NEIGHBORHOODS:
THE NEW ENVIRONMENT OF OLD AGE

Modernization and Neighborhoods

Just as modernization has transformed the structure of families and ethnicities, so it has meant an upheaval in the mediating structure of the local neighborhood. Old people have come to live in a dramatically different environment from the past, in suburban environments or in urban neighborhoods where the stability of the old neighborhood has been shattered. The neighborhood, like the family or ethnic group, has always been an important ingredient of the life world of old age. But that life world has been threatened by forces that have altered the local environment:

> For (decades), streets everywhere were at best passively abandoned and often . . . actively destroyed. Money and energy were rechanneled to the new highways and to the vast system of industrial parks, shopping centers and dormitory suburbs that the highways were opening up.. . . within the space of a generation, the street, which had always served to express dynamic and progressive modernity, now came to symbolize everything dingy, disorderly, sluggish, stagnant, worn-out, obsolete—everything that the dynamism and progress of modernity were supposed to leave behind.[38]

Above all, people who were "sluggish, stagnant, worn-out, obsolete"—the elderly—would be those who had to be left behind. The local life world began to disintegrate.

In the central cities, any sense of comfortable public space disappeared with rising fear of crime. The old could no longer walk or sit in comfort in public places. Social networks among the old were increasingly driven out of the public world and into private spaces—into informal support systems that were being progressively banished from the public world. This process, more than anything else, heightens the marginalization of the life world of old age in modern societies. Those elderly who have experienced the eclipse of shared public space suffer losses of meaning that are not easily calculated in cost-benefit terms.

This process was described poignantly by the late Barbara Myerhoff in *Number Our Days*, her study of the elderly Jews of Santa Monica in Southern California:

> Soon after the urban development project began, a marina was constructed at the southern end of the boardwalk. Property values soared. Older people could not pay taxes and many lost their homes. Rents quadrupled. Old hotels and apartments were torn down, and housing became the single most serious problem for the elderly who desperately wanted to remain in the area. While several thousand have managed to hang on, no new members are moving into the area because of the housing problem. Their Yiddish world, built up over a thirty-year period, is dying. . . .[39]

The enduring importance of the local urban neighborhood in the lives of old people reminds us that, contrary to the popular stereotype, the city environment can be a highly favorable one for older people. Gerontologists have documented the rich extent of informal support systems that sustain quality of life for the elderly in large cities.[40] Beneath its apparent disorder, the modern city conceals a complex order and thriving social network, an ecology of human relationships. There are the movement of people on sidewalks, a constant vision of eyes watching the street, and a galaxy of commercial, residential places available for people.[41] This complex public space stands in contrast to the safe, yet artificial environment of the senior housing complex or the retirement community. The retirement community, like the controlled artificial greenhouse, represents a loss of this complex ecology of urban life in which multiple generations live side by side.

On the one hand, this image of the city is a portrait of the rich multiplicity of the modern urban environment, its texture, its varieties, its possibilities for freedom, privacy, and individual autonomy. It is a celebration of local virtues—of family, neighborhood, and informal networks. But it is also a nostalgia for a place of refuge secure from the disturbing currents of modernity.[42]

This vision of modernity has a concrete meaning for the elderly. It is the American parable of progress, the saga of upward mobility. "Moving up" in the world means moving away, leaving the old neighborhood behind. The elderly Jews depicted in *Number Our Days* feel bittersweet emotions about the success of their children and grandchildren, who have now moved on and out beyond the old world and its limits. They are happy and proud of their children, but they also mourn the passing of the shared world. The mobility of successive generations means, finally, the erosion of those integrated mediating structures—family, neighborhood, ethnicity—that could have sustained old age in a traditional environment.[43] Family contacts are likely, of course, to be maintained. But intermittent contact is not the same thing as preserving the whole fabric of mediating structures: the overlapping ties of family, ethnicity, and neighborhood that reinforce one another.[44] These losses are real and undeniable.

A Policy Dilemma: Neighborhood Revitalization and the Elderly

Is there an alternative to those losses and an alternative to the decline of old neighborhoods? In the last two decades, many urban neighborhoods have reversed earlier patterns of decline and have become the center of a dramatic urban revitalization movement in this country.[45] The historic and neighborhood preservation movement has led to restoration of once declining neighborhoods: the Society Hill area of Philadelphia or Brooklyn Heights in New York, for example. In Boston, Charleston, St. Louis, and Washington, DC, and in cities all over the country a similar trend can be seen. Yet this trend has had mixed results for the elderly. Indeed, it poses a distinct policy dilemma for mediating structures in an aging society. On the one hand, revitalized older neighborhoods improve the quality of life and upgrade property values. On the other hand, older renters or homeowners in revitalized neighborhoods commonly find themselves faced with rising rents or tax rates, threats of condominium conversion, and, at the extreme, forcible displacement from a cherished and familiar neighborhood.[46]

A recent comprehensive study of neighborhood revitalization and aging confirmed the tendency of elderly to age in place.[47] The most important fact about housing for the aged is that more than 70% of heads of households over the age of 65 now live in homes that they own, and, of those homeowners, 80% own the home outright, with no mortgage. In urban areas persons over 65 tend to live in older housing with lower property values and they are likely candidates for gentrification, i.e., in-migration to central cities by middle-class groups. Residential reinvestment is driven by young, urban professionals seeking renovated housing or condominium conversions. In general, those forced to move by displacement will face higher living costs elsewhere.

The old have also been displaced from neighborhoods for "benevolent" reasons based on an ideology of social welfare paternalism. Social workers commonly report frustrating cases where frail elderly want to continue living in a neighborhood that has become dangerous. But if neighborhood decline is bad, it has sometimes proved the case that urban renewal or forced relocation is even worse. The policy problem is how to find ways to "improve neighborhoods, and, at the same time, shield [the elderly] from adverse impacts."[48] Exclusive focus on the gentrification/displacement model of urban revitalization has the drawback of promoting an unduly negative view of the impact even for the elderly neighborhood residents.

The mediating structures concept of neighborhood integrity offers a strong argument for resisting gentrification and displacement. Neighborhood life, after all, depends on a certain coherence. This quality made Hamtramack in Detroit a Polish neighborhood or New York's Harlem a black neighborhood. The mediating structures concept also suggests that instead of asking exclusively about the *needs* of the elderly, we ought to look also at the potential *contributions* of older neighborhood residents. Older people can be a stabilizing force in neighborhoods, helping to preserve local traditions, ethnic culture, social networks, and civic associations. Neighborhood revitalization, if successful, may safeguard stability but threaten older people in other ways. Rehabilitation of older neighborhoods drives up property values, thus raising rents and taxes. Eventually, the old may no longer be able to afford to live there. Thus, two policy goals—enhancing the independent living of the elderly and improving the quality of neighborhood life—can be in conflict.

In considering the policy dilemmas, we must distinguish two distinct forms of urban neighborhood revitalization, each with different results for older people. The most familiar form involves an influx of new home buyers, often young urban professionals. Another form of revitalization is the resurgence of neighborhood pride by long-standing residents, including older people themselves. This revitalization takes the form of social investment: e.g., creation of citizen's anticrime or neighborhood watch groups, home repair programs, and mobilization of neighbors against changes initiated by outside municipal or corporate interests. Unlike real estate investment, social investment demands some form of mutual self-help and collective action.

Both forms of neighborhood revitalization exhibit common themes of neighborhood conservation: recycling existing housing assets through rehabilitation; reliance on self-help, personal investment, or sweat equity; and working through local government rather than federal government.[49] But clear differences exist between the two forms of neighborhood revitalization. Policies favoring real estate investment focus on monetized gains and losses. By contrast, policies favoring social investment are likely to strengthen mediating structures and look to nonmonetized costs and benefits. Both approaches might foster something called neighborhood revitalization but with vastly different results for the aged.

The transition of America to an aging society will be accompanied by serious dilemmas of housing and living arrangements for older Americans. The mediating structure of the neighborhood represents a critical element of quality of life in old age because it reminds us of dimensions of the life world that are not readily captured by the conventional terms of policy analysis and debate. The most important point to be made here is that policy debates need to look beyond monetized transactions alone. Local citizenship, quality of life, and human development over the life-span will depend on the vitality of mediating structures that sustain the life world in the last stage of life.[50]

SUMMARY: REDISCOVERING MEDIATING STRUCTURES

A policy perspective favoring mediating structures needs to be seen in terms of a calculus of meaning, and not simply of a calculus of efficiency. In the literature of gerontology, mediating structures have too often been seen merely as vehicles for efficient care-giving or service delivery. Mediating structures, so understood, become simply a residual welfare function for care for the frail elderly but little more. Thus, informal support systems have been identified with the private world of family, friends, and neighbors, but not necessarily as a means of empowering people for a life of collective action.

Framed in conventional terms, the attitude of professional practice toward mediating structures is clear enough: the focus is on sickness, not health; on professional, not citizen, control; on separate, private individuals, not social institutions as part of an enduring public world. A covert negative ideology of old age is unwittingly reinforced, and the aged are viewed as weak and in need of expanded professional care-giving. This ideological stance leads to very specific policy prescriptions: decentralized social services, new techniques of case management designed to optimize informal support systems, and recruitment of volunteers who expand the size and control of nonprofit institutions without making new demands on the budget. But the results are very different from what the perspective of mediating structures might promise.

Until quite recently, as Harry Boyte writes, "large parts of the population sustained older traditions of place, religious identity and cultural heritage relatively intact." Movements for social change among workers, women, blacks and other minorities, "drew directly upon strong bonds of community life, voluntary organization, ethnicity and religion as the resources with which to mount challenges to concentrated power."[51] The problem today is that mass media, consumerism, geographic mobility, and the rising power of corporate and government bureaucracies have eroded that traditional sense of local power and control.

Both liberal and conservative political ideologies have responded to this erosion of local power but in different ways. Conservatives, appealing to distrust of the federal government, have sought to return power to local control. But conservative versions of local control in practice have actually meant return of power to local elites who could exercise domination free of scrutiny from the national government. The result has not necessarily been a strengthening of mediating structures.

In parallel fashion, an influential segment of contemporary liberalism has weakened the legitimacy of traditional mediating structures. The liberal ideology has favored values of equality and individualism over against the power of the church, the family, or neighborhood and communal cultures. Liberal policy proposals have sought to strengthen centralized state power. Against the power of the marketplace, liberals have struggled to put the power of government acting on behalf of the people. But this struggle can only have an ambivalent outcome if it contributes to an erosion of a sense of meaning embodied in mediating structures. And that sense of meaning is crucial for old age.

The enduring power of mediating structures in lives of Americans is one of the oldest traditions of the nation. American voluntarism reaches back to what Tocqueville already recognized in America in 1830, namely, civic involvement through the creation of voluntary associations. It was precisely this local experience of democracy that created a public space distinct from both individual privatism and the power of the market-place.

Civic involvement goes back to mutual self-help practices of many groups in America's past. It is rooted "in the legacy of gift-giving" among Native American Indian peoples, of mutual-aid societies and fraternal and so-roral orders within Black, Hispanic, and other ethnic ghettos, in quilting bees and barn raisings and voluntary fire departments in small farmer's communities . . .."[52] It is precisely these movements of the poor and dispossessed who have kept the principle of mutual aid alive as they strug-gled against the dominant local powers. Neighborhood groups, women's groups, and consumers' and environmental groups have all been part of this political struggle.

But the vitality of mediating structures also depends on actions of gov-ernment. Perhaps it is not surprising that, after taking office, the Reagan Administration sharply curtailed the use of VISTA volunteers working with many community groups. The Administration also cut back decen-tralized community planning under federal programs such as CETA, the Community Development Block Grants, home energy conservation, and local crime prevention. The same fate awaited national efforts such as the Home Mortgage Disclosure Act, the Neighborhood Self-Help Pro-gram, and the National Cooperative Bank, all of which sprang from the ethos of the neighborhood movement. At the same time, money for Fos-ter Grandparents and other volunteer programs was increased. Here we see the real policy agenda of the Reagan Administration concerning vol-untary action and mediating structures. Individual acts of charity or care-giving are applauded, while collective efforts that threaten political dom-ination are weakened.

There is a distinct role for older people in the revival and strengthen-ing of mediating structures. The elderly represent a community memory of past traditions of neighborhood, religious, and ethnic identity and cul-tural continuity. The dissolving forces of consumerism, media power, and modern bureaucratic values have not entirely melted away these pockets of community memory and tradition. Those who are in opposition to the dominant power groups need to make use of groups like older people who have a natural interest in maintaining local community against disruptive powers. Here we take note of a final paradox. Precisely because the elderly are likely to be culturally conservative, they may be natural allies for those progressive forces resisting disruption of communal life. Only by reflecting on this paradox, and on the historical dialectic it embodies, will it be possible to fashion policies that preserve meaningful quality of life in old age, while also supporting collective provision of social welfare in a pluralistic society.

9

Mutual Self-Help

"Help from without is often enfeebling in its effects. . . .
Whatever is done for men or classes, to a certain extent takes away
the stimulus and necessity of doing for themselves; and where men
are subjected to over-guidance and over-government, the inevitable
tendency is to render them comparatively helpless."
— Samuel Smiles, *Self Help* (1859)

THE SELF-HELP MOVEMENT

John Naisbitt called it one of the ten "megatrends" that are sweeping
America.[1] Alvin Toffler sees it in the rise of "pro-sumers" who are a sign
of the new postindustrial society. Frank Riessman counts 15 million
Americans who are already involved.

What are these observers describing? In different ways, they are point-
ing to a new boom in an old social movement: self-help. The term "self-
help" can mean many different things, ranging from individual self-care
to mutual-aid networks. Professionals in the field of aging are now rec-
ognizing that mutual self-help groups offer new possibilities for one of the
biggest challenges faced by America as it becomes an aging society: namely,
how to increase the availability and quality of services in a period when
government funding is tighter than ever. Self-help offers some answers,
and there is already a rich record of experience to learn from.

Any list of the problems faced by the elderly today would have to include health care, nutrition, crime prevention, and long-term care. These
are areas where government at all levels has tried to respond. But there
seems never to be enough money to provide services for all who need
them. In addition, in the bureaucratized environment of human service
providers, it is not always easy to respect individual independence and
autonomy.

Self-help could be a solution to these problems, yet public funding is hardly ever provided for helping older people do more for themselves. In health care, for example, we spend billions of dollars on those elderly in need but virtually nothing on teaching older people to care for themselves. This is the service strategy that promotes more and more services but never seems to be able to catch up to all the unmet needs. Yet a closer look at each of the big problems mentioned above—health, long-term care, crime, and nutrition—will show that mutual self-help is a strategy that makes sense for the solution of those problems.

The Service Strategy

One response to the coming of an aging society is a more ambitious service strategy to provide more and more human services to the expanding elderly population.[2] Another approach would be an incomes strategy: providing vouchers or direct transfer payments—for example, under Social Security or private pensions—allowing older people to purchase services themselves and encouraging privatization through the marketplace. What is important to see is that all positions on the policy spectrum— from total government provision to total reliance on the private market —start from a premise that old people are dependent and in need of services. Both liberals and conservatives share that key assumption, although they propose different policy prescriptions in response to it. Indeed, most scenarios of the future start from this same premise: an aging society means a more expansive service strategy.

Yet the previous chapters of this book have documented that all is not well in the service economy of an aging society. As more and more professionals provide services to the aging, the expense grows greater, yet there is dissatisfaction with the services provided. Is there a way out of this dilemma of greater needs and limited capacities, or must we face a "politics of triage" that leads either to privatization, on the one hand, or rationing of services, on the other?

One promising way out is to encourage more programs that will develop the capacity of older people to do more for themselves. This solution—the idea of mutual self-help—is the policy strategy examined in this chapter. The main line of argument is that many of the vital needs of the elderly—in health, crime prevention, nutrition, and long-term care—can be met by systematic programs of mutual self-help. The self-help alternative could reduce the overload of demands on the service system while at the same time improving quality of life and autonomy for older people themselves. It differs from the conventional service strategy developed in the welfare state, but it also departs from policies favoring privatization.

The Self-Help Ethos

The "self-help ethos," as Frank Riessman has called it, has grown rapidly in recent years as mutual self-help groups have proliferated.[3] By some estimates these groups involve more than 15 million people with 500,000 different groups at the local level. The best known self-help groups often deal with dramatic problems faced by people in crisis: Alcoholics Anonymous, for example, or Mended Hearts (for heart surgery patients). But the self-help phenomenon is not confined to isolated groups of victims or to people suffering from diseases. Communal solar greenhouses, Weight Watchers Group, and networks of personal computer users are very definitely "mainstream" activities that also express the self-help ethos.

There's another reason not to limit self-help to people who are victims. Self-help activities involve consumers in actually producing their own use values. In that sense, self-help is part of a growing self-service economy where more and more productive activities are taking place outside the monetized marketplace.

History and Recent Trends

Mutual self-help groups have a long history in the United States. The recent vogue for self-help reaches back to a style of citizen activism rooted in the American tradition.[4] The growth of labor movements emerged from nineteenth-century mutual-aid networks of workingmen. In the early twentieth century, immigrant populations turned to mutual-aid organizations in the face of indifference from the larger society. Among such groups, it was not a sense of individual moral failure but rather a need for a common front against hostile outside forces.

Quite different were other self-help efforts such as Alcoholics Anonymous or Gambler's Anonymous, where individual psychological problems were the focus. Still different, in turn, was the rise of political action groups and consumer groups, a phenomenon of the 1960s and 1970s in America. Mutual self-help encompasses all these varieties: social networks emerging from indigenous community groups, advocacy organizations promoting a cause, and groups formed to address a common individual problem, such as arthritis, or made up of families with victims of Alzheimer's disease.

Mutual self-help groups are typically informal. They are organized on a face-to-face basis through personal networks or contacts. Members of these groups can both give and receive help. In contrast to professionalized transactions, mutual self-help groups require giving help to others. That act of help-giving can be beneficial in itself. For the elderly person suffering from losses and perhaps feeling useless, involvement in mutual self-help can restore a sense of self-esteem that springs from the need to be needed. Finally, from a policy standpoint, mutual self-help groups represent a distinct departure from the way that human services have been defined and organized by the helping professions in the welfare state.

We need to recognize a political dimension of mutual self-help. Some critics see self-help groups as a retreat from broad social responsibility in favor of local or private concerns. Certainly rampant privatism is an important social trend, as a glance at the self-help section of any bookstore will demonstrate. But there is also the phenomenon of mutual self-help. This hybrid term is used in order to underscore the collective, interpersonal dimension of the phenomenon. Indeed, many mutual self-help groups have important ties to citizen activist movements. A group may begin with a local or private grievance, but before long that concern may take on a political dimension.

Autonomy

The self-help ethos includes a strong distrust of experts, skepticism about professionals, and rejection of control by outsiders. Whether in citizen activism or self-care for one's own body, self-help groups represent a demand for empowerment: for control over what is closest and most vital. But that strong motivation need not preclude interest in wider horizons. While local self-help groups are organized on a bottom-up basis, those same groups may be federated into larger, even national organizations that have distinct political goals and styles of operation.

This point is especially important in the field of aging. Borkman has raised the question of why gerontologists fail to appreciate mutual self-help.[5] She argues that what Kalish called the "New Ageism" is at work: old people are seen as weak, dependent, incapable of self-determination or problem-solving. We can see that ideology at work in the popularity of natural support systems in gerontology. There is a clear difference be-tween self-help groups, with their preoccupation with self-determina-tion, and informal support systems. Informal support systems are more easily integrated into, and controlled by, formal service providers and profes-sionals. Instead of a commitment to autonomy, natural support groups are more likely to exhibit professional attitudes of paternalism toward the old. This style of paternalism is obviously opposed to the ideal of auton-omy in the self-help ethos.

Orientation toward natural support groups has the consequence of tar-geting services precisely for those elderly who already are tied to existing groups: that is, to people who are known to families, friends, or neigh-bors. Those elderly who are isolated are unlikely to benefit from the nat-ural support strategy. There are some problems—in mental health, for example—where it appears that older people are reluctant to communi-cate their problems to either family members or professional helpers be-cause of stigma or sense of shame. Mutual self-help groups, such as those for widows, are able to reach older people who might not be reached by other means.[6]

But problems of equity and access remain. Mutual self-help, like the formal care-giving system, reaches only a small proportion of those who might benefit. Older people are underserved by self-help in about the same proportion as they are by professional services. Lower income groups tend not to participate, and self-help groups, like other forms of voluntary ac-tion, are likely to be dominated by middle-class, better educated persons. With the elderly, this would certainly mean those relatively well-off peo-ple who may be experiencing problems in old age but who also have a lifetime of confidence in their basic ability to solve problems. The chal-lenge is how to enable more older people to gain access.

Here is also the delicate question of the role of professionals, who may be called on to refer people to groups or to provide modest support. Sometimes the relationship between lay groups and professionals works smoothly. At other times, there is strain. Among members of self-help groups, there is fear that groups may be co-opted by professionals. On the other hand, professionals sometimes have the idea that self-help groups will discourage members from using professional services. Both views are mistaken. People who use self-help groups use professional services as well but apparently for different purposes. And many self-help groups in turn seem to be open to professional involvement.[7]

There is also a fear that self-help groups are essentially inward turning, feeding an ethos of localism, separatism, or even segregation according to the disease or problem that gives rise to the group. Self-help groups then appear as just one more sign of the progressive fragmentation of our society. In addition, the same inner cohesion that makes the group effective could also allow it to be dominated by charismatic personalities, as has happened in a few well-publicized instances (e.g., Synanon). As to the danger of segregation or "ghetto-ization" by illness, Katz suggests that goals of normalization seem to have lost none of their appeal. In fact, self-help groups favor democratization, demystification, and antielitism. As people gain experience in running groups, they may learn skills— problem solving, working with other people, public relations, risk-taking—that contribute to wider citizen participation beyond the life of the local group.

Much of the literature on mutual self-help stresses its role in social care-giving and psychological support, at times encouraging a political or advocacy role. This positive view of self-help is correct, but it is a view characteristic of health care providers or human service professionals. That is, it emphasizes mental health and the potential of client groups to serve as vocal allies of professionals demanding more services.

Quite different, however, is a view that sees self-help as an element of nonmonetized productivity: that is, as part of a growing self-service economy that appears to be a major component of postindustrial society. The problem with the social care-giving perspective is that it tends to see the elderly still in a dependent, needy role. A more exciting potential for self-help lies in its possibilities for encouraging older people and professionals alike to transform their image of what dependency or productivity in old age might mean.

The possibilities for mutual self-help are illustrated in four areas of concern to older Americans: crime prevention, nutrition, long-term care, and health care.

SELF-HELP AND CRIME PREVENTION

Fear of crime is a major problem among older people in our society. In the 1974 public opinion survey on aging conducted by Louis Harris and Associates, 47% of the over-65 population identified fear of crime as a major problem, while in the 1981 survey, the proportion increased to 52%.

Here again, public images make matters worse. The media routinely play up cases of violent crime against the elderly. Whereas the fear of crime is greater among older people, statistics indicate that the elderly are less likely to be crime victims than younger people. Yet in urban areas of our country, fear of becoming a crime victim has made the elderly virtual prisoners within their apartments. The popular image the elderly as crime victims may have actually made the problem worse by intensifying anxiety without providing any remedies.

One answer to the problem is to put more police on the streets. But budget limits for local governments make it more and more difficult to put a cop on every corner. A more productive response, particularly for the elderly, would be to organize mutual self-help on a community-wide scale.

In neighborhoods around New York City the SCAN Program (Senior Citizens Anti-Crime Network) has established mutual-aid groups to deal with the fear of crime and help older people take action on their own behalf. In Sun City, Arizona, activists have gone further. These local groups of elderly have established posses, complete with cars equipped with Citizens Band radios to keep in touch with the local sheriff's department, which cooperates with the elderly groups. In Oakland, California, a similar effort is led by a 74-year-old grandmother, Hazel Monica, who started the program five years ago after a family member was victimized. In that period she personally claims credit for more than 200 arrests and now commands a group of seniors, aged 60 to 84, who walk the neighborhoods and are praised by police and local residents for helping to improve safety and strengthen deterrence against crime.

The Sun City posse and the neighborhood walk are instances of the block watch and neighborhood watch concept long effective in many localities. This concept of neighborhood mobilization opens up new opportunities for older people in mutual self-help. Since retired people are often at home with time available, they can play a major role in such efforts. In Denmark, for example, it is not unusual to see elderly women sitting in the windows high above a street, equipped with special two-directional mirrors to monitor movement on the street below. The Citizens Band radio fills a similar role in Sun City. With appropriate support from local government, it might be possible to expand the neighborhood watch concept and make it into a far more elaborate mutual-aid network on behalf of the entire community. Instead of being victims, the elderly would become valued members of a community crime prevention force.

A still more active approach is followed by the Parkchester (suburban New York) "Court Watch," where older people are in contact with others who have been crime victims. These mutual-aid groups not only provide comfort to victims but also show up in court to let their voices be heard by the judge at trial and sentencing. The presence of elderly residents, including crime victims, helps focus the attention of the official criminal justice establishment, which is all too often overwhelmed by a growing caseload.

One approach to "self-help" in crime prevention aims at complete self-sufficiency: for example, through handguns or paying for private police forces. These gestures reflect a radical loss of confidence in public protection. Today, for example, total spending on private security forces of all kinds is now greater than public budgets for public police forces in the United States.

But a very different approach to self-help in crime prevention is also possible, one that reinvigorates public responsibility rather than undercutting it through privatization. This alternative approach to self-help in crime prevention seeks to hold public authorities accountable for providing the public services that are promised and expected. In the Sun City posse or in the local neighborhood watch, a self-help approach does not necessarily rely on older people to do the full job of protection from crime by themselves. In Oakland, Sun City, Parkchester, and other places around the country, groups of elders are cooperating with law enforcement officials. Rather than withdraw into enclaves, senior citizens become a new focal point for wider neighborhood revitalization. Mutual-aid groups bring older people together and help them see themselves no longer as passive victims but, increasingly, as people who can help determine their own destiny through collective action in the public sphere.[8]

SELF-HELP AND SUBSISTENCE PRODUCTION: GARDENS FOR ALL

Nutritional needs are high on the list of problems the Older American Act has tried to address. Despite the goal, only a minor proportion—less than 5 percent—of the elderly are actually served by either nutrition centers or Meals-on-Wheels programs. Yet more than half of the households in America are now raising food in their own backyards and local neighborhoods. The value of this home produce in 1981 totaled $16 billion—more than the entire federal Food Stamp program. Yet it is hard to find any discussion on subsistence production or nutrition for the elderly and rare to find examples where government has actively promoted it. This failure is discouraging because the potential for home food production is already proven. Among the rural poor in the South, home vegetable gardening has long been a significant contributor to nutrition. Among those engaged in home gardening, people over age 55 are the highest producers and spend the most time in this activity.

Self-help in food production among the elderly is alive and well, despite the absence of recognition or encouragement by the official service strategy. Self-help not only makes use of the nonmonetized labor power of the elderly but also helps build new community institutions that overcome isolation and give older people a sense of involvement in collective social contribution:

> In Middleberg, Pennsylvania, the local senior citizens center has a communal greenhouse where older people grow vegetables, bulbs, seedlings, and flowers. Operated successfully since 1980, the solar greenhouse reduces heating costs for buildings while generating food at the same time. It was built entirely with volunteer labor from the senior citizens center along with people from the local community. The greenhouse offers a convenient setting to provide education in gardening methods and produce vegetables to meet the nutritional needs of the elderly, while flowers and bulbs are sold for income to sustain the project.[9]

Creating communal gardens and greenhouses on the Middleberg model need not require vast resources, nor is it unprecedented. During World War II "victory gardens" were popular patriotic efforts of ordinary citizens, generating 40 percent of all the fresh vegetables produced during the War. Even today, the value of household vegetable subsistence production today is equal to about 40 percent of U.S. agricultural exports. But current public policy simply ignores the production that does not get measured in the marketplace.

The benefits of self-help in subsistence production go beyond nutrition or economics by themselves. Subsistence production can be a communal activity that can make new use of public spaces, bring age-groups together, and deliver direct benefits to those who are most impoverished.

In Cheyenne, Wyoming, another communal solar greenhouse incorporates the nonmonetized labor of the elderly but in an age-integrated community setting. Senior citizens are working side by side with children, the handicapped, juvenile offenders, and others from the local community. The Cheyenne area is not a natural agricultural area. The climate is rough; snow is seen as late as May and gardens have been destroyed by August hailstorms. The Cheyenne area imports 95 percent of its raw food supply. With many low-income residents, food stamps have been an important component of nutrition, but now a mutual self-help approach has become successful through the greenhouse. The elderly are heavily involved, but so are juvenile offenders. Frail older women in their eighties cultivate garden plots, while younger volunteers learn from the elderly about homemaking, recipes, and life in Wyoming during bygone days.[10]

A Gallup Survey conducted for Gardens for All, The National Association for Gardening, showed that more than half of people over age 55 have some kind of garden and more than 60 percent of the gardeners are motivated at least in part by the desire to same money. Gardens for All has estimated that there are about one million sites around the country where local governments are sponsoring community gardens. These communal gardens can appear virtually anywhere—on rooftops, in empty lots, on plots of land not being used for other purposes. Communal gardens help to reclaim wasted space and convert it into attractive neighborhood sites.[11] In New York City, for example, nearly 90 percent of these urban gardens are located in poverty areas.

In an era of high technology and agribusiness, subsistence production sounds like mere romanticism and nostalgia for a vanished past. It may be much more than that. In light of the new value of discretionary time and nonmonetized labor among older people, subsistence production offers tangible opportunities for self-help activities that can contribute to well-being. It suggests that there may be many more instances of hidden potentials for productivity in an aging population.

MUTUAL-AID TO PROTECT THE INSTITUTIONALIZED AGED

Anyone who has worked with older people knows that, along with fear of crime and fear of physical dependency from illness, another major fear is felt by old people: the fear of going into a nursing home. It is a fear of ultimate powerlessness and vulnerability. In the case of long-term care, the need for government intervention to protect the powerless seems indisputable. But more intervention, more regulation may not do the job. Despite repeated attempts at reform, at new legislation, we see nursing home scandals come to light at regular intervals. Old people and their families are more fearful than ever.

Countervailing Power and the Limits of Reform

There are limits to how far government can go in actually protecting the rights of the institutionalized elderly. For example, a nursing home patients "Bill of Rights" remains only a utopian ideal, if not a fraud, unless an enforcement mechanism can be found to make those rights a reality. But enforcement demands power. Only systems of actual countervailing power can effectively check the abuses that legal interventions were originally designed to correct. The difficulty is to find advocates who have power and are also independent and incorruptible. In long-term care, as in other fields of government regulation, the regulators easily become captives of the industry they are supposed to regulate. It may be that only a consumer grassroots self-help effort can, in the long run, provide the combination of independent and incorruptible power needed to spur actions by professionals and by government.

We need mutual self-help, then, not to *replace* government regulation, but to keep government honest and to keep officials attentive to the problems. Self-help efforts to protect the vulnerable elderly will need to draw strength from outside government in order to avoid the inevitable temptations of political power. Mutual-aid groups in long-term care settings will need to call on mediating structures, such as churches, voluntary associations, families, and other groups. This struggle is difficult, but examples of success point to the promise of mutual self-help in long term care.

Friends and Relatives of Institutionalized Aged. Founded in 1975 in the wake of a major nursing home scandal, Friends and Relatives of Institutionalized Aged (FRIA) is today the largest consumer self-help organization in the field of long-term care. After the 1975 scandals, the New York State Moreland Act Investigation Commission concluded that, without an organized consumer watchdog group, government regulators would not maintain enforcement of nursing home codes to protect the vulnerable elderly. Thus, FRIA was founded to organize friends and relatives concerned to keep up pressure on nursing homes, while preserving the anonymity of elderly residents who might otherwise be fearful of complaining about abuses. As a grassroots self-help organization, FRIA maintains its distance from both the private marketplace and government bureaucracies. This independence has proved essential through a series of adversarial campaigns: for example, in seeking to prevent weakening of government regulatory powers, in working to redress racial discrimination in nursing homes, and in efforts to upgrade long-term care services and protect the legal rights of institutionalized elderly.[12]

The self-help movement can be a potent political force, as the consumer movement in nursing home reform has demonstrated. Mutual self-help and government protection are not in opposition but can work together to make possible what the state alone could not achieve. In Michael Walzer's terms, self-help offers a means by which political power can be won again through new popular forces against the state.[13]

SELF-HELP AND HEALTH CARE FOR THE ELDERLY

Background: Crisis and Reform in Health Care for the Aging

The American health care system, as it exists today, is poorly designed for the health care needs of an aging society.[14] The current system is too often concerned with responding to symptoms rather than with emphasizing prevention or treatment of chronic conditions.

Against this background, self-help approaches to geriatric health care have special appeal and are attracting greater interest.[15] Self-help activities are likely to have particular value for chronic ailments, and self-help offers more opportunities for individualized care and personal autonomy than is to be found in the formal health care system. The challenge for the future will be to integrate self-help and self-care into a more comprehensive geriatric health care system for an aging society.

Chronic Illness

As medical science enables more and more people to reach advanced old age, the incidence of chronic illness and physical disability will grow. Not only do chronic conditions occur more frequently among the elderly; they also persist for longer periods and interfere with activities of daily living. For many of these conditions, curing is not a reasonable option, but caring and coping skills remain critical. Self-help for chronic illness has shown particular promise for chronic conditions such as arthritis, heart ailments, hypertension, visual impairment, and diabetes—all conditions more likely to affect older people. Several chronic conditions among the elderly lead to limitations of activity and are thus threatening to quality of life. Chronic illness poses a difficult challenge for the prevailing health care system, which has evolved in response to needs of a younger population.[16]

In a period of cost containment, health care budgets will be hard pressed to cover the rising demands of care that require hands-on management of chronic illness and physical disability in an aging population. For this reason, mutual self-help groups could have a special role to play in chronic illnesses that affect the growing elderly population.[17] From a cost-effectiveness point of view, mutual self-help has already shown itself to be an attractive policy option. But to realize the potential gains from a self-help strategy in geriatric health care, professionals and policymakers will need to take seriously the role of self-help groups.

Self-help groups can be effective in the daily management of chronic illness, in rehabilitation and coping with functional deficits, in patient compliance with medical regimen, and in health education and preventive health maintenance.[18] Even in a high-tech atmosphere of contemporary health care, the high-touch perspective of self-help retains its importance. For example, the use of new technology such as prosthetic devices, biofeedback, and electronic communication systems can often be made effective only by relying on patient education and self-help. Some of these innovations—such as self-administered diagnostic tests in place of medical laboratory procedures—offer the promise of cutting health costs while increasing patient autonomy at the same time.

Technologies of Self-Care. Self-help activities are likely to be accelerated by innovations of technology that make sophisticated self-
care in the home far more feasible than it was in the past. A study
by the Congressional Office of Technology Assessment confirmed
that there are bright prospects for the development of user-friendly
self-care technologies that will be available to the homebound elderly. These technologies range from the tube feeding and infusion
therapies to sophisticated wheelchairs and home diagnostic tests.
Examples include blood pressure monitoring devices, "chem-strips"
for testing blood sugar levels and urinary tract infections, biofeedback equipment (for control of stress, migraine headache, etc.), home
kidney dialysis equipment, and microprocessor-driven electronic
prostheses, including new robotics technology, to enable the handicapped to live at home. Major problems of the elderly such as diabetes, hypertension, stroke, and kidney failure could benefit from
the use of new technologies for self-care.[19]

The private marketplace is already aggressively gearing up for a new
boom in self-help technologies and in related home care services. As cost
containment pressures force earlier discharge of patients from hospitals,
the trend toward home-based care is likely to grow in the future. By some
estimates, that self-care market could reach $6 billion by the end of the
decade. But without consumer education and participation, self-help and
home care easily lend themselves to fraud and abuse. Critical policy questions will not be resolved by technology or the marketplace alone. We
need to ask: what additional steps—such as consumer education, preventive health maintenance programs, or provision of supportive services—
are needed?

The postindustrial economy, with greater decentralization, telecommunications, and technological innovation, offers great promise for an
older population faced with chronic disease and limited mobility. Yet we
can also see that postindustrial technology itself is not the full solution.
In health care, the technology of curing or coping is usually not the best
answer. It is far better to prevent disease in the first place. Diabetes, for
example, one of the great scourges of the elderly, often results in blindness or amputation of limbs. We can certainly imagine how robotics and
prosthetic devices could enhance the lives of the elderly blind or disabled. But it would be far better to prevent the onset of diabetes than to
manage the disease more efficiently through home-based technology. The

same point can be made about other chronic conditions of old age. Primary prevention—stopping the onset of disease—is preferable, with secondary or tertiary prevention—early detection and management—strictly a second-best alternative.[20]

Self-help and self-care has a role to play at all levels of prevention. Indeed, in all three modes of prevention, behavioral changes are likely to play the key role, more so than exotic new types of hardware. Overall, there is need for greater emphasis on preventive health maintenance— through diet, exercise, and eliminating poor health habits—all areas where mutual self-help can play an essential role. For both prevention and for coping with the chronic diseases of old age, self-help will be crucial in an aging society.

The cornerstone of self-help in health lies with self-care.[21] Self-care involves a hierarchy of activities ranging from maintaining proper nutrition to using knowledge to note symptoms of illness to the highest level of actually taking over functions that have been performed by medical professionals, such as monitoring blood pressure or giving self-injections.[22] What is fundamental to all forms of medical self-help is a motivational element (confidence, desire for self-control, etc.), which goes hand in hand with a cognitive element (information and training). Both are necessary for effective medical self-help.

Both self-care and mutual aid have a place in care for the aging, but social networks offer particularly promising channels for policy-based intervention. Some elderly are isolated and cannot be reached through groups; others in the same condition can flourish only if new social support networks are made available to them. The distinction is crucial in developing interventions that promote self-help for health promotion. We know that elderly are more likely than others to live alone. But isolation can be dangerous to health. In a study of mortality in a sample of 7,000 adults, it was discovered that the risk of death was more than twice as great for those with smaller rather than larger social networks.[23] Advanced aged typically brings bereavement and loss of social networks, leading to greater isolation. Loneliness and depression easily lead to neglect of self-care or proper nutrition, with dangers of mortality. Hence, new intentional networks—such as mutual self-help groups—could play a role in reducing mortality.

Self-help is not an all-purpose solution for the health problems of old age. Self-care may even be part of the problem rather than part of the solution. Self-medication, after all, is probably the most common version of self-care that exists. Indeed, one problem of self-care among the elderly is that old people living alone are likely to fall into habits of taking multiple medication, sometimes with disastrous consequences.[24] There is clearly a need for balance among self-care, mutual aid, and professional intervention.

Neglect of Self-Help

In view of the potential importance of mutual self-help in health care, we are led to a natural question: why has the self-help alternative in health care for the aged been persistently ignored in recent discussions of health policy reform? To put it bluntly, the current system offers few incentives for patients to contribute to their own health. On the contrary, commercial interests, reimbursement systems, professional education, and the structure of health care systems generally discourage self-help. The elderly, as major consumers of health care, are now becoming victims of a new fiscal crisis, most notably in Medicare. The health care system oscillates between expansion (creating more services or facilities than necessary) and contraction (refusing to supply basic needs of chronically ill elderly).

An alternative policy approach is conceivable. By stressing health promotion and disease prevention we would both improve older people's indepedence and reduce costs, while promoting greater quality of life at the same time. The problem with this policy shift is that it runs against the strong vested interests of major health providers: hospitals and nursing homes, pharmaceutical companies, the insurance industry, and associations of professionals whose income depends on expansion of the current disease-based system.[25] The prevailing "medical-industrial complex" looks not to health but to disease and dependency.[26] The incentives point in the wrong direction. Health promotion and disease prevention are not goals consistent with the political economy of health care in America today.

There are some helpful signs on the horizon—for example, the spread of health maintenance organizations (HMOs), which certainly could have a larger role in health promotion for an aging population. But for the moment, the looming crisis in financing Medicare and long-term care dominates policy discussions today and excludes alternatives that might point beyond our current preoccupation with monetized costs and benefits.[27] We are already seeing the results of policy paralysis tied to fiscal austerity and covert cost-shifting.[28] As the health care system now exists, in other words, there is little subsidy or encouragement for those nonmonetized services that are in fact already a major building block for health promotion and self-care among the aged. Without acknowledging and promoting nonmonetized transactions, including self-help, the monetized system faces few alternatives but to move toward crisis, cutbacks, and rationing.

The alternative scenario is to build on the experience of success, including the hidden success represented by the remarkable health gains of today's elderly population. A major cause of declines in mortality and morbidity in the aging population over the last fifteen years has been behavioral changes in preventive health maintenance, exercise, diet, decrease in smoking, etc. These life-style changes have already had enormous impact on cardiovascular mortality rates by reducing the impact of diabetes, hypertension, obesity, and other conditions. Such chronic conditions are precisely those likely to be most amenable to a self-help strategy.

But prevailing policy proposals, both liberal and conservative, tend to be preoccupied with access and monetized services alone. Life-style concerns and nonmonetized service alternatives, such as self-help, are ignored. Single vision is simply blind to what is not measured or registered in conventional accounting. For geriatric health policy, single vision is already proving to be a disaster. Under present policies chronic illness and dependency are only likely to increase in the future, while financial resources remain inadequate to rising demands. In health care as in other policy areas, this version of an aging society evokes the specter of decline.

SELF-HELP: CODE WORD OR STRATEGY FOR HUMAN DEVELOPMENT?

When we think of self-help and public policy, the term "self-help"often serves as a code word for benign neglect: for cutting budgets for direct services and suggesting that government ought to pay less attention to social problems. It is a familiar argument that government does best to leave initiative to private individuals who solve their own problems. For conservatives, then, any substantive government policy on self-help is simply a mistake. Interference in individual self-help efforts, regardless of benevolent intent, is wrong.

The whole thrust of this book is against this view of self-help as benign neglect. In aging policy, no less than in welfare reform, we certainly need attention to self-help. But by itself, self-help is not an answer; it does not stand alone or in opposition to professional assistance, and it should not a synonym for cost-cutting or cost-shifting. For aging policy, self-help deserves serious attention as a strategy on behalf of traditional social welfare goals. But those goals must now be enlarged to include autonomy and social productivity. For the elderly, what is needed is dignity, quality of life, and a measure of autonomy and personal responsibility: precisely the values too easily overlooked by the bureaucracy and professionalization of the welfare state. Instead of benign neglect, what is called for is an affirmative strategy for promoting human development over the lifespan.

Self-Help and Policy Analysis

But this positive picture of the self-help ethos raises a critical question. To what extent can mutual self-help groups be a legitimate object of policy when their own anarchic, bottom up style keeps them at a distance from the policy arena? Can we even discuss an explicit policy for activities that elude measurement and control? Finally, even if modest steps toward management of self-help group were possible, is such management actually desirable? Are not self-help groups, and the self-help ethos in general, better served by a hands-off policy on the part of public officials and government agencies? Is it possible that formulations of policy in the field of self-help would threaten the very qualities of informal spontaneity that make self-groups effective in what they do?

These objections are worth taking seriously, but they do not call into question the need for affirmative policies on behalf of self-help. Many areas of daily life do not become explicit objects of formal public policy, yet these same activities can be profoundly affected by policy decisions nonetheless. The best example is the family. The United States has no formal or explicit family policy.[29] Yet few would doubt that other matters of public policy—for example, divorce, child labor, public education, or day care, to mention only a few—have a profound effect on the quality of family life.

The same analogy can be applied to public policy on self-help groups. As with family life, in a free society, government has no authority to make policy for such matters. Yet the alternative is not benign neglect. Policy decisions will, of necessity, have their impact on the flourishing of self-help groups. Indeed, some analysts would argue that the very proliferation of self-help groups in recent years is a symptom of, and perhaps a constructive response to, the failure of government and professionalized interventions in the human services. The rise of the self-help ethos is a symptom of this wider legitimation crisis.

ISSUES IN SELF-HELP AND AGING

If we expect a serious public commitment for mutual self-help in an aging society, then policy analysis must address the following questions in the future.

1. *Scale, impact, and benefit.* What are the numbers of older people involved in mutual self-help activities? How do we measure success or results? Does self-help reduce or increase demand for services? Self-help groups need not reduce efforts to encourage government involvement in preventive health services.[30] On the contrary, self-help efforts often stimulate more effective advocacy for public funding.

2. *Older people and self-help.* What makes self-help groups for the aged different from self-help groups for other age-groups? Some self-help groups (e.g., Stroke clubs) obviously have a more aged membership. There is evidence that the current generation of elderly is more reluctant to use professional mental health service because of fear of stigma associated with mental illness. Does reluctance to use the formal service system mean that self-help groups for the aged could be a more effective approach or will the same reluctance prevent involvement in mutual-aid activities?

3. *Dependency and self-determination.* Self-help groups are characterized by an ideology of self-determination and suspicion of experts. Must that ideology prevent professionals from collaborating effectively with self-help groups of older people? Where can aging service institutions play a role in encouraging self-help activities? What are the implications of mutual self-help groups in aging for the training of geriatric professionals in fields such as medicine, social work, and nursing?[31]

4. *Supporting mutual self-help.* The great disadvantage of self-help groups lies in the intangible qualities that give them strength, namely, their spontaneous and informal structure. What kind of institu-

tional supports do mutual self-help groups need to maintain their own continuity? For the elderly, there is the additional problem that high mortality rates can disrupt the continuity of leadership and membership in the group. For older people self-help groups could be more effective if they had institutional ties to provide some elements of support while still respecting autonomy and self-determination.

TAKING SELF-HELP SERIOUSLY

Finally, there are larger questions to consider, questions about self-help and the welfare state. The rise of the welfare state has been accompanied by the progressive commodification of interpersonal lfie. What was once an informal exchange of reciprocity becomes absorbed into the cash nexus and the domination of professional services. This commodification of interpersonal life is unchanged even if it is the state rather than the marketplace that manages the process of employment, whether in schools, hospitals, or nursing homes:

> It is difficult to see how things could be otherwise in a society in which the development of the productive forces has ensured that every activity is socialized, technicized and articulated with other activities through the mediation of the state apparatus. No consumption, production, communication, transportation, illness, health care, death, learning or exchange occurs without the intervention of centralized administrations of professionalized agencies. The concentration of capital has destroyed the social fabric at its roots by destroying every possibility of autonomous production, consumption and exchange, whether for individuals, groups or communities.[32]

But Gorz's pessimistic conclusion follows only if we overlook those vital spaces of cultural autonomy and self-development that still exist. Among the most important of these are mutual self-help groups.

CONCLUSION: BEYOND SINGLE VISION

In the Soviet Union one can buy maps of Leningrad that are accurate except for one peculiar blind spot: the churches of Leningrad never appear anywhere on maps sold by the authorities. Acknowledgment of existence of the churches on an official map would somehow violate the ideological view of the government authorities, so the buildings are simply left off.

Ideological blindness to self-help takes many forms. One side of the covert ideology of old age stresses the failure model. For those who see the elderly weak, frail, and unable to care for themselves, a self-help strategy holds little appeal. Many left-wing analysts have been notably blind to the possibilities of self-help. Left-wing critics tend to conflate self-help with outdated forms of subsistence production that have declined with the rise of competitive and monopoly capitalism.[33]

But this analysis clearly shortchanges the potential of the elderly for productive roles in society. The economic importance of nonmonetized subsistence production of services by the elderly is likely to be far in excess of the subsistence production of goods. In the self-service economy of postindustrial society still more opportunities for nonmonetized productivity will be possible. Further, there are dimensions of the self-help phenomenon that elude the categories of economic measurement but may have important consequences for personal well-being or even political empowerment. For example, mutual-aid activities promoting mental health may have decisive implications for family life, for health status, for consumer behavior, and even for political mobilization. Food cooperatives, voter registration drives, and women's mutual-aid groups have all proven politically significant.

The deepest error of the left lies in an ideological blindness that persists in equating ideas of personal responsibility and self-reliance with the competitive self-interest of the marketplace.[34] Tragically, the left has taken on the very categories of the right, who have appropriated the language of self-help and individual responsibility on behalf of the ideology of capitalism. The task of forging a new social policy for an aging society is to reconstitute the bond between public provision and private initiative, between the welfare state and the ethos of self-help. There is no better place to begin than with self-help and no better group to start with than the dependent elderly who have repeatedly been viewed as irrelevant to the productivity of society.

Mutual self-help for the aging is not a panacea or a substitute for all the services that old people need in an advanced industrial society. Other problems—income, health care, and social services—must be addressed in their own terms, and those problems require solutions through collective action and political struggle. Yet nothing could be more mistaken than to pose centralization and decentralization as opposing or mutually exclusive strategies for political change. The whole point is that the coming of an aging society and a postindustrial society will require policies that promote new contributive roles and new forms of productivity for the older population. Mutual self-help offers an alternative strategy toward achieving those goals and toward sustaining the quality of life in the last stage of life.

10

Late-Life Education

EDUCATION IN THE AGING SOCIETY

The emergence of the United States as an aging society has profound implications for the role of education in society. Beginning a century ago, public policy in America has supported mass education for children and young people, first through secondary education, more recently through a principle of universal access to higher education. By 1900, this American principle of universal education was already helping create an educated and highly skilled labor force. Compulsory schooling along with laws prohibiting child labor were quickly coupled with rising educational requirements by employers. The result was that education became the normative activity for the first part of the life cycle. This emerging pattern constituted a decisive "modernization of the life cycle" that linked education to the mass industrial economy and enforced sharp boundaries between the stages of life.[1] The modernized economy assigned education to youth, work to adulthood, and leisure to old age.

The demography of an aging society has begun to challenge this familiar linear life plan. First, education is no longer tied exclusively to youth and there is a declining population of young people among age-groups traditionally served by schools and colleges. Higher education has adapted with modest steps toward nontraditional learning but with relatively few changes in fundamental structure, financing, or curriculum. But the coming of an aging society will demand further changes. Gains in productivity in the future will depend in critical ways on the retraining of adults and older workers to adapt to a postindustrial economy. The challenge to education for an aging society will be a new emphasis on lifelong learning among late-life groups: people in their fifties, sixties, and beyond.

To respond to the new demographic and economic realities, educational institutions will have to develop new roles in recycling human resources in later life. In a postindustrial economy, human capital formation on a lifespan basis now becomes strategically important. In fact, the recycling of human resources in the second half of life has already begun. Higher education is beginning to play a role in retraining older workers or displaced homemakers, in teaching new life skills to cope with late-life problems (e.g., health care for chronic illness), and in offering opportunities for personal enrichment through culture and the liberal arts. Demonstration programs in many countries have shown the feasibility of such late-life education in reducing unnecessary dependency in old age. Whether public and private policies will support such initiatives is a question for the future.

Education and the Information Economy

The key to understanding the role of education in an aging society lies in the movement of American society toward a postindustrial information economy. The pivotal role of the production and distribution of knowledge constitutes the economic basis for postindustrial growth. The new knowledge industry can be distinguished into three major segments:

- the formal education system, the largest sector of the human services and the principal occupation for most people during the first quarter of their lives;

- a parallel but invisible instructional system sponsored by business and industry, now operating at a scale that nearly equals total expenditures for formal higher education;

- the still more informal and widely dispersed learning systems identified with publishing, mass media, culture, entertainment, and the communications industry.

Each of these segments of the knowledge industry promotes learning over the lifespan, but each does so in very different ways. Roughly speaking, each of these subsectors of the knowledge industry can be correlated with the modernized life cycle: that is, with the life stages of youth, mid-life, and old age. In the linear life plan, the formal education system holds a near-monopoly on the uses of time at the beginning of the life course, while corporate education and training concentrates on people in the middle years. Finally, we have the informal learning system that occupies an increasing part of most people's lives. Older people are linked to the knowledge industry chiefly through mass media. The advent of an information economy has so far not fundamentally altered the modernized life cycle and the segmentation of activities—education, work, and leisure —over the life course. Yet changes are now underway that may alter that pattern in the future.

The Growth of Late-Life Learning

In recent years, lifelong learning has begun to grow dramatically in popularity[2] for several reasons:

- Rising educational levels in the adult population. Prior educational level is still the best predictor of continued interest in lifelong learning.

- Popularity of self-initiated learning projects undertaken outside the formal education system.[3]

- Leisure time opportunities through mass media, culture, and the arts. The informal learning system is rapidly expanding through telecommunications technology such as home computers and videocassette.

- Lifelong learning is made necessary by career changes and obsolescence of skills from rapid technological change in the job market.[4]

- Changes by educational institutions give more support to nontraditional education, i.e., flexibility allowing for wider access by the adult population.[5]

At the same time, education for older adults has increased dramatically in the last decade and a half, as shown by the following examples.

- In a twelve-year period ending in 1981, the number of persons over 65 participating in adult education nearly tripled, growing at an average rate of 30 percent every three years (in contrast to 12 percent for adult participants of all ages).

• The participation rate of the elderly population is still small but is growing: up from 2.4 percent in 1978 to 3.1 percent in 1981.[6]

• The 1974 Louis Harris National Survey recorded only 2 percent of the elderly as being enrolled in courses, but by 1981, the figure had grown to 5 percent.[7]

All surveys show a strong correlation between years of prior schooling and participation in adult education. While only 2 percent of persons over 65 without a high school diploma were engaged in education, the figure rises to 16 percent for those graduating from college, with higher levels of formal education for each succeeding cohort of elderly.[8] Thus, there will almost certainly be a substantial expansion in the desire for older adults to participate in educational activities, if those opportunities are available. Conditions on the demand side of late-life education are undergoing rapid and favorable change, a trend likely to continue in the foreseeable future.

EDUCATION FOR OLDER ADULTS

Despite recent growth and rapid change, there is still a persistent negative stereotype that the elderly are too old to learn. Old people themselves accept the stereotype. In the Harris Survey this was the reason often cited when older people were asked why they did not participate in educational activities. But today there is abundant evidence that people can continue to learn at any age.[9] Cognitive abilities with most relevance in the daily lives of older people are precisely those that show the least decline with age.[10]

The potential for late-life learning in the future can already be seen in the variety of programs available today. But this same variety also frustrates any effort at systematic policy analysis in older adult education. Difficulties arise from lack of clear definition, absence of reliable statistics, variety of funding sources, and diversity of agencies and institutions that support the programs. Most of all, the difficulty springs from the lack of institutionalization of older adult education, which has flourished on the margins of higher education rather than in the mainstream. Some of the most innovative educational programs are not located in educational institutions at all. Education programs in senior citizens centers or other agencies of the aging network lack connection with academic institutions, and hence, they often languish for lack of educational leadership.

Learning among older adults shares many characteristics of adult education generally.[11] Education for older people is offered in a variety of settings, generally by organizations that do not have education as their primary purpose: for example, a social agency or a health care provider. The flexibility and informality of the nonacademic setting encourages participation by older people, who have been out of school for many decades and have anxiety about returning to the classroom. These nonacademic institutions can often prove to be better sites for late-life learning because they do not need to be bound by conventional styles, as schools and colleges must.[12]

In fact, the interests of older and younger adult learners are likely to be very different.[13] Older learners tend not to be interested in credentials or degrees; they do not want tests, grades, or competition. On the contrary, they tend to be interested in participative learning that can promote immediate understanding or practical application. Older people cannot wait for a distant future. Yet for the older adult this pragmatic learning may mean something quite different from coping skills or narrow job preparation, as it often does for younger people. Learning in late life may be learning that enables people to grasp the meaning of their lives through history, philosophy, religion, or literature.

The breadth of programming of educational activities for older people is very wide. Some is in the area of coping with social change, preretirement preparation, physical health needs. Very popular are programs for personal growth, hobbies, self-understanding, or the arts. The learning style of older people is shaped by prior life experience, including their involvement with educational institutions. Reliance on prior experience is both a strength and a weakness; it offers the possibility of cumulative growth of learning over a lifespan, but at the same time it presents a risk of rigidity when circumstances have changed.[14]

Modal Patterns in Education and Aging

Looking at the broad field of older adult learning presents a contradictory picture, pragmatic motivation combined with intense questions of personal meaning; demand for strong leadership combined with participatory engagement; and above all, a restless experimentalism so common in all adult continuing education in America today. This diversity of older adult education calls for analysis of broad patterns that might guide developments in the field.

Modal Pattern	Characteristics	Basic Attitude
1. Rejection	Age segregation; forced retirement neglect; isolation	Repression, avoidance
2. Social services	Transfer payments; professionalized services; education to fill time	Liberal welfare state
3. Participation	Second careers; life skills; contributive roles	Normalization
4. Self-actualization	Individuation, psychological growth	Ego integrity

Education for older adults is a recent innovation in the history of education.[15] There are few precedents for it, so it is perplexing to think about what kind of institutional change would be required in an aging society. Yet certain modal patterns are evident in the attitudes toward education for older adults,[16] as indicated in table 10.1. Stage 1, rejection and neglect of the aged, corresponds roughly to the negative position of the elderly brought about by modernization and industrialization. Stage 2 is correlated with liberal policies of the welfare state designed to ameliorate those conditions. Stage 3 evokes the goals of the Gray Panthers and those who urge the normalization of old age in an age-irrelevant society. Finally, Stage 4 envisages possibilities of humanistic psychological growth in old age that today may seem utopian.

1. **Rejection.** The first modal pattern is based on the linear life plan, which amounts to the "obsolescence of old age."[17] If education is viewed as an investment in human capital, then investment in old people makes little sense on economic grounds; the life of the asset is too short, depreciation is too far advanced. Better to write off the worn-out asset and start over with younger people. The purpose of education is justified by goals outside the educational process itself. This instrumental view of learning sees people as instruments to be set aside and discarded when their usefulness is at an end.

2. **Social Services.** In Stage 2, the liberal welfare state, the elderly are seen as a dependent group in need of services, and education is one more service provided them. This attitude is common among

professionals in the aging network. Education is just one more way to fill time for private leisure; it has no justification beyond private individual preference. According to this view, the key problem is one of access and opportunity. Older people should have the option for late-life learning, but whether they take advantage of it ultimately has no wider significance. Thus, tuition-free/space-available policies are the natural expression of a view that sees late-life education as a low-cost, low-priority option for individual use of leisure time.

3. **Participation.** A more radical view is to see education as a way for the old to participate fully in community life. In Stage 3, the old are to be given the chance to learn the skills required for self-sufficiency, whether in the workplace or in self-help groups. Education becomes a way of attacking the structured dependency of old age and creating an age-integrated society. On this view, old age is not to be separated from other stages of life or other age-groups. Instead, development is seen as a lifelong process, where social contribution represents its highest fulfillment.

4. **Self-Actualization.** The psychologist Abraham Maslow held that self-actualization—the highest peak of psychological functioning— was more likely to be found in older people than in younger people.[18] Ideals like self-actualization or wisdom represent unique possibilities for education in the last stage of life: what Rosenmayr called the "late freedom."[19] These ideals raise far-reaching questions about late-life learning. Is there anything about the older adult's learning capacity that points to special strengths for education to consider? Should we be satisfied with a normalization model that encourages the old to be just like everyone else regardless of age? Our current educational system almost completely neglects these value issues and offers little encouragement to larger questions about the meaning and purpose of education itself. But the highest stage of older adult education could well offer a promise of ego integrity in the final stage of life.

POLICY GOALS FOR LATE-LIFE EDUCATION

When we turn from this framework of modal patterns to public policy, many problems immediately present themselves. A basic question is unavoidable. Regardless of the philosophical purpose of late-life learning, why should public policy support such a purpose? What rationale in public policy can be found for extending education into later life? A point of departure here can be found in the policy recommendations of the 1981 White House Conference on Aging, which devoted a special miniconference to educational needs of older adults[20] and offered a four-part rationale for education in old age:

• *Surviving*: learning for economic necessity

• *Coping*: learning for practical life-skills

• *Giving*: learning for community contributions

• *Growing*: learning for self-realization

There is a parallel between the goals enunciated at the White House Conferences in 1971 and 1981. But perhaps more important is the theme chosen by the 1981 Miniconference on Lifelong Learning and Aging: "Self-Sufficiency." Clearly, the decade of the 1970s had brought a shift in the outlook among those committed to lifelong learning for older adults. While still sentimentally attached to the earlier, utopian goals, by the 1980s there was now an understanding that educational progress for older people would not come through federal money or new programs. During the 1970s there had been a hopefulness that greeted the 1976 Lifelong Learning Act— introduced by then-Senator Walter Mondale. But that hope gave way to realism when the Lifelong Learning Act was passed but never funded. By the time of the Reagan domestic budget cutbacks of the early 1980s, few defenders of bold new domestic policy initiatives could be found. As the mood of liberal hopes cooled, there was understanding of the new political and economic environment in which adult education programs would exist in the foreseeable future:

• *The economic problem*: high unemployment among older workers and lack of retraining for jobs in growth sectors of industry

• *The social service problem*: excessive dependency on social services provision that cannot meet the demands for trained personnel and services.

• *The political problem*: lack of opportunity for empowerment of the elderly, especially the poor, in decisions affecting their lives

• *The existential problem*: increases in longevity unmatched by any clear sense of the purpose or meaning of this lengthening of old age

When we examine each of these problems identified here, we can find the elements of a new rationale for late-life learning, a rationale more in tune with the political and economic realities of the years ahead.

Retraining of Older Workers

In the remaining years of this century, demographers predict declining numbers of youth and younger workers, while the number of middle-aged and older workers will rise. The economy and the labor market seem certain to remain volatile in response to disruptions of technology, international trade, and the obsolescence of skills. Yet, to date, neither employers nor educational institutions have been eager to involve older workers in retraining to equip them with skills for the new growth industries of the future. The economic challenge—lifelong learning for economic survival—has a strong claim for serious attention from public policy in the United States.[21]

Education in Coping Skills

The last decade has seen an upsurge in services for the elderly: nutrition, social services, health care, and so on. Yet as these service sector jobs have expanded, the human service providers have done virtually nothing to educate their elderly clients in how to do more for themselves. Public policy unfortunately encourages a service strategy, not learning for self-reliance. Instead of education for self-sufficiency, the service strategy has promoted still further dependency among the elderly.

Education for Citizenship and Empowerment

The Older Americans Act calls for involvement of older people in planning for services. Yet the actual operation of advisory boards for area agencies has often been little more than window dressing. Older people often have more time for involvement or contribution in community activities. Yet there have been few efforts to encourage serious education or training for citizen participation among older people except as a "silver-haired lobby" on behalf of narrowly defined needs.

Liberal Education

One bright spot over the last decade has been the growth of programs for leisure-time and liberal arts education for retired persons: for example, in Elderhostel or the Institutes for Retired Professionals. Yet all these programs have been organized in such a way as to guarantee that they remain outside the mainstream of higher education. Their success has been confined to an elite elderly group who have been fortunate enough to have access to those learning opportunities. The success of liberal education programs poses something of a paradox: education for self-fulfillment has a powerful claim as a humanistic ideal, yet it has a weak claim on public resources. Any vision of the good life in an aging society should certainly include provision of opportunities for self-fulfillment. Yet it remains a real question how public policy should respond to this ideal.

OLDER ADULT EDUCATION FOR LIFE SKILLS

Older adult education should occupy a central position as part of a broader strategy to enhance the life skills and capacities of older people themselves. Such an educational strategy demands a much broader approach than education for aging has had in the past. In particular, it is necessary to go beyond a limited academic approach and give greater attention to experiential learning that builds on strengths of life experience. That new style requires collaboration among educators and service providers in the aging network. Instead of a traditional academic model, we need a piggyback approach that incorporates older adult learning throughout the human service system—in nutrition programs, senior centers, health clinics, and other community locations. Older adult education should be tied to self-help opportunities.

The Self-Help Alternative

The growth of self-help represents a distinctive form of lifelong learning and poses a challenge to our concept of education in an aging society.[22] Instead of educational institutions setting the agenda, individuals and groups set their own learning goals in mutual collaboration. For older people a key feature of mutual self-help groups is the style of experiential learning in such groups.[23] These groups not only provide services; they also promote learning of new skills based on exchange of personal experience among members of the group.

Education for Self-Help. Education in later life can help older people learn skills for self-sufficiency and coping with problems of aging. An impressive example here is the Senior Health and Peer Counseling Center of Santa Monica, California, where older adult education is combined with self-help groups.

Classes and workshops are focused on blood pressure control, nutrition, stress management, exercise, and health education. Health screening and referral services, linked to nearby hospitals, are also available. The Santa Monica Center is nationally known for recruiting and training peer counselors: elderly people who work with other older people in emotional distress.

The Santa Monica program illustrates a striking demonstration of the piggyback model of late-life education for coping skills. Education is integrated with concrete services in health and mental health: physical and emotional needs are both incorporated. Instead of a "hard path" of constantly expanding services and entitlements for a dependent population, here we have a "soft path" where education for mutual self-help builds coping skills along with self-esteem.

Health care is not the only area where education and self-help can collaborate to build the capacity of older people. Another area of importance is nutrition.

Peer Nutrition for the Elderly. Nutrition services have been a cornerstone of the Older Americans Act since the early 1970s. The mutual-aid approach to nutrition education is illustrated by the Peer Nutrition for the Elderly program developed in 1978 in conjunction with the University of Arizona Cooperative Extension Service. The project is aimed at older people participating at 44 senior centers served by the local Area Agency on Aging in Phoenix, Arizona. Nutrition education classes are offered twice a month at each senior center by trained senior aides. These are paraprofessionals, all 55 or older, who are themselves trained by the project director and who in turn present nutrition classes to other older people. It is an instance of the well-established "each one/teach one" philosophy.

Nutrition classes themselves last just under a half hour and are given an hour before the congregate meal at lunchtime in order to reach the maximum audience. Classes cover topics such as nutritional concepts, consumer education, meal-planning, and health issues related to diet. The classes make use of a range of teaching techniques, including group discussion, slides, games, films, cooking demonstrations, individual counseling, and opportunities for questions and answers. Follow-up is provided through a regular newsletter to participants.

The local elderly are directly involved in planning the program through an advisory board that sets goals and monitors progress. A professional in the home economics extension agency of the University of Arizona Cooperative Service is responsible for technical preparation and training the aides. Funding for the program has come from Titles III and V of the Older Americans Act.[24]

The striking aspects of the Phoenix Peer Nutrition Education Program are its astonishing success in linking the mutual-aid model to life skills education and its ability to do so at extremely low cost (less than six dollars per participant per year). The potential of the "soft path" for education for self-help among older people has yet to be tapped. Part of the success of the Peer Nutrition Program springs from the combination of a self-help model with resources available from higher education. The same combination has also proved successful in life skills education for displaced homemakers.

Education and Retraining Displaced Homemakers. In 1976 the Vocational Education Act for the first time focused on the educational needs of middle-aged displaced homemakers.[25] "Displaced homemaker" refers to the person who, through divorce or separation, or the death or disability of a spouse, finds herself needing to move back into the job market at the age of 40 or beyond. In the years since its inception, this national effort at retraining displaced homemakers has demonstrated the feasibility of public initiatives to build on the capacities of age and experience.

The successful programs have provided practical life skills training —for example, in personal financial management or job search techniques. Another element has been helping older women translate knowledge from life experience in homemaking or volunteer work into paid employment. As in other self-help efforts, experiential learning for these women means both learning new skills and building on prior experience in order to transfer those skills to new applications. Local chapters of the Older Women's League, often in collaboration with community colleges, now offer training programs on financial and retirement planning, housing, health needs, and family life, and they also influence skills acquired in leadership development and advocacy training.

Education for displaced homemakers is crucial because older women, as a group, still exhibit rates of poverty far higher than the average. Many steps are needed to eliminate that poverty, but one of the most important is giving older women the skills to prevent impoverishment by enhancing their income-earning capacity. The education initiatives of the Older Women's League demonstrate that this approach is feasible. But, as with other self-help efforts, the need for support from government or the educational system is also evident.

The effectiveness of all these programs for late-life learning stands in contrast to conventional policies based on old-age dependency. Instead of proliferating services and transfer payments, these programs build on the life experience and strength of older people. Today, as funds for health care and social services are being cut, clients and patients are vulnerable because they lack skills of self-sufficiency. Gerontological professionals have not been trained in how to educate older people for such life-skills. The elderly, in particular, have been seen as a group for whom only services, not education, is appropriate.

An alternative approach would favor older adult education through participation and normalization—Stage 3 of the model proposed earlier. This alternative is based on a model of lifespan development firmly anchored in expectations for personal responsibility and community contribution. Mutual self-help, tied to educational opportunity, offers promising hope in this direction. But without public investment in building skills and capacity—that is, education—for the older population this promise will not be fulfilled.

HIGHER EDUCATION IN THE AGING SOCIETY

Some of the most exciting initiatives in older adult learning have taken place outside the mainstream of our colleges and universities. Yet the higher education system itself remains crucial and its potential for late-life learning has barely begun to be explored. A new role for higher education becomes necessary at a time when higher education institutions themselves are now adapting to an aging society. Colleges and universities are already being forced to cope with demographic fluctuations, such as the declining number of 18-year-olds and with the spread of aging, "tenured-in" faculties in a period when institutional survival puts a premium on flexibility and change.

The coming of an aging society is likely to accelerate a trend toward nontraditional higher education[26] if only because of institutional self-interest. The future will mean more older students and fewer young people in the population. So far, colleges and universities have weathered the impact of the 1980's "baby bust" by enlarging their clientele through modest changes, more flexible programs, and aggressive marketing to recruit students. American higher education has demonstrated impressive flexibility in scheduling and outreach, in providing credit for life experience, and in offering counseling for adult learners. In some cases, separate programs—evening programs or weekend colleges—have brought education to sites beyond the traditional campus.[27] But these separate programs never quite achieve parity with the standard educational offerings. They always remain examples of "learning at the backdoor."[28]

Beyond Access

Most policy discussion on education for older adults has been centered on issues of access: how to make the current higher education system more available to older people. But in thinking about older learners, other issues may be more important than promoting access. For example, the pedagogical traditions of the university are not compatible with the active learning interests and individual learning styles of adults. With the process of aging, individuals become more, not less, diverse. Individualized learning based on life experience is more appropriate than the teaching style of conventional education. In short, there are basic conflicts between the expectations of experienced adults and the curriculum of postsecondary institutions. This situation calls for much more innovation by institutions themselves, not just to respond to existing demand but to create imaginative programs for a better educated aging population in the future.[29]

In thinking about lifelong learning for an aging society, we can easily be deceived by needs assessment tied to the status quo. Surveys of perceived educational needs are always dependent on a respondent's prior experience with education. But people do not really have a sense of what

the need or demand for education might be until actually offered a concrete alternative program. The successful experience of the Open University in Great Britain has demonstrated this point.[30] Educational innovation for an aging society demands not merely access to a predetermined
product but redesign of the product itself to meet the needs of learners
who bring with them special strengths of age and experience.

An outstanding example of innovative design was the creation of Elderhostel, a summer educational program for older people.[31]

> **Elderhostel.** Elderhostel was founded in 1975 as a short-term resi-
> dential college program for people over sixty. Courses are noncredit
> and in the liberal arts and sciences; sponsoring institutions are largely
> four-year colleges and universities, but about 10 percent are other
> educational institutions such as environmental study centers, sci-
> entific research stations, or conference centers. By 1985 more than
> 100,000 students annually were enrolled.

A 1984 national survey confirmed that the Elderhostel population
is generally not a disadvantaged group. Their income and educational status are certainly above average for those over 60; 75 percent of Elderhostelers have attended college in contrast to 15 percent of the general U.S. aged population. A key feature of Elderhostel
is the residential format. The residential program offers a degree of
intimacy and socialization that is an important part of the package.
Elderhostel is also noncredit; participants enroll just for the joy of
learning. Finally, there is a travel aspect to Elderhostel that fits into
a new retirement life-style. Elderhostel is a learning network available for individuals to use as they wish: a unique combination of
socialization, travel, and continuing education.

Why has Elderhostel been such a phenomenal success story? In large
part because it offers a new retirement life-style that reinforces self-re-
spect. But Elderhostel also works because it promotes morale among campus staff. Today there are common complaints from college faculty about
declining skills, poor motivation, and career orientation on the part of
younger students. But at many campuses professors fight to teach in Elderhostel because older students are an ideal audience for liberal education. Faculty enthusiasm in turn reinforces the feeling of self-worth on
the part of Elderhostel participants. Innovation is sustained to a degree
far beyond what would be possible through either the marketplace or policies of mandated access.

But the reasons for success are deeper. William Berkeley, Elderhostel's president, points to founder Marty Knowlton's creative insight in 1975. In the mid-1970s, it was a radical idea to think of the elderly as a resource, as people with a potential for growth and continued learning. In retrospect, Elderhostel seems obvious. Elderhostel was not an idea whose time had come but rather an idea that was long overdue.

But most institutions at that time did not see the elderly as a positive market. Public rhetoric was dominated by a negative picture of old age; 1975 was the year Robert Butler's book on aging, ominously titled *Why Survive?* won the Pulitzer Prize and called wide attention to the plight of the elderly in America. Ironically, even at the time, that negative image was quickly becoming out of date. One could already point to a sizable group of nonpoor, healthy, well-educated elderly interested in educational opportunities. But there were few institutions to meet that need. Gerontologists and higher education institutions were preoccupied with turning out social workers and health care professionals to care for the ills of old age. Few adult educators bothered to think of lifelong learning as continuing past age 65. When they did so, they thought, not in terms of innovation, but in terms of the traditional liberal idea of open access.

Reduced-Tuition/Space-Available Programs

Open access has been the dominant policy principle in public higher education for older people. Along those lines, the most important public policy initiative promoting late-life education has been the tuition waiver programs that have become popular in the United States. The basic idea behind the policy was simple and appealing. In publicly supported colleges and universities, senior citizens would be eligible to enroll in any class if there was space available in that class after the regular enrollment was completed. Enrollment of older students in the classroom, apparently, would cost nothing extra but would open up access to education for older people. In state after state, legislatures authorized tuition reduction or tuition-free access for senior citizens who wish to enroll in institutions of higher education. A 1979 survey of 2,400 colleges and universities found that 63 percent of community colleges and 43 percent of all four-year colleges and universities offered space-available/reduced-tuition plans for senior citizens.[32]

Despite this remarkable growth, the number of senior citizens who enroll in the tuition-waiver plan has been disappointingly small. It is rare that more than a hundred or so will attend classes on a campus of ten thousand or more students. The reasons for lack of enrollment include the fact that many people do not know about the program, others lack transportation, and still others find the campus environment intimidating. But probably the most important reason is that older people simply do not want the kind of learning offered by conventional higher education. Tuition waiver policies were based on the premise that financial need was the fundamental barrier to access by older people. If the financial barrier were removed, by eliminating tuition, then greater access would be achieved. The fact that large enrollment gains have not followed suggests that the premise is mistaken.[33]

The credit-based/degree-bound education offered in mainstream higher education is simply not what most older people themselves actually want. They may accept it, because it is cost-free, but the style of teaching and learning offered in the mainstream is almost entirely at odds with everything known about older adult education. Regular courses involve testing, grades, and competition. They generally make no provision for drawing on the life experience of students or allowing time for extended discussion, reflection, or self-paced learning. Peterson puts it bluntly: "The expectation that older people will enroll in the institution's regular courses is doomed to failure."[34] And K. Patricia Cross comments:

> Such tuition-waiver programs appear to fly in the face of . . . the evidence offered in the needs assessments. . . . Courses designed for academic credit are not likely to meet the identified needs of the elderly, and they are likely to be conducted in a competitive atmosphere, even if the adult learner is not a direct competitor. Moreover, classroom lectures or other traditional methods of instruction do not utilize the experience of older learners and their desire to contribute to the discussion. . . . Finally, free tuition, while nice, does not appear to remove a major barrier to learning for older people.[35]

The Pattern of Success

A contrasting approach is found in Elderhostel and also in successful ventures such as the Institute for Retired Professionals (IRP), which was founded in 1962 at the New School but has since spread to twenty other institutions, including Duke, Temple, and Harvard Universities.[36] Unlike Elderhostel, the IRP and similar programs draw on the skills and experience of older adults themselves as teachers. It is a mutual-aid model applied to liberal education in later life. Parallels to the IRP model can be found internationally in the spread of the University of the Third Age, which offers late-life learning in proximity to higher education institutions but uses nontraditional methods.[37] The University of the Third Age has flourished in France, Spain, and Scandinavia and is now appearing in other countries. Like the IRP, the Universities of the Third Age draw on the local culture and resources of higher education but use those resources in nontraditional ways.

We need not conclude that liberal education for older adults must be confined to an elite group, as the IRP programs have been. Comparable off-campus instruction in the liberal arts has been demonstrated by the Institute of Study for Older Adults based in Brooklyn, New York. Under the Institute's program, members of senior centers help design their own courses, primarily in the liberal arts, while local community colleges send instructors to the local senior center and offer classes in a congenial environment. Even among the poor and less educated elderly, courses in the liberal arts, as well as life skills, are among the most popular.

Those who are comfortable coming to a college campus—Elderhostelers or IRP members, for instance—are typically well-educated people with positive prior experiences with education. But campus-based learning is not for everyone. For other older people, access to higher education may have to come through the local senior center, or the church or synogogue, or perhaps even through store fronts or nursing homes. Successful ventures suggest that late-life education in the liberal arts does not have to be restricted to the elite. By using cassettes and large-print books, by drawing on volunteers, by bringing programs into senior centers or community sites, it is possible to vastly enlarge the audience for liberal education in retirement.

The pattern of successful ventures of higher education for older adults suggests why conventional approaches—such as tuition waiver policies —are not working. A more effective approach involves something more than opening up access by older people to conventional credential-based education. Higher education could make a much larger contribution to late-life learning, if public policies were fashioned to provide incentives in that direction. Today, college administrators are not eager to advertise the availability of space-available/reduced-tuition policies, because that would increase enrollment in a situation where reimbursement does not cover costs of instruction or administration. By contrast, where reimbursement formulas provide the proper incentives, the situation can be dramatically different. For instance, Saddleback Community College in California draws fully 20 percent of its student body from senior citizens, chiefly because it offers off-campus classes at nearby Leisure World, with its 22,000 retirees who are eager participants in adult education. At Saddleback, reimbursement formulas for enrollment levels provide appropriate institutional incentives.

The numbers of people of traditional college age (18 to 24) will decline by the end of the 1980s.[38] As higher education seeks a new clientele of students, it may move to look more seriously at retired persons. But such a move would involve major changes in curriculum, teaching methods, and financing, far more so than the modest shift toward more nontraditional programs in the 1970s. Neither higher education nor the aging service network have exercised leadership in designing policies that would offer real opportunities for late-life education on any significant scale. Without that leadership, even promising ventures such as Elderhostel, the IRP, or Universities of the Third Age will remain on the sidelines, far from the mainstream of higher education. Higher education has a strategic role in promoting lifespan development in an aging society. But the challenge of fashioning public policies toward that goal is a task for the future.

Lifespan Development or Market Imperatives?

American society has prized education but has favored it for reasons linked to America's image of itself as a youth culture. According to that popular image, education offers hope for the next generation, a promise of upward mobility, or a means of building economic progress. These are all purposes that command enthusiasm and that have evoked public policies in support of those goals. When higher education has attempted to address adult development it has been through nontraditional learning or through market-driven programs in continuing education, rarely through a comprehensive vision that draws on what is already known about adult lifespan development. Until recently neither educational institutions nor the public at large have given any serious support to late-life education.

Our traditional images of youth and age tell us that youth, not age, is the time for learning. Even the weakening of the linear life plan has not fundamentally changed this assumption. The new boom in nontraditional learning has not challenged the traditional image. Instead we have expanded our image of youth into middle adulthood. Continuing education has introduced market imperatives while driving out human development goals at every turn.

The effect of market imperatives has been to extend the domain of credentialism over the entire life course. When middle-aged executives or housewives go back to college or attend special seminars, then adult learners take up the position of youth: they are resocialized for new roles and new skills. But this is not human development so much as it is defensive education in a competitive job market. In a period of rapid social and technological change, this middle-class style of lifelong learning is increasingly becoming obligatory for more and more segments of the population.

But this popular style of lifelong learning may not find much place for older learners, since older adults are less and less required for tasks within the economic system. Old people may pursue education, but it is strictly a private pursuit of leisure-time activity, without any larger meaning or purpose. Here is a view of old age as a phase of life cut off from any shared future, cut off from past and future generations.

These considerations not only explain why education for older people tends to have low priority. They also suggest why, at the outset, we have no clear basis for what public policy should be in this domain. Educators and gerontologists may wax enthusiastic over demonstration programs that show what is possible. But demonstrating the feasibility of older adult education does not tell us why, as a matter of social policy, educational opportunities ought to be provided to older people. There is a basic contradiction here: old people are becoming a "surplus population" or perhaps, a "new clientele" for higher learning. But our policy framework can find no real reason for supporting older adult education in the first place.

Late-Life Education: The Missed Opportunity

Robert Hutchins, in The Learning Society, invokes the Athenian vision of a society where all citizens aim at the full development of their highest powers.[39] This full development of human life was called Paidea or what we might loosely translate as "lifelong development through education." This vision of Paidea—the learning society—today could be one that includes late-late education as a path for lifespan development. The coming of an aging society seems to offer a new historical foundation for achieving this vision of lifelong learning. Optimistic forecasts assure us that we are entering an era when lifelong learning and lifespan development will become institutionalized throughout society. The growing numbers of older people would constitute a new clientele for higher education.

But reality has fallen far short of this lofty vision. Why is it that when we look at education for older adults over the last decade we see such a disparity between the promise and the achievement? Why have such good ideas as older worker retraining, life skills education, citizenship partici- pation, and liberal education for older people failed to take root—even after demonstration projects have shown over and over again how they can meet the clear needs and desires of older people?

When we look at the development of educational gerontology itself, a dismal picture takes shape. Back in 1974, the Academy for Educational Development published a series of monographs, beginning with *You Are Never Too Old To Learn*.[40] These monographs documented the impres- sive programmatic diversity and creativity of new educational offerings for older people at American colleges and universities. When we look today we can still find impressive programmatic descriptions, for in- stance, of retraining programs for older workers or liberal arts education for retired persons. But the programs never become the basis for changes in educational policy. It is as if the very existence of inspiring programs —or the demonstration that such programs are possible—is enough.

Celebrations of the coming of a learning society sometimes sound as if the mere existence of demonstration programs will somehow pave the way for acceptance in a utopian future. But the utopian impulse fails to con- front embedded ideologies and vested interests that block serious change. So the next step—policies to anchor those programs in the fabric of in- stitutional life—never gets taken. That failure is not simply a matter of institutional self-interest but also a failure of imagination among the very proponents of lifelong learning.

In the first instance, it is necessary to examine critically the incentives of the educational system as a political and economic structure in itself. Why does the currency of the higher education economy—the credit system—impoverish the learning of older adults? What are the vulnera- bilities of the higher education system today and where are the openings for change? In a new environment of heightened competition for the lei- sure-time market of the young-old, we are likely to see educational pro- grams competing with travel, recreation, entertainment, and other activ- ities as marketplace imperatives dictate the shape of noncredit learning.

We also need to look at the question of who pays and who benefits from the arrangement of learning opportunities available in society. With education of older people, we need to ask which groups of elderly receive benefits of education and which groups might receive benefits under alternative political conditions. For example, it is generally accepted that, under the prevailing conditions, both market and nonmarket factors insure that the highest educated and most affluent groups have the highest participation rates in adult education. This seems to be the pattern, not only for fee-based programs, like Elderhostel, but also for open programs, like the tuition-free programs at state universities.

This participation pattern presents a dilemma. Most adult educators believe that the elderly poor have the greatest need for education in self-help, job retraining, or political empowerment. Yet the programs that exist are not reaching the poor. Statistics repeatedly show that both fee-based and tuition-free programs fail to reach those with the greatest needs for education. It is hard to escape the conclusion that the present distribution of resources guarantees that the affluent, well-educated elderly are receiving the lion's share of opportunities, while little or nothing is done for the poor. But the formal educational system itself is in no position to change this, since education for older people attracts little attention in the youth-oriented education system that now prevails.

The solution to this problem will not come through the popular idea of access. The more educational opportunity is made available, the wider grows the gap between the people who have education and those who do not. What counts is motivation, not just opportunity or capacity. Simply providing more options means that well-educated people will take advantage of the opportunities. Poorly educated people, which today means people over 65, are falling further behind as adult education opportunities expand.[41] Will this pattern persist in the future? Until fairly recently, the elderly have been, on average, severely disadvantaged in comparison with younger adults. But with rising education levels of successive cohorts of elderly and with general population aging, all industrialized societies are becoming increasingly homogeneous with respect to levels of educational attainment. This shift is an important development, but in itself it will not eliminate the inequity in access among subgroups within the elderly population today or in the future.

Research and practical experience have confirmed the capacity of older adults to learn and public policy has offered modest opportunities. But this prescription does not go far enough. There certainly ought to be many options and multiple auspices, locations, and types of programs available. But if programs are to be coordinated and not totally fragmented, it may demand some public response to see that resources get driven to places that the free market does not take care of.

The policy question is always who pays and who benefits. If only a limited group of older people benefit for strictly private purposes, then it is hard to argue with those who insist that older people should come on a pay-as-you-go basis. But if we have an image of education in late life as the systematic development of human capacities, if we can design programs to address problems of increasing literacy, improving health care, maintaining nutrition, retraining people for jobs, enlisting the talents of volunteers, helping younger generations, and contributing to the common good of society, then there is far less trouble selling the idea of older adult education to legislators, to departments of higher education, to the taxpayers, and to the public. These are the terms in which the policy debate must be cast.[42]

The starting point of this book is a conviction that education can contribute dramatically to quality of life in old age. To make a case for a wider public policy supporting late-life education, we need to see quality-of-life issues in a broader context. Today public policy—as symbolized by the tuition-free/space-available programs—still looks on education of old people as a frill, as inessential, strictly as a matter of private decisions, and, above all, as something that does not cost any money and certainly is not worth spending any money on. How would we feel if health care or the education of children were seen that way? We need to take late-life education with more seriousness instead of seeing it as a way of filling up time for the old folks. In the future, as cohorts of older people become increasingly better educated, there is likely to be an increase in those who could take advantage of adult education programs if the opportunities were provided. The potential for lifespan development through education is clear. But what remains unclear is whether our major social institutions will move toward providing these opportunities in the years to come.

11

Retraining Older Workers

The coming of an aging society means a population with a growing number of middle-aged and older workers. If the aging society of the future is to maintain or increase the level of productivity of the past, it will be necessary to engage the productivity of older workers, who represent a human resource largely wasted or ignored in the past.[1] To make use of that human resource will mean changes in retirement policies and incentives that have historically reduced the labor market participation by older workers in favor of earlier retirement.[2] What is needed are not simply prowork policies but something more imaginative. Indeed, some voices have called for a revision in our conventional concept of the life course so that in the third quarter of life—roughly, age 50 to 75—there would be greater opportunities for more flexible participation in the labor force.[3]

But in a rapidly evolving postindustrial economy, these goals will not be easily achieved. Changes in technology, international trade, and the composition of the labor market make it necessary to retrain workers for jobs that did not exist in the past. For years gerontologists and specialists in adult education or human resource management have called for retraining of older workers, but such proposals were not taken seriously. Serious policy debates on work and retirement revolved around Social Security and pension policies, where large public expenditures were at stake. Retraining and other human development policies were seen as "soft" options related only to quality of life.

Today there are new conditions that could reverse that history of neglect for worker retraining:

- Technological change—for example, the impact of computers and automation—is dramatically reshaping the workplace. Worker retraining is becoming a necessity for individual and organizational survival.

- New federal manpower initiatives, such as the Job Training Partnership Act, are actively involving the private sector and represent a departure from manpower policies of the past.

- Changing demographic structure of the labor force: through the remainder of this century there will be declining numbers of younger workers and growing numbers of middle-aged and older workers.

- New interest in work-life extension, prompted by elimination of mandatory retirement, a higher age of eligibility for Social Security, and desire for personal financial security.

- Concern for sagging U.S. productivity and competition in the international economy, prompting steps to improve the quality of the work force over the entire lifespan.

These trends represent a challenge and an opportunity for the future. But behind the trends there is a human story of unemployment and despair being enacted in America's old industrial communities as jobs disappear and industries decline. One illustration is the story unfolding in Youngstown, Ohio, in response to industrial dislocation.

CASE STUDY: YOUNGSTOWN, OHIO

Youngstown, Ohio, is a classic illustration of the painful transition from smokestack industries to the uncertain postindustrial economy of the future.

Youngstown has historically been a blue-collar, unionized town. But in the last decade, the city has been hard hit by plant closings in the rubber, automobile, and sheet metal industries. One of the most devastating of these was the closing of the steel mills in Youngstown in 1977, which put more than 5000 workers out of their jobs.[4] The impact of plant closings and unemployment varies greatly according to the age of employees—primarily because of the "last hired/first fired" seniority rules of labor unions. Seniority rules help some older workers (those over 55)

but hurt others (those 40 to 55). Workers over 55 not only enjoy seniority but can also go on early retirement and in any case are likely to own
their own homes.

In this environment older workers sometimes feel guilty while younger
workers (25 to 40) who have recently been laid off are likely to be bitter.
Unions are caught in the middle and may encourage older blue-collar
workers, who often have good pensions, to leave early, opening up positions for younger workers who are the future of the union. An older worker
who leaves may apply for disability. Workers Compensation pays better
than early retirement, and so older workers who leave early can stay on
disability until age 60 or 65. Many officially "retired" workers, and workers on disability as well, work at cash jobs (electrical repair, home building, painting, plumbing, etc.). The underground cash economy cushions
some of the casualties created by competition between older and younger
workers for the declining jobs in Youngstown's industrial sector.

In the scramble to hold on to jobs in declining industries, we see some
unpleasant dilemmas of generational equity: for example, the conflict between seniority and solidarity in the labor movement. Will retraining of
older workers improve mobility and soften the intergenerational conflict
for jobs? Retraining efforts are just beginning, but Youngstown's industries are cooperating. Perhaps two-thirds of workers to be retrained are in
their thirties; the rest are older workers, often fearful about retraining.
Some are retrained for high-technology jobs—to repair robots or computers. These jobs require higher skills, yet there are fewer of these positions than there are jobs eliminated. Jobs in growing industries are likely
to be located elsewhere in the country, but unemployed older workers in
Youngstown are reluctant to leave. Strong family ties among the Polish,
Slovak, or Italian ethnic groups keep people from looking elsewhere, and
in any case, it is difficult to sell houses or to find jobs that match skills
or previous pay scales.[5]

The impact of industrial change in Youngstown during the 1970s was
particularly severe on the older worker: more than a third of those displaced by plant closings or shutdowns ended up on early retirement with
a loss of more than half their previous wage level. Those displaced workers who did find other jobs generally took positions at far less money and
with a degradation of skills: retail trade, fast food, or other low skill/low
pay service fields. Others still hang on—hoping for industrial recovery,
fearful of the deskilling and downward mobility that the future seems to
hold.

But the situation may not be hopeless. Against the gloom of the

Youngstown case, we may cite one of many examples where industrial change has been accompanied by successful retraining of older workers.

EXAMPLE OF AER LINGUS

Aer Lingus, the Irish national airline, was faced with the need to modify operation of its major cargo warehouse by transforming it into an automated facility using computer-controlled management of freight linked to an information management system for the entire unit. In doing so, the company faced a major choice. Would older workers be let go or would they be retrained for the new operation? The company chose retraining, and the gamble paid off.

The Aer Lingus retraining effort was divided into three stages. First, workers were thoroughly oriented to the changes about to take place in the warehouse. Next, they received information about the new system and became familiar with new methods and problems. Finally, workers were retrained to manage the system using the "Discovery Method" pioneered in Britain by the Belbins in their extensive studies of worker retraining. Retraining built on prior experience but adapted that earlier experience to new, more productive technology: a classic example of the "value-added" approach to older worker retraining.[6]

THE NEW POLITICS OF OLDER WORKER
RETRAINING

The choice of retraining or layoffs is one thing when that choice is made in a single company. The choice becomes quite different when an entire industry—steel, textiles, shipbuilding—is faced with industrial decline. The scenario in Youngstown—and in Buffalo, Detroit, Cleveland, and other cities across the country—has become familiar. Economic change, we are told, always has winners and losers. If the balance comes out on the side of net growth and economic advance, then shrinkage of "mature" industries may not be a bad thing. It simply becomes one more chapter in the history of the "creative destruction" that identified with the dynamic movement of capitalism: no gain without pain. In fact, by mid-1980s, even in the "frost-belt" cities of Boston, New York, and Philadelphia, there were signs of resurgent regional economic growth, no longer in the old smokestack industries, but in new service industries tied to the postindustrial economy.[7] Creative destruction seemed to be working.

But creative destruction is not policy that will make an aging work force productive. Still less does it address the issues of equity—the human losses—entailed by industrial decline. Deindustrialization is likely to leave the losers behind. Workers who lose their jobs in declining sectors are not the same ones who get jobs in growing industries. In the process of change, older workers may be at a particular disadvantage.

George Maddox once observed that our society cultivates a "no deposit, no return" attitude toward older people. The "throwaway" culture not only discards empty bottles or obsolete machinery; it also discards human beings in a process of creative destruction led by the economic cycle of boom and bust or rising and declining industries.[8] That harsh economic image is the exact opposite of an ecological vision in which generations succeed each other in a balanced cycle of renewal. The ecological vision includes an image of recycling that might inspire in us the ideal of renewing all our resources, including people, rather than throw them away and then wonder how to dispose of them properly.[9]

In a growing number of cases, "retirement" actually becomes a euphemism for discouraged or dislocated workers in the U.S. economy. The group called "at-risk" includes older workers. Here the aging of the population is linked to the aging of declining industries in the American economy: older workers are more likely to be found in older industries. Persons over 55 are more likely to have worked in automobiles and steel, rubber and durable goods and much less likely to have worked in growth fields such as computers, electronics, or financial services. A study by the Congressional Budget Office (CBO) estimates that, during the coming decade, 15 percent of all manufacturing jobs will be eliminated. This translates into 3 million displaced workers in the present decade and, by the end of the century, 7 million.[10] As defined by the CBO study, approximately half of displaced workers are over age 45. If we add to these figures the ranks of displaced homemakers—a major cause of poverty among single women in old age—then the numbers would be even higher.

As Harrington notes, what is new today is not the cyclical unemployment that has disproportionately affected minority groups, for example. Rather, it is a structural unemployment striking at the industrial heartland. Even the optimistic forecasts of the Reagan Administration estimate that unemployment will remain at high levels for years to come, as it has in the recent past.

Because of the threat of unemployment to older workers, it is not surprising that older workers insist on seniority rules and push for policies to protect their jobs and preserve existing industries. They feel they have no alternative. It is a defensive response, like trade protectionism to keep out foreign imports. But protectionism, in the form of seniority rules, is strictly a short-run solution. It has a serious long-run cost to the older worker:

> Protection erodes his employability, without offering him real security. He is safe during mild contractions of the market and from the effects of the pruning of labor when companies introduce labor-saving devices, but he is still subject to the shake-out which throws him mercilessly on to the labor market when whole units have to be closed down. Then his long-standing service may count for little. . . .[11]

The result of protectionist policies may be to preserve jobs for dwindling numbers of older workers while long-term decline continues unchecked: precisely what happened to thousands of jobs among longshoremen during the long decline of the ports of New York and San Francisco. Today an aging, and dwindling, band of longshoremen preside over a declining American shipping industry. Protectionism "worked" for those who managed to hold on to jobs. But this zero-sum solution was not an effective response to the problem. Is this a forecast of things to come in other sectors of the economy? Demands for protectionism are rising today: shoes, apparel, electronics, steel, machine tools, appliances—the list is endless. Instead of retraining the work force for postindustrial growth, we are tempted by a policy of protecting and defending the past.

As Mancur Olson has warned, when key interest groups move into a position to veto innovation, economic growth comes to a halt.[12] Older workers could be in precisely such a position. But older workers—workers aged 40 to 60 and beyond—will soon be a critical element in the American labor force. By the end of the century, the bulk of the American labor force will consist of middle-aged or older workers. They are not disposable containers that can simply be discarded when their usefulness is at an end. But there are a variety of responses in regard to how best to cope with the new economic environment.

One response is found in the prescriptions of old-time liberals who look to the tradition of the New Deal. They see the answer to older worker employment in the expansion of public service employment opportunities on the model of the WPA or CETA. Government becomes the employer of last resort and accepts the responsibility to create jobs for older workers who cannot find employment in private industry. For older people, Title V of the Older Americans Act provides such public service employment.

Unlike old-time liberals, corporate liberals prefer to see older workers employed, not by government make-work programs, but by the private sector. Earlier job training sponsored by the National Alliance of Businessmen embodied the corporate liberal viewpoint. Corporate liberals would favor a strategy of job development, through tax credits, attacking age discrimination, or other means to encourage corporations to hire older workers. If retraining for jobs is necessary, this task could be undertaken by the private sector, by educational institutions, or by government, in cooperation with others. Corporate liberal thinking is prominently reflected in the current Job Training Partnership Act, where older workers are singled out for a modest set-aside of training funds.

Neoliberals

Finally, there are those often described as neoliberals.[13] Old-time liberalism was concerned with redistribution, whereas neoliberals put more emphasis on economic growth and perhaps on industrial policy to achieve that growth.

The logic favoring a national industrial policy is based on a concept of market failure. Certain investments—e.g., basic research or worker training—are public goods that can benefit all, yet will not be promoted by individual companies. Some changes—such as plant closings entailed by competition—may have long-range benefits, but these changes also have immediate negative consequences for workers and additional costs borne by society as a whole (e.g., higher welfare costs). In short, because of market failure to respond to such costs and opportunities, government must step in. Specific government initiatives for retraining older workers would be justified because the failure of the marketplace can be corrected only in this way.

But neoliberal proponents of industrial policy disagree on specific policy initiatives. Industrial policy may call for a "preservationist" strategy —as Felix Rohatyn does in proposing a new Reconstruction Finance Corporation to support declining industries.[14] Or industrial policy may call for an "accelerationist" strategy—as Lester Thurow does in proposing to accept the decline of older industries and instead seek to encourage the new, "sunrise" industries of the future (computers, biotechnology).[15]

Robert Reich advocates a policy reminiscent of corporate paternalism where-in individual companies become responsible, perhaps legally, for retraining displaced workers for jobs in the new growth sectors.[16]

Conflicting Strategies

All varieties of liberals—old-time liberals, corporate liberals, and neoliberals—start by acknowledging the deficiencies of the marketplace. But beyond that point, disagreement arises. There is disagreement on the causes, and hence the cures, for unemployment of older workers. Old-time liberals look to government, not to private industry, to provide jobs for older workers. The old-time liberal view is dominant among aging interest groups (NCOA, AARP, National Council of Senior Citizens) whose own advocacy position is matched by sizeable Title V contracts that now comprise a substantial share of their organizational budgets. The old-time liberal view also finds a vocal constituency among nonprofit agencies who benefit from subsidized employment of older workers. It is one of the few examples of public service employment that retain visible support in Congress, which rejected the Reagan Administration's effort in 1982 to cut Title V funding at the same time that CETA was eliminated.

In the past many elements in the old-time liberal coalition have been unenthusiastic about retraining of older workers as a policy goal. From the inception of Social Security through the Great Society and the CETA program, the liberal priority has always been jobs for youth. Labor has shared these attitudes, and some unions have been distinctly ambivalent about ending mandatory retirement. Seniority protection for older workers was tied to a fixed retirement age and supported by pensions negotiated by labor leaders. This, in essence, was labor's version of the linear life plan, which long proved congenial to all parties.

Recently, union leadership has had to deal with the difficult issue of competition between older and younger workers.[17] For example, seniority issues have surfaced in the form of two-tier wage structures—one for older workers with seniority, a much lower wage for new, younger workers. Such plans have been put into effect in the automobile industry, in the postal system, and in the airlines. Two-tier wage schemes, like other forms of rationing, represent the erosion of solidarity and productivity in favor of protectionism. Some unions have acknowledged the need for employee retraining, but ambivalence remains. For many in the old-time liberal coalition, retraining is not a vital issue. Aging network professionals who

are involved with Title V, for example, often see the retraining requirements of the law as irrelevant; they see themselves as administering a
means-tested jobs program for unemployed older workers, a program that
is justified in its own right.

For at least one element in the old-time liberal coalition—organized
labor—retraining of older workers can actually have directly negative
consequences. If older union members are retrained for jobs in new, often
nonunionized industries, then there is a danger of eroding still further the
membership base of the union. Moreover, high-tech industries tend to
offer mostly low-skill, low-wage work in environments typically nonunionized. Then too, labor is well aware that retraining can be a political
gesture that seems to address problems of unemployment without actually
creating jobs.[18] With older workers, retraining alone may equally prove
to be a dead-end policy option.

The case of the neoliberals presents a mixed picture for aging policy
because of conflicting views on whether government should try to protect
the jobs of older workers in older, declining, "sunset" industries. A strictly
preservationist strategy in fact would offer little support for retraining older
workers. The result would be not very different from how the Trade Adjustment Act has worked out in practice. We would hear rhetoric about
reindustrialization, but the reality would be rear-guard protectionism. By
contrast, accelerationist neoliberals like Thurow and Reich favor incentives to develop new technologies and industries of the future. In an aging society, an accelerationist strategy means a commitment to retraining
experienced workers—that is, recycling human resources through a "value-
added" approach to manpower development over the lifespan.

Some Doubts About the Retraining Strategy

But will the accelerationist strategy actually allow us to recycle the human resources represented by an aging work force? Studies of displaced
older workers show that nearly 60 percent experience a drop in occupational status. Downward mobility was not confined to blue-collar workers: professionals and managers were also forced into lower positions. Some
would argue that such declines are only temporary, that people can bounce
back and find new openings. But it is far easier to start over at 25 or 35
than it is at age 45 or 55. Data on age discrimination assembled by the
U.S. Civil Rights Commission and by other researchers demonstrate that
ageism takes a toll in the labor market.[19] Today, under the Equal Em-

ployment Opportunity Commission (EEOC) the largest category of cases filed for discrimination are those based on age rather than on sex or other categories.

But the real point is that structural factors in the postindustrial economy require policies more far-reaching than equal opportunity or elimination of age discrimination. The service economy and high-technology industries are likely to offer lower pay than traditional manufacturing jobs; services now account for seven out of ten of the lowest paying American industries. And according to forecasts of the Bureau of Labor Statistics, the service jobs likely to expand in the future are those such as janitors, food service workers, hospital orderlies, and secretaries. The overall impact of microelectronics on industry will probably be an accelerating loss of jobs; that, after all, is the whole point of introducing automation and labor-saving devices in the first place.[20] The advent of the information economy means the deskilling of the very occupations that are growing in size. Bank tellers, computer operators, keypunchers, and retail clerks will all use computer technology but at ever lower levels of skill.

In this new economic environment, we need to look critically at proposals for work-life extension for older workers. It is doubtful that celebrated proposals for job flexibility—part-time, flex-time, phased retirement—can contribute much here. Proposals to "end the linear life plan" introduce marginal flexibility but fail to come to grips with the political economy and the reality of the dual labor market. "Flexibility" sounds appealing, but job flexibility and part-time positions for the elderly may actually end up pitting old people against other needy groups: women, minorities, and the working poor. Economic pressures have prompted employers to seek part-time workers who are less costly since they draw fewer fringe benefits than full-time workers. Between 1970 and 1982, the number of part-time workers, voluntary and involuntary, grew dramatically: from 11.5 million to 18.2 million workers. Concealed in this aggregate growth is the fact that *involuntary* part-time employment grew at a rate more than five times as fast as the voluntary sector.[21]

Labor Market Segmentation

Labor market segmentation is a complex phenomenon in which industrial change, age, education, and public policy all play a role. For example, educational credentials play a part in the new stratification of the labor market, which is increasingly divided between good jobs and bad.

Younger workers and recent graduates are likely to be more advantageously positioned with educational credentials than older workers are.

Increasingly, older workers, like workers of all ages, must cope with a dual labor market. On the one hand, high-tech, upscale positions are open to mobile professionals and technical specialists; at the same time, low-paying jobs are available in trade and services. The dual economy weakens middle-range jobs and tends to separate workers into two contrasting groups. The primary labor market includes heavy manufacturing, construction, utilities, and other sectors that often have strong unions and higher pay scales. The secondary labor market includes retail trade, office services, and certain manufacturing sectors, such as textiles, where more intense competition results in high employee turnover and lower wage levels.[22] These structural features of the labor market set the stage for the downward mobility of workers displaced from their jobs. It is a problem that reindustrialization has not been able to solve:

> For those displaced from the old mill-based industries, reindustrialization has created a serious problem. With a "missing middle" in the economy, the loss of a mill job has meant that the newly unemployed worker either had to make the leap up to the higher-skill jobs in the top end of the labor market or settle for work that is lower-skill, lower-wage, and more unstable. Making the transition to the new jobs in computer programming, systems installation, and technical consulting has not proven easy for many of them. . . . At best, reindustrialization . . . seems to have created jobs for the sons and daughters of those (workers) displaced, but not for the generation that actually worked in the (textile) mills.[23]

Under these conditions some retired workers will actually prefer part-time or unstable employment. Such retired persons who are prepared to work for low wages beneath the Social Security earnings limit are simply likely to depress wages for other older workers who need stable positions. The advent of home computer terminals and telecommuting could make it possible for still more retired persons to enter the secondary labor market and be employed on a piecework basis in the "electronic cottage" of the future.

One of the most depressing facts about the current deindustrialization of the American economy is that vulnerable groups are pitted against one another. Women, minorities, younger workers, and older workers are especially vulnerable. For some of these vulnerable groups, it is possible to be retrained and move on to new opportunities, but, as Bluestone and

Harrison put it, older workers face the prospect of being "too old to find new work, but too young to die."[24]

The solution to these problems will not be found in macroeconomic policies that ignore the structure of the lifespan or the dual labor market. Moreover, the single vision of economic calculus overlooks the human wreckage produced by policies to promote economic growth. In appraising these policies, social costs and benefits must also be taken into account, and older displaced workers will often end up paying those costs. But social accounting need not become a code word for protectionism or for the politics of distributional coalitions (special interests) who promote their own advantage against the public interest, whether by age and seniority or by some other criterion. Instead, social accounting ought to signify a balance between legitimate competing concerns. When social policy takes account of that balance—as it does, for example, in Sweden— then it is even possible for disinvestment in sunset industries to take place more quickly. Equity and growth can coexist, and neither younger nor older workers need to be sacrificed.[25]

Ironically, as Kuttner argues persuasively, more balanced attention to social, as well as economic calculus, may be indispensable for economic growth itself. Today opposition to risk and change is a powerful force supporting those distributional coalitions, whether among unions or among ailing corporations. Older workers, in particular, are simply not in a position to take risks that the young may shoulder more easily; for example, to move to the sunbelt looking for hypothetical jobs in fast-growth industries. Older workers, facing retirement or the aging of their own parents, need a margin of security, not to mention recognition of the non-monetized exchanges that are part of lifelong social networks and mediating structures. It is this social reality that single vision repeatedly overlooks. When change must come, all workers need confidence that they can be retrained for new jobs, not just thrown onto the scrap heap. Age does make a difference, and a humane industrial policy would take account of lifespan development and life stage differences among workers.

Potential for Retraining

There can no longer be doubt about the feasibility of retraining. But there are serious doubts about whether companies and industries will include older workers in their normal retraining opportunities. Employers' preference for hiring and training younger workers is well known, and that preference need not be seen as irrational or as the result of age discrimination. It may not be ageism but simply a judgment about return on investment.[26]

There are other countries, such as Japan, that take a longer range view of retraining and worker development, but that long-range view of human resource development is rare in America. Business and industry see training and retraining from a much narrower point of view than the educational system. As Reich observes:

> The vast majority of . . . programs . . . provide training in narrow jobs or in processes unique to the company rather than in broadly applicable skills. There is an obvious reason for this. Broader training would render employees much more marketable, and therefore require that the firm pay them a higher wage in order to retrain them. Few firms are so generous (or foolish) as to want to bid up the wages of their work force in this way.[27]

It would be a mistake to expect business and industry on their own to provide this kind of lifespan educational perspective—the broad-gauged skills applicable to new and emerging industries of the postindustrial society. Policy initiatives, such as the Job Training Partnership, that entrust retraining to private industry will not adequately address this problem. If this is the case, then American workers—above all, older workers—will be faced not only with skills obsolescence but also with declining opportunities to retool for opportunities in the years ahead.[28]

A crucial responsibility, therefore, falls to the educational system, particularly higher education, which, at least in its mission, has the goal of developing broad-gauged learning that could enable older workers to make use of earlier skills and adapt them with flexibility to new opportunities. There are some hopeful signs that higher education, working with government, can meet the challenge. In California and North Carolina, for example, state governments have moved imaginatively to make use of the community colleges acting in close cooperation with needs of businesses for job training.[29]

Unfortunately, with these few exceptions, the higher education system has shown little interest in the retraining needs of older workers. Despite talk of nontraditional instruction, educational opportunities remain directed at youth or younger adults. If resources for worker retraining are distributed by the existing educational system, then we can expect the youth bias of the existing educational system to have its pervasive effect. We should not be misled by expressions of interest by colleges and universities in enrolling older students. When colleges speak of older students, they mean people between 30 and 40. Retraining of workers over 50 by institutions of higher education is negligible. Without specific policy initiatives to link industry and higher education in efforts targeted at retraining older workers, we cannot expect the educational system to make much contribution to the problem discussed here.

HISTORY OF WORKER-RETRAINING POLICIES

Until very recently the task of retraining workers has not been taken seriously by policymakers in business, labor, or education. Each sector with its single vision, has disregarded the possibility of recycling human resources in the older worker. On the contrary, each sector has seen the older worker as a candidate for retirement. Companies, unions, and public officials have all acquiesced in this policy. The result has been that job-training programs have been directed at unskilled workers, typically youth. Apart from modest demonstration efforts, public policy has not supported programs that would retrain older workers whose skills are obsolete.[30]

Yet precedents for successful retraining efforts exist in the past. American policies for retraining go back to the Morrill Act (1862) and the Hughes Act (1917) providing vocational education. The New Deal saw the Civilian Conservation Corps and, during World War II, the Vocational Education for National Defense program. The wartime effort involved not just young people but adults of all ages in serious retraining opportunities. The policy focus on adult education continued later, in the postwar period, when the G.I. bill during its first decade enrolled more than 7 million veterans.

By the 1960s new social concerns had arisen and government retraining policies responded in the Manpower Development and Training Act (1962) and the Trade Expansion Act (1962) with its Worker Adjustment Assistance provisions. But the conflict between *welfare* goals and *human development* goals remained unresolved. Retraining concerns in the 1960s reflected two major policy goals: the war on poverty concern with a goal of training minority poor for employment and the goal of assisting workers displaced from their jobs by automation. One goal was responsive to youth, the other to middle-aged and older workers.

Despite limitations, these programs helped large numbers of workers of different ages. By the late 1970s a range of federal government employ-ment and training programs were enrolling well over 5 million adults. These included on-the-job training programs, institutional training pro-grams for job skills, vocational rehabilitation programs, work experience programs, and public service employment.[31]

The CETA program quickly became a political pork-barrel operation to provide public service employment and help out cities with their bud-get problems. Serious retraining efforts were neglected, even as CETA was becoming tainted as a "welfare" program. Local government failed to adequately involve the private sector and used CETA funds to cover la-bor costs for temporary positions. In the old-time liberal tradition, re-training was merely a matter of lip service.[32] These developments laid the basis for the Reagan Administration to eliminate CETA and replace it with the Job Training Partnership Act (JTPA).

The same failures in the area of training and human resource devel-opment occurred in another program—the Trade Adjustment Act—de-signed to help workers who lose their jobs because of foreign imports. But instead of paying serious attention to human resource development, the Trade Adjustment Act funds became another form of unemployment compensation. Since 1974 the Worker Adjustment Assistance Program has reached more than 400,000 workers. But only 3.7 percent of these received any retraining and less than 1 percent received relocation ben-efits.[33] In 1981, $1.5 billion in benefits was paid out, but training monies came to barely a *tenth of one percent.*[34] On the political level, the Trade Adjustment Act, like CETA, became vulnerable to the charge that it was merely a "handout" program, transferring income without retraining workers or making them more productive. In 1981 the Reagan Admin-istration acted to reduce benefit levels under the Worker Adjustment As-sistance Program—this at a time when unprecedented numbers of work-ers were feeling the impact of recession and job losses from imports.

Need for New Policy Approach

In both CETA and the Trade Adjustment Act, conservatives attacked programs that lost sight of their original policy goals. But in the attack, conservatives cut the budgets while continuing the narrow focus of poli-cies so that human development over the lifespan is even less likely. What is called for is investment in developing human capacities, not just in youth but over the life course, including middle age and later life.[35] Here we see the limits of the current JTPA, which continues an earlier CETA pattern of decentralization, now no longer under political control but through Private Industry Councils incorporating representives from many segments of the community. The problem with retraining older workers is that the costs and benefits must be assessed on a basis wider than an individual firm or industry or locality. Policymaking needs to take a broader view of the externalities involved in decisions to invest in human capital.

These facts go far in explaining the inadequacy of corporate liberalism in addressing problems of retraining older workers. Over the past decade, most of the research, demonstration projects, and public policy thinking on employment for older workers has centered on the activity of large corporations—the dominant actors in the American industrial economy. We have seen initiatives for senior employment agencies to place older workers, for new job development, for steps combating ageism, and—at a broader macroeconomic scale—for tax or investment policies to promote retention and hiring of older worker.[36] At the same time, public policy has tried to attack age discrimination and mandatory retirement. In other words, we have cautiously experimented with a corporate liberal strategy, while preserving some modest older worker jobs programs, such as Title V, that were part of the old-time liberal agenda.

This orientation has had its virtues, but two crucial areas have been overlooked. First, the emphasis on large corporations has neglected the experience of smaller companies, particularly those in fast-growing and entrepreneurial industries. And, second, the stress on placing older workers in jobs has neglected the fact that jobs in many industries—the so-called smokestack or declining industries—are now disappearing. At the same time, new industries—in microelectronics or biotechnology, for example—are growing rapidly, but older workers are not trained for jobs that become available in those growing fields. Thus, the emphasis on placing older workers in jobs is likely to fail unless it is linked to training for new jobs emerging in faster growing small businesses. Older worker employment development has generally missed the target here. Neoliberal critics correctly diagnose the problem but offer conflicting advice on policy options for the future.

Industrial Policy and Retraining

Several policy proposals have sought to overcome the defects of earlier national manpower policies. Most of these proposals are consistent with some version of industrial policy, but they are generally more modest in scope and therefore not susceptible to the criticisms that have repeatedly been made of proposals advanced under the rubric of comprehensive industrial policy.

One example is Pat Choate's concept of an Individual Training Account, financed by joining contributions from worker and company. The account could be drawn upon if the worker were displaced from a job. The funds would then constitute a voucher to be used at certified retraining institutions, on the model of the G.I. bill. A problem with Choate's proposal is that it depends on tax and savings incentives, which are likely to be more remote from low-income workers threatened with displacement.[37]

In addition, there is the fact that experience with corporate tuition reimbursement plans shows that, even with 100 percent reimbursement for college courses taken, only a tiny proportion of employees can ever make use of this fringe benefit. People tend to think of retraining, like health care, only when a problem has already presented itself. Finally, relocation assistance, along with retraining, is vital for those older workers who have built up equity in home ownership but now face high mortgage rates if they try to move and buy a new home.

Major retraining of older workers, then, demands broad changes in public manpower training policy. But action need not await national policy changes. Some unions, such as District 1199 of the Hospital Workers Union, have already embraced the idea of worker retraining. Since 1969 their Training and Upgrading Fund has been supported by an assessment of workers' payroll earnings. In 1982 the United Auto Workers and Ford opened a National Development and Training Center in Michigan to provide worker retraining. In 1984, in settlement of the UAW strike against General Motors, the company agreed to guarantee job security and provide retraining opportunities for workers whose jobs were threatened.

Policies to soften the life-cycle impact of automation and job displacement will not be easy to implement. On the one side are conservatives who believe that traditional laissez-faire capitalism will solve the dilemmas created by the impact of technology or international trade. On the other side are those calling for policies of active government intervention on behalf of threatened groups. It remains unclear whether these policies can avoid the dangers of protectionism.

TOWARD A NEW POLICY FOR RETRAINING OLDER WORKERS

Work, Aging and Postindustrial Society

Beyond disputes over industrial policy, there are larger questions here about the future of an aging society. There is deep pessimism about future job growth in advanced industrialized economies. On the one hand, new technology is needed to insure productivity growth. On the other hand, an aging work force is threatened by skill obsolescence or the vanishing of jobs altogether. These conflicts are likely to be exacerbated by the coming of an aging society. There will be problems of resistance to innovation, high and inelastic salary levels, job rationing by age and seniority, and reluctance to take risks.

As we move away from the linear life plan, we also move away from security and predictability. One response to an unpredictable world is some variety of protectionism. This defensive response sets old against the young, haves against have-nots. Another response would be to promote skills of adaptation and development over the entire life course. Instead of seeing older workers as an unproductive burden, we would invest in retraining to offer them contributive roles in many different settings.

The shift to a postindustrial economy threatens the interest of major groups—large industrial corporations, organized labor, and older workers whose skills are heavily invested in economic sectors doomed to slow decline. Those large interest groups that are threatened will only reluctantly accept the need for massive changes. In such an environment, the only alternative to obsolescence and decline will be the continuous recycling of human resources attuned to growth sectors of the postindustrial economy of tomorrow. Corporate liberal and old-time liberal policies generally fail to address that challenge because they look to big government or big business, not the small business sector where high job growth is to be found.

Small Business and Training Resources

A study by David Birch of MIT indicated that, during the 1970s, almost two thirds of the new jobs generated in the United States were created by small businesses—those that employ fewer than twenty people.

By contrast, among the largest corporations in America (the Fortune 1000), there was minimal job growth during the same period.[38] These firms generating jobs were, overwhelmingly, new, young companies. The age of companies, not just size, was important: a conclusion especially important for the issue of employment of older workers.

Birch's conclusions underscore a major policy dilemma for hopes of retraining older workers to take advantage of new jobs created in growth sectors of the economy. The problem is that the major resources for employee training and retraining are located in corporate training units of these same large corporations. Who then is to provide the training? Industrial training for older workers could be provided by the large corporations, but the new job growth is not found there. In small businesses, where the job growth is found, incentives for training or retraining older workers are not available.

The basic reason for this is simple. Small businesses generally exist in competitive industries undergoing rapid growth and change. For a company to invest heavily in training, there is risk that the benefits of the investment will be lost if the trained employee leaves to work for a competitor. But if all the companies in a specific sector were to get together and jointly support a common training institute that would provide trained employees whom any of them could hire, such an arrangement might be to the benefit of all involved.

The structural divisions between small business and large corporations, like the divisions of the dual labor market, point the way for policy initiatives in the future. What is needed, clearly, is a way to gain the advantages of pooling the cost and risk of investment, while maintaining the flexibility of small business initiative. If older workers generate lower turnover costs, then the marketplace itself might solve the job placement end of the problem.[39] But since individual companies in isolation cannot take on the risks of older worker retraining, the solution here would necessarily involve some form of industry-wide consortia. Some projects have already shown the feasibility of such an approach.

Ford Foundation Sponsorship of Retraining for Small Business. The Ford Foundation has undertaken support for consortia along the lines suggested here. An exemplary project, for example, is now underway in Michigan, where the decline of the automobile industry is the most visible sign of a wave of deindustrialization that in the last few years has eliminated nearly a half a million jobs, more than 80 percent in manufacturing or construction. At the same time, small businesses continue to start up. Yet these small firms typically require skills that displaced workers are not likely to have. Under Ford sponsorship, the Michigan Investment Fund is providing private venture capital for small companies who will hire displaced workers. The companies work in partnership with community organizations that provide retraining, counseling, and job placement.[40]

In such consortia of smaller companies, higher education institutions could have an important role. Colleges can be expected to take on that role if they see a potential market of new students. But for higher education to become involved in older worker retraining, there would need to be changes in financial aid policies and in curriculum design to reflect closer cooperation with business and industry. By aligning consortia of smaller companies with higher education institutions, perhaps including state government and regional economic development interests, there may well be a constituency to support more active steps for retraining of older workers along the lines proposed here.

By itself, the marketplace alone will not respond to the problem of retraining older workers. But under a collaborative approach, success is possible. There are many precedents for such successful collaboration at the local level among industry, education, and labor.[41] The irony here is that, in the fast-growing industrial sectors of the economy, the market has a role in solving many of the problems of jobs for older workers. Yet because of the competitive structure of that same marketplace, disincentives to older worker retraining cannot be overcome unless a broader system of industry-wide cooperation is achieved.

But the leadership—for consortia, for investment in worker retraining, for demonstration programs—will have to come from the public sector. Enough experience already exists to point the way; as the following examples show.

- In Delaware, the State Division on Aging runs an employment program to retrain older workers for jobs in the hotel and restaurant field. The program is jointly managed by the Widener University School of Hotel and Restaurant Management and staff of the Sheraton-Brandywine Inn in Delaware.

- In Montana, CETA funds were used to train a group of older workers as job counselors, who were later placed in the State Employment Service. These positions make use of the age and life experience of retrained older workers.

- Some jobs require relatively advanced technical training; for example, the program of the U.S. Forest Service to train low-income elderly in photography, cartography, and the use of aerial photographs in surveying and mapmaking.[42]

- Not all jobs in the restaurant industry need be dead-end jobs. "Meal-in-A-Minute" Corporation is a national fast-food chain employing more than 14,000 persons in 900 local units. Its Career Advancement Program encourages displaced homemakers and other mature workers to prepare for advancement opportunities in management, for example, in quality control specialties.[43]

- In Missouri, the State Office on Aging designed a specialized training program in the use of microcomputers for persons over age 55. Older workers were retrained in skills of word processing, data base management, and spreadsheet analysis for accounting. A major computer equipment producer donated equipment, and more than two thirds of the older people initially enrolled successfully completed the program, a large proportion receiving jobs within two weeks of the end of the training.[44]

- A university-based research laboratory has been retraining its older machinists to work with numerically controlled equipment recently upgraded by manufacturers. As new technology is introduced, senior machinists are sent to the factory, where they learn the new technology and then return to the laboratory to teach other older machinists in small groups. Worker retraining has become an expected part of the job at this facility.[45]

NEED FOR NEW POLICIES
FOR OLDER WORKER RETRAINING

Retraining older workers for a high-growth postindustrial economy represents a positive direction for the future of an aging society. This policy approach stands in stark contrast to the failed policies of the past. The conventional approach, too often, amounts to sheer protectionism—defending job security at any cost—or, failing that, it calls for aggressive placement and job development. These efforts amount to a zero-sum game—cutting up the pie in different ways, where my gain comes at your loss.

But these responses do not try to increase the productive capacity of older workers. An alternative approach would be to give priority to preparing older workers for new opportunities and new productive roles. Ideally, the national government would include population aging as part of a far-reaching industrial policy where lifespan development would be the key to economic growth in the future. Models for such an integrated approach do exist in other countries.

Retraining in Other Countries

At any given time, one tenth of one percent of the U.S. labor force is engaged in training or retraining; the comparable figure for other industrial economies, such as Germany, Sweden, France, or Japan, is ten to fifteen times higher. Japan is well known for its attention to retraining workers in depressed industries. Workers there receive job training and unemployment compensation with help in finding a new job with greater security. The Japanese style of lifetime employment security obviously reinforces this expectation by employees and gives management an incentive to make workers more productive. West Germany, too, has had extensive systems for retraining workers. Both those currently employed and those unemployed may be trained or retrained for a period of up to two years.[46]

RETRAINING FOR LIFESPAN PRODUCTIVITY: BEYOND SINGLE VISION

Training and retraining of the work force are critical in the transition to the postindustrial economy of the future.[47] Today we are only at the beginning of serious efforts in older worker retraining.[48] Future initiatives will have to include, not only displaced workers, but those who have been continuously employed but now need to update skills threatened by the danger of obsolescence.[49]

Public policy response to this situation has been inadequate and even misdirected. Federal retraining initiatives, such as the Trade Adjustment Act, have largely failed, and little retraining of older workers has even been attempted. It is not clear what current federal policy can actually accomplish unless it provides serious incentives such as training subsidies, tax credits, new adult retraining services, or other programs. But conventional policies simply fail to address these questions. In essence, we are subsidizing protectionism and ratifying the linear life plan.[50]

The disincentives are built into labor markets and educational policies and are reinforced by tax policy and housing policy as well. Without looking at this total picture, retraining by itself will not solve the problems. The result is the immobility of an aging labor force:

> A large part of the problem is that much of the American work force is now immobile. Workers feel too insecure to leave family, friends, and familiar territory; they are unable to finance their own retraining; and they are uncertain where new jobs are located and for what jobs training should be sought. . . .[51]

The contradictions in our present policies do not help to solve the problem. For example, the federal tax code prohibits educational deduction for those engaged in retraining for a new occupation, while permitting deductions for those who improve their skills within their present occupation. The tax system in effect supports lifespan development of human capital only to meet the requirements of the current employer. A middle-aged or older worker threatened with the loss of a job who tries to be retrained for another one cannot deduct the cost of retraining. What we have in effect is a tax code that subsidizes the mobility of financial capital but not the mobility or development of human capital. A company can take a tax loss on physical capital when a plant is closed, but the unemployed labor left behind is ignored. The tax code then reinforces an inherent bias toward the status quo: keeping people in their current jobs.

Because of the historical geographical mobility of the American labor force, private firms and local governments have underinvested in education and training in comparison with other industrialized countries.[52] In the past, such underinvestment was tolerated because companies could recruit younger workers who had acquired the necessary skill levels through public education. Our current policies reinforce this pattern. It is simply unrealistic to expect private firms or local government to make investments in human capital if they cannot expect to recoup the benefits. Still worse, in a period of hypermobility of international capital, it becomes all too easy for industries to simply abandon a local area when human resource costs become excessive. Aging workers are simply written off and left behind.

In effect, our current national policy offers incentives for economic dependency in retirement, while local or private policy bears the entire burden to offer incentives for enhancing productivity through human capital investment. It is not surprising that individuals and private firms opt for publicly subsidized dependency while avoiding risky human capital investments in retraining older workers. The aging society, then, confronts a contradiction: increased longevity means an abundance of life in the later years, yet the political economy channels older people away from productive roles in the workplace. If the abundance of life in an aging postindustrial society is to fulfill its promise—for both productivity and lifespan development—then economic policies must insure that these two goals support each other.

12

Culture, Leisure, and Lifespan Development

"At first we want life to be romantic; later to be bearable; finally, to be understandable."

—Louise Bogan

LEISURE, THE BASIS OF CULTURE

The modernized life cycle is divided into separate life stages: youth, midlife, and old age, each with its characteristic activities and purpose. In this view, later life is for retirement, for letting go of the serious demands of life in favor of enjoyment and leisure. But what is this leisure and what is the purpose of the free time made available in the last stage of life? The expansion of empty time in late life can be distinctly problematic. It opens up a kind of psychic vacuum to be invaded by forces that convert empty time into a new market for commodified leisure: the colonization of private life by the structures of industrial society.[1] For older people, this empty time poses a deeper threat: the loss of meaning when the self is detached from any larger purpose. The great danger of old age in a culture of narcissism is the danger of self-absorption and despair about the future.[2] The privatism of old age represents the loss of a shared sense of the public world.

To what extent does our present-day culture of late-life leisure contribute to this danger? The answer depends on the activities that are expected to fill the last stage of life. Participation in deeper culture forms can contribute to self-discovery and self-transcendence. But much of what passes for leisure time in retirement is simply an escape from self-development, let alone concern for a wider social world. Late-life leisure presents itself as purely private entertainment: a time for distraction, not self-development. Old people are encouraged to bury themselves in private pleasures or empty activities to fill the time available until death. The hope is that life can be made bearable since it is not understandable. This pointless exercise of false activism is what feeds our secret despair about the last stage of life. Is there an alternative?

There is a tradition reaching back to both the ancient Greeks and Hebrews that holds out a different possibility for the end of life. This alternative was the ideal of culture as the foundation for self-development.[3] On this view, leisure is not simply empty time left over when other activities are finished. On the contrary, the leisure of old age takes on a positive content that corresponds to the actual possibility of self-development. Culture, in this sense, is, to paraphrase Louise Bogan's remark, what makes life understandable. Leisure as free time offers that indispensable margin of existence that allows human beings to participate in symbolic forms that give intelligibility to their lives.

KEEPING BUSY OR FINDING MEANING?

It follows that quality of life in old age depends on something more than the availability of social activities in clubs, senior centers, or community organizations. The Older Americans Act has endeavored, with some success, to encourage these opportunities for life enrichment, and that is all to the good. Social gerontologists have emphasized the importance of such opportunities for socialization and group activity. Still these activities do not reach the deepest levels of meaning.

In many respects American social gerontology, in both theory and practice, has unwittingly reinforced an image of the "other-directed" side of old age. In senior centers and affluent retirement communities, a common ethos of activity can be seen. How much of this feverish activity, often fervently supported by younger staff members, is actually a disguised denial of old age, a response to the cultural vacuum at the center of life? Late life is hailed as a time to keep busy, to remain involved with others, engaged in activities. But vigorous activity and sustained meaning are not the same thing. In fact, frenzy of activity can simply mask an emptiness of shared meaning. This is perhaps the reason why so many activity programs in senior centers seem hollow, as if participants are merely going through motions that have lost their purpose. Something deeper is missing.[4]

This deeper dimension of life, a dimension of meaning, is to be found elsewhere: in those cultural forms—of ritual and contintuity between generations—that give intelligibility to the last stage of life. Without those symbolic forms of culture, old age is in danger of becoming a time when life no longer points beyond itself but sinks back into self-absorption veiled by outer distraction. A deeper understanding of leisure demands a distinctive view of old age. Instead of a period of empty time—after work and before death—old age becomes invested with a positive meaning and direction. Old age becomes a period for participation in cultural forms that express the continuity to life: the heritage of the past and of a world that will endure beyond me.[5]

This perspective offers a basis for growth and development in the last stage of life. This conviction has been the basis of every chapter in this book, namely, the hope that the abundance of life promised by increased longevity can be matched by a corresponding abundance of meaning.

Education, mediating structures, self-help, and retraining each have a part to play in late-life development. But these activities, each in their own way, take on an instrumental character. They are means, not necessarily ends in themselves. Retraining and mutual aid depend on shared cultural assumptions: the importance of productivity, for example, or the value of helping others. As life expectancy increases, these shared cultural values are simply prolonged into old age. A good age, then, comes to mean nothing more than an extension of the values of middle age into the last stage of life.[6]

CULTURE AND SELF-DEVELOPMENT

But culture and leisure in old age represent a different order altogether. Culture and leisure have no goal beyond themselves. They are not instrumental activities. The arts and culture are activities that are ends in themselves, undertaken, as we say, for their own sake. Without those cultural forms, we face a world where continued meaning in old age lies only in productivity of some form or other. How often do we hear the cheerful advice that satisfaction in old age depends on the need to be needed? Do those who give this upbeat advice ever ask themselves what happens when, because of frailty or isolation, people are in fact no longer needed by others? Does this activist view of life explain perhaps something about those old people, at all levels of society, who are profoundly depressed because they feel useless?

The entire thrust of this book has been to argue that the structure of human needs and the forms of productivity have radically changed in postindustrial societies. It would be an error to design social policies that anchor the meaning of old age entirely on contributive roles in society. This point remains valid even in a world where larger numbers of young-old have higher levels of health, education, and personal resources and thus may be able to contribute more in the future. But there are also the old-old whose opportunities for social contribution may be far more limited. Yet individual development and meaningful living remain possible nonetheless.

The whole question hangs on the balance between an ethic of productivity and an ethic of self-development. In this balance, the symbolic forms of culture are crucial. Take away those forms of culture, and old age without productivity becomes just empty time. More ominously, an individual life becomes a precarious period of waiting for extinction. Without culture, old age will eventually be felt as purely private time deprived of wider purpose and meaning.

CULTURE, AGING, AND THE PUBLIC WORLD

Self-Fulfillment in Later Life

Christopher Lasch is one of many critics who castigated American life for an excess of self-absorption and privatism. The critics had a point, but what they failed to see was the positive aspect of an ethos of self-fulfillment. They forgot that the cherished goals of personal development were intimately tied to the quest for self-fulfillment. Peter Clecak, commenting on critics of privatism in American life, chalks up a measure of self-absorption as one of the unavoidable casualties of the quest for self-fulfillment. Clecak sees this quest for self-fulfillment as a valuable and salutary trend of the last two decades.[7] Surely he is right to insist that the gloomy portrait since the 1970s has been overdrawn.

The leisure of old age offers an instructive case in point. Privatized leisure has many advantages to old people. The material basis for leisure has opened up unprecedented possibilities for self-fulfillment. Higher pensions, earlier retirement, the means for recreation and travel—these have provided the current generation of elderly with opportunities not available to previous generations beyond a small elite. Privatism, being able to "do your own thing," proved as attractive for the old as for the young. For a generation of elderly who had earlier experienced the Depression, this newfound leisure seemed a luxury to be savored. For the working class especially, retirement was experienced, not as oppression, but as liberation.

But in the cultural area, the picture is more mixed. Privatism and the erosion of the public world have had ambivalent consequences for old age. Retirement made possible free time for personal development. But the expansion of time was matched by the shrinking of common cultural institutions that might support an image of positive development over the lifespan, a sense of meaning and continuity across generations. In place of a common culture, old age was given over to new institutions that would fill the free time available. The most pervasive of these has been mass media.

The world of television and other forms of media, invading the home and enveloping everyday life, has progressively eroded clear-cut boundaries between the public and private spheres of life. Old people spend more time watching television than any other age-group does. Television newscasters, evangelists, and talk show hosts become "friends," part of their everyday world. This was a major new development and, to some observers, a disturbing one. One might ask whether television is an adequate vehicle for a common public world. Does the image of millions of elderly people staring day after day into the television screen really constitute our best answer to what the new abundance of life in old age can mean?

Over the last two decades the loss of shared public space has had profound consequences for quality of life in old age. In cities the elderly have been imprisoned in their own homes by fear of crime. In the suburbs, other forces diminished the sense of shared public space among the old, for example, the separation between suburbs and central cities and the dominance of private automobile transportation, both the result of longstanding public policies. Privatism in transportation policy creates barriers to cultural participation and thus decisively affects the quality of life in old age.

The grim portrait should not be overdrawn. Loss of cultural continuity is not the same thing as social isolation or abandonment of elders. Surveys do show that families generally maintain contact across generations, even with geographic distance. But family contact is not matched by cultural continuity. The effect of privatization in living spaces, transportation, mass media, and the use of leisure time has made it more difficult to sustain shared norms of meaning in old age. In place of those norms, there has appeared an ersatz public space of television. It contributes an illusory intimacy that masks the emptiness of social life.

AGING IN THE CULTURE OF TELEVISION

The dominance of television in the lives of old people constitutes the triumph of commodity production in the realm of leisure.[8] Throughout advanced industrial societies traditional forms of folk or popular culture have been weakened or absorbed into a new consumer culture that can be manipulated as a commodity: television, film, records, electronic equipment, commercial sports. Television represents the domination of late-life leisure through one-way communication that reduces the last stage of life to silence:

> Mass art is a one-way communication and thus takes on the character of domination. The social impact of its production consists not only in its ideological content . . . but in its pervasive intervention into the existential time and . . . psychic space of the person.[8]

With the advance of one-way communication, over the last half century Americans have more and more lost the capacity to produce popular arts. In this respect the role of the elderly today may be unique: as a living link with earlier cultural capacities to make art and to transmit coherent cultural traditions in ways that make experience intelligible.[10]

Television is distinctly powerful in the leisure time of old people today. Beyond its manifest role as a means of structuring leisure time, television has latent dimensions that are easily overlooked. In particular, I want to argue that the culture of television has had a far-reaching effect on the image of old age. This latent effect is more subtle but more pervasive than any stereotypes or negative images of old age on the television screen. The latent effect of television in the lives of the old is tied to the transformation of the life cycle brought about by the electronic culture of television.[11]

Most gerontological critics of television have focused on the negative stereotypes of the elderly promulgated in the media: by comedy shows, by entertainment programming, and by commercials.[12] The content of television programming overwhelmingly casts a negative light on old age.[13] Old age is the period of life when richness of experience and reflective judgment might be most highly prized. But television has no place for such old-fashioned values. Television occupies a perpetual present: "What is the effect of a medium that is entirely centered on the present, that has no capability of revealing the continuity of time? What is the effect of a medium that always asks for an immediate, emotional response?"[14]

In a world that prizes novelty, the culture of television must undercut the authority and finally the meaning of old age: "In our present situation, adulthood has lost much of its authority and aura, and the idea of deference to one who is older has become ridiculous."[15] Cultures that see old age as a period of fulfillment and meaning tend to prize the old as links in a historical chain that reaches back to the ancestors. But the culture of televison shatters historical time: ". . . all events on TV come completely devoid of historical continuity or any other context, and in such fragmented and rapid succession that they wash over our minds in an undifferentiated stream."[16]

This present-centered sensibility is reinforced and multiplied today through the all-enveloping environment of mass media and mass culture. Mass culture, disseminated first through printing, later through cinema and broadcasting, has progressively eroded traditional and folk culture. More than anything else, electronic mass culture intrudes between old and young, sustaining the youth culture of adolescence and the fashion culture of midlife. Since youth culture and fashion must change with obligatory rapidity, the hegemony and prestige of mass culture enforce an irremediable generation gap that makes the culture of old age a remnant or vestige of obsolete memories and values.

Faced with the dichotomy between mass culture versus elite culture, any ideal of cultural policy tied to lifespan development seems impossible.[17] On the one hand, in mass culture, individual or local differences becomes homogenized or volatilized into electronic media. On the other hand, in elite, especially avant-garde culture, the structures of individual history become abstracted or dissolved into forms unintelligible to lived experience, e.g., abstract art, modern music, contemporary poetry. The common result in both cases is the progressive deconstruction of the self. Cumulative life history, the basis for lifespan development, simply disappears.

In the present mood of cultural pessimism, one must remember that the current hegemony of mass communications may not necessarily endure forever. Technology and culture are susceptible to change. Toffler[18] and others have suggested that new information technology is leading to "de-massification" in the information society. At the local level, this decentralized information technology opens up new possibilities. For example, tape recorders and videocassette/camera units, combined with low-cost microcomputers, make it possible for small groups or individuals to generate and distribute their own cultural products: publications in exotic languages, in-depth documentation of vanishing local life-styles.[19] Inexpensive, small-scale information technology, increasingly user-friendly, could allow the elderly to achieve new possibilities of cultural expression and communication: just the opposite of the "massified" cultural dominance of passive television watching. Access to this new telecommunications technology—"tools of conviviality," in Ivan Illich's phrase—should be a major item on the agenda of cultural policy for an aging society.[20]

The goal should be the development of a new technological infrastructure within public policies that would put new tools of conviviality in the hands of people in ways that enhance, not erode, cultural autonomy.[21] One example is low-power television, where instead of broadcasting, we would move to "narrow-casting." Audiences and groups that would otherwise be too small or unprofitable for mass marketing could come into their own. Since older people represent the remaining vestige of ethnic or immigrant groups of former years, such technological communication could be especially important for them. There would also be a place for interactive communication, not necessarily through television, but by simpler devices, such as the telephone, the postal system, and the provision of books and materials. The model for this has been pioneered by the British Open University.

The seeds for these alternatives already exist in the heritage of traditional cultures: in religion, family life, folk arts. These spaces of autonomy are not wholly dominated by the power of mass culture or the engines of modernization. What in the Third World would be called a "revitalization movement" also has its counterpart within postindustrial societies. The elderly, links to the ancestral past, may be the key group in such cultural revitalization. Here the fate of the old and the fate of our wider culture are intertwined. What we so desperately need is a form of collective memory that can survive the onslaught of a present-centered medium that absorbs into itself that last remembrance of what a meaningful cycle of life might be. This principle of culture as collective memory can serve as a touchstone for more positive options of cultural policy in an aging society. It is toward these more positive options that I want to turn now.

Cultural Programs for the Aging

The last decade has witnessed a remarkable proliferation of programs designed for life enrichment of older people. Cultural institutions such as

libraries, museums, theatres, musical organizations, and historical societies have been active, often in collaboration with social agencies serving
the elderly. Many of these initiatives were organized at the local level.
But the federal government, too, played a role, principally through the
National Endowments for the Arts and Humanities and the aging network supported by the Administration on Aging.

In early surveys older Americans were identified as an "unrealized audience" or a "new constituency" for the arts.[22] The elderly have resources
available—time, skills, life experience—and the arts could help develop
more positive images of aging. Museums, musical groups, and other performance organizations supported the idea, and outreach efforts began to
grow. In time, older adults were soon seen to be not merely an audience
for the arts but as themselves potential creators of the arts.

There are now examples of well-designed source books for program ideas
and techniques[23] and books for administrators of arts and aging programs.[24] There are proven methods in different media such as ceramics,
drawing, painting, sculpture, and other forms.[25] Museums—such as the
Brooklyn Museum, the Metropolitan Museum of Art in New York, or the
Baltimore Museum of Art—have mounted nationally prominent programs to involve older people in their programs.[26]

Other cultural initiatives have been organized on a local level. For example, drama groups in senior citizens centers[27] have proven popular and
have given creative dramatics a solid niche in the aging network. The
same is true for creative writing groups, which have been successful in
nursing home settings.[28] A recurrent motif in such writing groups, as well
as in the theatre groups, has been the use of reminiscence to draw on life
experience.[29]

Similar success has been demonstrated with other art forms. Among
nonverbal arts, dance has a prominent place in activity programs for the
elderly because of its benefits for health and therapy.[30] The same holds
true of music, which has been shown to play a powerful therapeutic role,[31]
particularly when linked with dance and movement. As a nonverbal medium of emotional intensity, music can reach nursing home residents who
are confused or withdrawn.[32]

The visual arts, including painting and photography, have also been
immensely popular. Especially noteworthy in the art of old age has been
folk art and so-called naive art[33] forms wherein the artist often draws on
reminiscence to invoke a world of childhood memory. Grandma Moses
and Grandma Layton are only the most celebrated of many late-life painters
in this style.[34] Folk art has been closely tied to the traditional crafts

movement, which maintains its vitality in the United States. Older people are well situated to preserve the continuity of vanishing craft traditions. The Elder Craftsman stores, now active in many states in this country, provide a retail outlet that helps encourage older people to preserve craft traditions. In addition, commercial craft fairs, frequently of high quality, offer a new retirement life style, blending artistic expression with travel and income potential.[35]

This explosion of late-life involvement in the arts by older people is a promising sign for the future. Demonstrated capacities for late-life creativity could point the way to a new quality of life for an aging society. Over the last decade, with the rise of what Bernice Neugarten labeled the "young-old," we seem to be witnessing the appearance of demographic and social conditions for greater numbers of "Ulyssean Adults," that is, individuals whose retirement years mark a second career, whether in the arts or other creative activities. What is becoming clear is that earlier pessimistic conclusions about declining creativity with age were mistaken. This pessimism failed to adequately consider the role of the social environment, which includes stereotypes and expectations that discourage creativity in later life. Far too many older people have been victims of this self-fulfilling prophecy of decline. But as environmental conditions change, that tendency could become reversed. Cultural programs for older people have been a step in that direction.

Aging and Cultural Policy

In the early 1970s cultural programs designed for older people were rare. By the 1980s, they had become common. This proliferation of programs was partly the result of new interest by professionals in the field of aging, who began to recognize the importance of culture and life enrichment programs. But the new interest was also backed by modest government initiatives aimed at special constituencies and underserved groups, of whom the elderly were a primary example. During the boom years of the 1970s, the budgets of the National Endowments for the Arts and Humanities grew rapidly. At the state and local level, there was expansion of the work of arts councils, local cultural activities, and educational programs that involved colleges and universities in cultural activities for older people. What happened during the growth years of the 1970s is that older people became a legitimate constituency for cultural programs in much the same way that the older learner became a new clientele for lifelong learning and adult education.

Does this growth promise a more aggressive cultural policy for an aging society in the future? The potential exists, but there is doubt whether the promise will be fulfilled. Despite rapid growth of cultural programming, the idea of a cultural policy for aging seems doubtful to many.[36] Some analysts, such as Edward Banfield, would argue that in a free society the very concept of cultural policy is misconceived.[37] They would be opposed to an active role for government in providing cultural programs for special segments of the population, such as older people.

The broader question of government support for the arts and culture will not be argued here.[38] But it seems undeniable that we are operating under a de facto cultural policy evolving since 1965, the year when both the Administration on Aging (AoA) and the two Endowments were established. Moreover, acting under the authorizing legislation of the National Endowments for the Arts and Humanities, as well as under the Older Americans Act, the nation has been committing public funds to providing services and programs to meet special needs of older persons as a group. In 1981, the Endowments and AoA signed an interagency memorandum defining new terms of cooperative activity, putting issues of cultural policy and aging on a formal level of discussion for the future.[39] The reality is that, over the last decade, government funding, and private initiatives stimulated by it, have already created a broad pattern of support for cultural policy on behalf of the elderly.[40]

But the role of government agencies, important as it is, should be seen as part of a more complex pattern of support. In the discussion that follows, the question of cultural policy is seen from this broader perspective: one that includes private initiatives and the role of the private, nonprofit sector where museums, libraries, historical societies, and arts organizations make their decisions apart from what federal policymakers may decide. In other words, cultural policy is taken to mean all policy decisions of institutional actors in the humanities, arts, and aging. This broader approach to cultural policy seems justified in terms of the intergovernmental policy agenda of the Older Americans Act. The mandate of the aging network from the federal Administration on Aging down to local senior centers is precisely one of coordination and pooling of resources in the community at large. Cultural resources—in museums, libraries, performance groups, and institutions of higher education—represent an important contribution to quality of life in old age. In fact, some of the most successful examples of cultural policy initiatives in aging have not involved federal dollars but have come about through the leadership by local groups drawing on the resources of their communities.

RECENT TRENDS IN
CULTURAL ACTIVITIES AND AGING

Older people have participated in the upsurge of interest in cultural activities in the United States over the last decade. The most reliable data on participation by older Americans in cultural activities come from the national surveys conducted in 1975 and 1980 by Louis Harris and Associates and commissioned by the American Council for the Arts and the National Committee for Cultural Resources.[41] The Harris data point to impressive growth of involvement by the elderly in cultural activities and the identification of barriers to increased participation.

Trends in Recent Participation

The most important finding of the Harris studies is documentation of the growing participation by older Americans in artistic activities, both as audience and as creators. This growth is reflected among older persons in favorable attitudes toward the arts. For example, 86% of older respondents regarded cultural institutions (museums, theatres, concert halls) as important for the quality of life of the community. Even more significant, between 1975 and 1980, those older people who saw cultural institutions as very important grew to 65%. Positive attitudes were accompanied by rising levels of participation. Attendance at live performances of the arts grew during the second half of the 1970s, doubling from 22% to 44% for those over sixty-five reporting attending theatre in the last year. Comparable figures were shown for those attending museums and art galleries.

What factors account for this upsurge of interest in cultural activities by older Americans? First, the increased participation parallels similar growth by the wider public of all age-groups, but the over-65 age-group still exhibits greater gains in appreciation and sharper increases in participation rates. We are seeing an upsurge of cultural involvement among all Americans, which suggests that future cohorts of elderly are likely to continue the pace of involvement. Second, the current group of older persons is more educated than earlier cohorts, a trend that is continuing: average educational attainment for tomorrow's elderly will be even higher than today. Since educational level is the most important predictor of involvement in the arts and culture, this trend has positive implications for the future.

Finally, during the last decade there were major policy initiatives by cultural institutions, including leadership exerted by public agencies such as the National Endowments for the Arts and Humanities. These policy initiatives were designed to promote outreach and enhance participation by underserved audiences—such as the elderly. Those initiatives have undoubtedly played some part in raising participation levels. From a policy standpoint, the crucial question is to examine the comparative importance of these initiatives in contrast to the general background factors of rising education levels, higher levels of discretionary income, and wider public interest in the arts. This question becomes critical in assessing specific proposals designed to remove barriers or promote access by older persons to cultural programs.

The success of outreach efforts has been to challenge stereotypes of ageism and to open up new opportunities. An important lesson has been to show that cultural programs, when properly designed, can reach many different subgroups of the older population, including minorities, rural elders, the frail, and even the old-old, including nursing home residents. Cultural activities need not be confined to those who are active, educated, and mobile. But the stimulus for those efforts has often been linked to government funding. Now, during a period when funding has dropped and all programs are subject to scrutiny, it is important to appraise what has been learned from the rich results of the last decade.[42]

During the period ahead, it is likely that transportation costs and performance costs will continue to rise. Declining government subsidies for mass transit and cultural programs mean upward pressure on costs. But it is unlikely that government funding for life enrichment programs for the elderly will rise. Cultural institutions will be under pressure to reexamine discount policies and outreach policies that were inaugurated earlier and that may have played a role in increasing participation by older people. The impact of austerity will be to reopen questions of access versus excellence at a time when many cultural institutions cannot afford to support both of these policy goals.

Despite documented successes, there has been little serious attention to the policy questions that have emerged.[43] This is dangerous for the present period. When budget cutbacks come, cultural programs are often the first slated for cutbacks, even though the total amounts of money expended are small. Cutbacks have occurred repeatedly, for example, in local public libraries, even though libraries can be lifelines for those elderly who love to read and who are limited in mobility. At a time when not all worthwhile programs can be supported by government, it is more important than ever to examine the policy rationale behind cultural programs in aging. That reexamination is the focus of this discussion.

THE CONFLICT
BETWEEN ELITISM AND POPULISM

Cultural policy often involves decisions on the competing values of access versus excellence, an issue that has become familiar as the elitist-populist debate. Elitism in cultural policy means that the arts and humanities should stress quality and excellence—a principle likely to be upheld by long-established cultural institutions such as major museums, libraries, and symphony orchestras. By contrast, populists seek wider access to cultural activities. Populists are often supporters of folk art, minority and ethnic culture, regional crafts traditions, and other forms of culture not always well represented in established cultural institutions.

As the elitist-populist debate unfolded, opposing positions became polarized. Elitists were charged with being undemocratic snobs who favored only establishment cultural institutions, while populists were charged with debasing high culture and sacrificing standards in favor of politicized criteria, for example, by awarding grants based on geography or ethnic quotas. When the Reagan Administration came into office, its agenda on cultural issues was hostile to the populist position in all its forms. Though the public debate has subsided, tension between the opposing positions has not been resolved.

Elitism, Populism, and Aging

For the strict elitist, the cultural interests or concerns of the elderly would not be an important matter for public policy at all. On an elitist view, the elderly are bound to appear as one more special constituency —like the poor, minorities, the handicapped, and so on. In fact, the elderly were initially grouped together with these other groups in the office of special constituencies at the National Endowment for the Arts. To critics, cultural programming for the elderly begins to sound like another version of interest-group liberalism gaining a foothold in the arts and humanities.

Regardless of ideology, cultural programs for older people have continued to prosper in the 1980s, if not to grow at the same rate as they did earlier. Part of the reason includes the leadership of state-based government initiatives. Originally, the state-based humanities committees, by congressional mandate, were specifically encouraged to address public policy issues. The state arts councils have been called on to reach out to new underserved constituencies, including older people, who have sometimes been ignored by more elite cultural institutions. The results have been important for cultural policy and aging.

In Oregon, the State Arts Commission is using video technology as a vehicle to reach older adults and inform them of the arts activities available to them in their own communities.

In Minnesota, the St. Paul Council on the Arts and Sciences has organized a consortium of individuals, including older persons, humanities scholars, artists, and agencies serving the fields of the arts, humanities, and aging. The consortium is holding a series of statewide forums, has initiated a newsletter to promote better communications, and has scheduled a major state conference.

Sponsored by the Vermont Arts Council, the University of Vermont's Fleming Museum has developed a cultural volunteer training program for older adults, convened a major symposium on aging and creativity, and compiled a resource list of older Vermont artists available for placement as artists in the schools.[44]

The Need for National Leadership

These examples suggest what a comparatively modest investment of public resources can achieve on behalf of quality of life in old age. But there is a problem with state-based initiatives and leadership. Decentralization has advantages, yet the responsive and innovative programs developed in one state may not be quickly disseminated to other states where similar program opportunities are missed. If a special constituency such as the elderly has been a focal point for exemplary program development, then information about those programs should be made readily available to other groups around the country.

There are other issues, however, where more difficult choices must be made: above all, the problem of access by older people to cultural programs.

People-to-Programs Approach

Recognition that older people face problems of transportation and access to cultural activities has prompted a number of arts organizations to institute people-to-programs policies. These policies have taken many different forms.

The people-to-programs approach is illustrated by the successful "Cultural Vouchers" program, which distributes either vouchers exchangeable for tickets or actual discounted tickets to groups of elderly. For example, the Theatre Development Fund, Inc. in New York provides dance vouchers and ticket subsidies for persons on a fixed or low income. Large numbers of elderly have benefited from these opportunities.

New Stage, Inc., in Jackson, Mississippi, provides theater experiences to 2,000 low-income elderly citizens of Jackson and neighboring counties.

The Des Moines Symphony in Iowa serves the local region by sponsoring special matinee performances for older people and making transportation available to them.

Some of these programs are targeted at the elderly poor; others, at both the elderly and handicapped. The assumption is that the elderly are an impoverished and deserving group who could not afford to attend cultural programs without a subsidy of discounted admission tickets. This is the familiar failure model of aging so commonly used to justify special age-based subsidies.

Some policy analysts doubt whether the public is actually well served by subsidies that, in effect, support cultural institutions themselves in the guise of aiding specific constituency audiences. Netzer, for example, has argued that providing subsidies to symphonies, ballet performances, or theatre primarily benefits artists whose salaries rise and prompt further increases in ticket prices. If the groups of elderly who attend such performances would have gone anyway or could have paid for the tickets on their own, then it is hard to see the justification for a policy of public subsidy.[45]

Empirical studies of attendance at museums and performing arts activities have indicated that those participating in these forms of cultural life are primarily well-educated and upper income professionals. And despite accelerating public subsidies for cultural institutions during the 1960s and

1970s, the audience for elite arts institutions did not become more diverse during that period.

It appears that those who take most advantage of existing people-to-programs subsidies for the aged are primarily the affluent elderly or the genteel poor, i.e., retired librarians, schoolteachers, social workers, and clergy. If this profile is correct, then the audience would resemble the audience of the national Elderhostel program, which also receives indirect subsidies from participating educational institutions.

In light of this participation pattern, one can raise a legitimate question about the equity of public funding. Everyone assumes that helping the elderly and helping the arts are self-evidently a good thing, so programs that accomplish both goals at the same time are obviously desirable. But enthusiasm for subsidies neglects the reality that the elderly poor are almost entirely left out by such age-based cultural policies.

Transportation Barriers

Along with discounted admission tickets, there is also an alternate people-to-programs approach that operates in a very different fashion, namely, steps to overcome transportation barriers. Probably the most important policy initiative here is the general policy of half-fare for the elderly on mass transit systems around the country—a program often begun under the leadership of Area Agencies on Aging. But transportation subsidies implemented through mass transit systems, even where combined with discounted admission tickets, are not always sufficient to overcome barriers to participation. Some older people are inhibited by physical mobility problems, by fear of crime, or by distance from mass transit access points. To overcome those barriers would require extra subsidy in the form of direct transportation in vans and minibuses, either from a congregate location such as senior center or from their own homes.

A comprehensive people-to-programs policy for cultural access could well involve sizable subsidies for admission, mass transit, and special transportation systems. A reasonable policy question arises about why scarce resources should be assigned to subsidize access to cultural programs instead of access to other activities. Why not subsidize general educational activities for older people or educational programs that enhance life skills and contributive roles in society?

Age-based discount programs raise all the equity questions of age versus need, whether they are initiated under public or private auspices.[47] Aside from means-testing subsidies for cultural programs, there may be other, more creative ways of targeting benefits, public or private, at the least advantaged elderly. But by focusing on chronological age alone, rather than on problems of mobility, income, education, or social class, one overlooks the crucial question of who is being helped by age-based discount policies embodied in the people-to-programs approach.

Programs-to-People Approach

There are sizeable subgroups among the elderly who have limited education, or whose cultural preferences are not reflected in high culture, and they will inevitably feel out of place in our elite cultural institutions. Why should we assume that the problem of access lies in overcoming barriers that are entirely physical or financial?

Here we recognize the advantages in a programs-to-people approach, which has proven highly effective with arts organizations:

The Eugene Symphony Association in Oregon engages professional musicians in a string quartet and a woodwind quintet to perform in local senior citizens centers.

The Oakland Museum in California continues to offer its "Museums-on-Wheels," which serves senior centers, schools and hospitals.

The Toledo Symphony Orchestra in Ohio brings seven small ensembles from the orchestra to perform in nursing homes and mental health centers in the Toledo area.

Those older people who might feel uncomfortable in unfamiliar settings have much more effective access to cultural programs in their own neighborhoods. In several instances, planners have found cost-effective ways of bringing the humanities and arts to older people in diversified environments closer to home.

Senior Center Humanities Program. Another illustration of the programs-to-people approach is the success of the Senior Center Humanities programs administered by the National Council on the Aging under support from the National Endowment for the Humanities. These programs rely on local discussion groups conducted by voluntary leaders in senior centers, nursing homes, nutrition sites, and other community locations. Groups focus on subjects such as "The Remembered Past: 1914 to 1945," "The Search for Meaning," and "Exploring Local History." Nationally edited anthologies serve as the basic text for discussions and include selections from literature, philosophy, autobiography, folklore, and the arts.

Since its inception in 1976, the program has brought humanities discussion groups, led by local volunteers, to more than 75,000 older people whose economic and educational backgrounds represent a cross-section of America's aging population.[48]

Hospital Audiences, Inc. Another example of the programs-to-people approach has been the work of Hospital Audiences, Incorporated (HAI). Beginning with hospital patients, HAI has expanded its work to bring live performances of theatre, music, and dance to nursing home residents and frail elderly in chronic care facilities. Hospital Audiences has received support from the National Endowment for the Arts for its unique approach to overcoming barriers that prevent groups of elderly from participating in cultural activities.

Instead of bringing diverse audiences to a central location to receive a uniform product, the programs-to-people approach enhances values of relevance, pluralism, and participation. Can it be said that programs-to-people activities for the elderly involve diminished standards? Based on experience to date, there is no reason to think so. There have been instances where standards of excellence are compromised: for example, where discussion groups degenerate into rambling conversations or where artistic performances are embarrassingly bad. But most programs involving professionals in the arts or humanities meet the minimalist criterion and some are truly excellent.

Some critics have charged that senior centers have offered a meager or even insulting diet of arts and crafts activities. One problem is that the prevalence of arts and crafts activities in senior centers can deter upper middle-class older people who tend to look down on crafts in favor of high culture. As long as cultural activities reflect narrow, elite values of status, exclusivity, and superiority, genuine pluralism may prove impossible.

But snobbish dismissal of arts and crafts fails to recognize the genuine value of craft activities. The same snobbism that rejects popular crafts activities too easily assumes that those elderly who lack formal education are foreclosed from ever appreciating the higher learning represented by the humanities. Yet the experience of successful public programs in the humanities has shown that this cultural pessimism and snobbism is short-sighted. Demystifying culture need not mean degrading it. Demystifying high culture ought to be a legitimate goal of cultural policy in a democracy, and the outreach activities of cultural programs in aging have contributed significantly to that goal.

A balanced position would recognize validity in both the elitist and populist views on cultural policy and aging. The demands and the rewards of the great cultural traditions need not be avoided because of fear of populism. The challenge is to create conditions for democratic participation in cultural life that can make available the excellence of higher culture to groups excluded from it in the past, while at the same time encouraging high standards of folk arts, ethnic arts, and traditional cultural achievements—all areas likely to be rich with meaning for the oldest members of a community.

The concept of the life world in old age underscores the significance of cultural forms as vehicles for interpersonal communication and gives a new importance to culture, as Habermas has emphasized. Supporting the cultural life world of old age means "the safeguarding of realms of experience and forms of life that are threatened with being eroded, undermined, and washed away by the dynamics of economic growth and bureaucratization."[49] Old people as a group are to be seen as the bearers of cultural content—a collective memory, as it were—that tends to be suppressed by dominant cultural powers. The challenge is to use that collective memory as a bridge across generations of young and old.

Intergenerational Programs

One of the most important efforts at bridging the gulf between young and old has been intergenerational cultural programs. This type of activity is especially attractive because it involves older persons both as providers and as recipients of services, as, for example, in oral history programs with school children.

The HISTOP: History-Sharing Through Our Photographs program, originating in two elementary schools in Oakland County, Michigan, served as an intergenerational sharing of history through family photographs and taught both the old and young participants the importance of photographs as historical documents. The project was modeled on a similar initiative in China, where older persons are placed in schools as roving historians teaching local history from their own experiences.

The Teaching-Learning Communities (TLC) of Ann Arbor, Michigan, has brought elementary school children and older adults together in an integrated arts program in schools and various community settings. The project is structured in an apprentice-like relationship where endeavors in creative activities such as poetry workshops, woodworking, drawing, stitchery, music and dance are informally shared.

These programs make use of older volunteers for enrichment purposes and activities that draw on the unique talents and abilities of older people such as their knowledge of local history. The indirect effect of these age-integrated programs is to offer children role models of older people exhibiting special strengths associated with old age and thus help to overcome negative stereotypes and build positive intergenerational relationships.

In these programs, public sponsorship and the spirit of volunteerism need not be in conflict. On the contrary, the proper partnership can result in benefits amply justifying the modest amount of public dollars invested. But the real rationale must be sought in the effort to provide quality of life and human development over the lifespan, including the last stage of life.

CONCLUSION: TOWARD A CULTURE OF LIFESPAN DEVELOPMENT

There have been historical traditions where cultural activity in old age was expected and encouraged, and in these settings late-life creativity has often flourished. It was not assumed that old people were automatically uncreative. In traditional China, for example, it was a natural expectation that, upon retirement, high government officials would take up calligraphy and landscape painting—esteemed cultural activities that were part of a task of self-cultivation and contemplation. "A Confucian in office, a Taoist in retirement," as the Chinese phrase put it. In other oriental societies, the culture of lifespan development in old age was by no means limited to an elite group. Folk art in Japan constitutes an interesting case that spans the higher and lower levels of society. The elite art forms of Japan have existed on a continuum with popular activities widely practiced and appreciated by the population at large: for example, flower-arranging, calligraphy, the tea ceremony, and the martial arts.[50]

The culture of lifespan development in the East was solidly embedded in a wider social context. In such cultural traditions, late-life creativity involved the transmission of meaning across generations. The bonsai plant cultivated by successive generations had its parallel in the statues carved by multiple generations in African societies or the parables and folk tales passed down through families in other cultures. In traditional cultural worlds, intergenerational transmission and late-life creativity were bound together.

Here we see a difference between the position of old age in traditional culture in contrast to the culture of modernity. In traditional culture the place of the artist and the storyteller is secure.[51] Tradition is what gives the older artist a framework for understanding the meaning of time—above all, in works of art that transcend a single generation, as in the medieval cathedral builders or West African tribes who carve ancestor statues. This form of cultural transmission stands in contrast to our con-temporary obsession with individuality and with our image of the artist as a romantic or isolated figure. In traditional societies creativity was seen as a sacred gift: the voice of the Muses, the expression of the whole so-ciety (e.g., Shamanism). In traditions of folklore, collective understand-ing of creativity takes precedence over individual self-expression. What would be more natural than for the older artist, at the end of the life course, to reach back to these voices of the past?

For old people today, creativity is also linked to the remembered past: to storytelling and reminiscence, to the recovery of meaning through the stories of forgotten times. For people whose cultural survival is at stake, such as American Indian tribes, late-life creativity can perform a vital function in the continuity and integrity of the group. In recent years, gerontology has been rediscovering the importance of narrative in the meaning of old age.[52] That importance has always been at the heart of traditional cultures, where the transmission of narratives and life stories has contributed to positive respect and dignity for old age.

It is a condition of modern life that the remembered culture and life experience of old age are constantly rendered obsolete by the culture of modernity. Mass media are only a heightened version of this condition. The obsolescence of old age has far-reaching consequences for old peo-ple, who are likely to lose confidence in their own capacity as culture bearers or culture creators. Perhaps partly in compensation for this loss, large numbers turn to mass media while smaller numbers are attracted to elite sources of high culture in which age and experience need not be a barrier. Yet the high culture of modernism seems inhospitable toward old age, while mass culture in turn merely reinforces passivity and distraction.

Here we can observe that both high and mass culture, on the one hand, are opposed to folk art, which proves to be the natural art of old age. Some folk art of course can appear unsophisticated, yet it can also be highly complex. In any case, it responds to a search for meaning and a need for continuity through intergenerational memory. Folk art grows from below while mass culture, and elite culture too, are imposed from above.[53] Today cultural policy seems polarized between opposing ideals of excellence and access, while ignoring the deeper question about the active roles of old people as culture bearers and culture creators. In folk art, at least, these active roles may be more available, as they were in traditional societies.

The primary task of cultural policy in an aging society is not primarily a matter of access to opera performances or setting up dance groups in senior centers. Access and group activities are important, but they are only a means to a larger purpose. That purpose is to help older people recover their identity as culture bearers and culture creators. To accomplish this purpose requires something more than simply opening up access to opportunities in the arts. For many older people the task may require a supportive environment to counteract those self-protective mechanisms that inhibit risk-taking necessary for creativity in old age. The task is not impossible. Local arts and humanities programs in senior centers have demonstrated how to construct such an environment and how to nurture the creativity of elders in it. Crafts, writing, creative drama and countless other forms offer a way of "unmasking of the self" and going beyond previous roles by exploring new values that progressively express deeper aspects of the self. The impact of these experiences can be extraordinary.[54]

A major message of this chapter, and of this book, is that the possibilities for late-life development for "ordinary" people are far greater than we have imagined. It was the great art historian Ananda Coomaraswamy who said, "It is not that the artist is a special kind of man. It is that every man is a special kind of artist." There are fruitful models for this philosophy in folk art and in the so-called primitive work of untutored older artists. Among the Pueblo Indians of the American Southwest, for example, nearly 90 percent of the elderly women are pottery makers. Yet the tribal women recognize different standards of excellence achieved within their craft.

What these cultural traditions demonstrate, finally, is how irrelevant policy debates about access versus excellence really are. The central point has nothing to do with elite versus popular culture or the utility of art as a form of therapy. The central point is the kind of cultural environment is required so that old age will be, not empty time, but rather a time of abundance. "Life," wrote the poet W. B. Yeats, "is a preparation for something that never happens." His words are a haunting image, a negative image, of what old age may turn out to be. The depression and loss of self-worth so often found among older people are bound up with the wider cultural environment in which we live. In the throwaway culture of modernity, the life experiences of old people are obsolete; they have no meaning. It is no wonder that our cultural image of an aging society is filled with gloom or with the desperate quest for perpetual youth.

But this negative image is not the only alternative, any more than the future of an aging society must be a specter of decline. Whether the aging society will be an opportunity for lifespan development and whether our social policies will call forth the latent strengths and capacities of age and experience remain open questions. These questions will not receive a satisfactory answer from benign neglect by the public sector. Without investment of public resources in developing capacities for growth, including the arts and culture, the aging of America will mean failing to capitalize on the strengths of life experience. We need new cultural images of what it could mean to develop human capacities over the entire lifespan. A culture of lifespan development is a culture where memories and lessons of the past are not forgotten and where hope for a common future is transmitted to the next generation.

Conclusion:
Which Path for an
Aging Society?

Public policy toward aging in America has, in many ways, achieved phenomenal success, more so than social policies in any other sphere. But
aging policies have also generated deep contradictions, and with the coming
of population aging, these contradictions are becoming inescapable. Along
with the contradictions, whole dimensions of human experience have been
disregarded by single vision. Quality of life, the uses of time, and personal
development over the lifespan have simply been ignored by aging policy.

In reviewing the history of American values and aging in the twentieth
century, I suggested what I think is the crucial question for public policy
in aging today, namely, where to find elements in the American tradition that give cause for concern or grounds for hope in the coming transition to an aging society. The causes for concern have been the themes
of the first half of this book: ideological dogmas, utopian illusion, and a
tendency to suppress uncomfortable facts about social class and the political economy of old age. These trends are all too familiar. They amount
to a pervasive false consciousness about old age in America today, shared
by the public and advocates alike.

This false consciousness is what makes human development in the last
stage of life nearly impossible for us to imagine. The false consciousness
also prevents us from acknowledging the contradictions of present policies that perpetuate the problems. A refusal to face up to contradictions
leads to underestimating costs, to getting carried away by quick-fix solu-

tions, and to a separation of social idealism from material interests. The cycle of idealism and cynicism is familiar in American history, in domestic no less than in foreign policy. A crusade to make the world safe for democracy is succeeded by isolationism. The call for a War on Poverty is followed by disillusionment and a mistaken belief that all efforts were a failure.

Along with these familiar trends, we may add a further element, quite specific to the contradictions of aging policy in America, namely, a refusal to accept old age, in its finitude and limits, as an intrinsic part of the human condition. For Americans, old age is a threat to autonomy, independence, and hopefulness about the future—all cherished American values. Here we confront another limit to our social policies that conventional liberalism cannot easily overcome. Liberalism hopes for solutions to the ills that vex our society. But the needs of old age will never be entirely resolved by the strategy that liberal policies would prescribe for us. Old age is not like poverty, pollution, or unemployment. There is a tragic element in the last stage of human life that cannot be entirely eliminated by any public policy we could devise.

This existential truth needs to be kept in mind in every debate over aging policy, its possibilities, and its limits. But awareness of limits or acknowledgment of the tragic sense of life is not a basis for hopelessness, still less for acquiescence in the sufferings of old age as an inevitable ingredient of the nature of things. On the contrary, if we want to foster quality of life in the last stage of life, then collective efforts depend upon a measure of realism and a sense of the limits of intervention, whether that intervention is on the medical, technological, economic, or political plane.

This stubborn fact—the residual existential tragedy of old age and death—is what makes the problems of aging resistant to any complete solution in the policy arena. The existential limit and the demand for public provision both exist in a precarious tension. Too much stress on tragic limits tempts us to benign neglect, while too much stress on public intervention gives rise to false hopes followed by disillusionment. Once disillusioned, we are likely to forget America's hidden success, whether in extending life expectancy or in reducing poverty in old age. In social policy, as in geriatric medicine, therapeutic omnipotence and therapeutic nihilism are equally to be avoided. What is needed is a dialectical balance between the two. Indeed, only a dialectical standpoint is capable of making sense of what development and quality of life in old age might ultimately mean.

This is the story I have tried to tell in this book. In telling that story, I have not forgotten that public policy must address itself to grounds for hope as much as causes for concern. The causes for concern are spelled out in the critique of ideology in the first half of the book. The grounds for hope are found in those forms of collective action that contain seeds for a new culture of lifespan development. This flowering of lifespan development holds unsuspected possibilities for the uses of time in old age and could give new meaning to the idea of growth and development at every stage of life. Let me stress again that these grounds of hope are not utopian in the sense of being imaginary or hypothetical. On the contrary, the grounds for hope emerge from the tangible experience of grassroots activities by older people themselves—in self-help groups, in cultural revivals, and in programs for late-life education.

Critics in contemporary society—critics of modernity, of capitalism, or of technology—too often ignore grounds for hope in the future. Instead, they point to what Max Weber called the "iron cage" of modernity, and then, on the basis of that image, draw pessimistic conclusions about the future. In the case of old age, pessimistic forecasts of the future simply feed upon the uncritical pessimism that most Americans feel about growing old in the first place. Individual fear of growing old becomes projected into an imaginary future: the specter of decline. But this image overlooks the lived experience of growth and community already found throughout America today. Family care-giving and religion are alive and well; mutual self-help groups flourish; lifelong learning spreads into ever newer forms; cultural activities become accessible to more groups in the population. Like the tiny plants that push up through concrete and asphalt in our central cities, these forms of life persist and grow, producing new shoots even when we imagine that they are crushed beneath the weight of institutional inertia.

Once having recognized such sources of life beneath the crust of conventional institutions, we are left with difficult questions about how to nurture such sources of lifespan growth and development. These are the questions of public policy, and they cannot be left to merely private initiative. All of these alternative approaches—self-help, education, retraining, and so on—have their limits and their drawbacks, which I have tried to acknowledge. At the same time, we can think of each of these forms of collective action as openings promising an escape from the iron cage that limits our imagination. Instead of a zero-sum game where we fight over redistribution of limited resources, we can begin to identify new possibilities for productivity in old age. Instead of pessimism or the specter of decline, we can fashion collective solutions that offer grounds for optimism and hope.

The criterion for an effective resolution of the contradictions of an aging society lies precisely in this path. Instead of suppressing contradictions, instead of taking resources from one group to redistribute resources to others, we may find it possible to identify those spaces in the public world where social action can encompass contradictions without either suppression or evasion. Examples like a community vegetable garden or mutual-help groups for widows sound like small, down-to-earth instances of American voluntarism. But the importance of examples like these should not be neglected. Extended to a collective scale, such instances of voluntary action offer grounds for hope. It is a hope, not based on illusory utopianism, but growing out of grassroots experience. We can see many signs of hope flourishing around us once we begin to look for them. These forms of voluntary action give a benchmark, show what is imaginable, challenge us to examine how far human development in later life might be possible if only artifical barriers were swept away.

These benchmarks for hope have never been more needed. Liberalism, in particular, needs to call upon these images of hope if it is to be possible once again to mobilize the power of government on behalf of human needs and purposes. In a time of doubt about the future, examples of experienced hope can have extraordinary importance. They offer an escape from the despair of privatism into which our political life tends to sink. By highlighting human possibilities, these realistic utopias give guidance for individual action and open up new paths for social policy. The aged, who are a prime constituency for the modern welfare state, must be at the center of this debate over alternative social policy.

Two Roads Diverged

Can we expect that the emergence of America as an aging society will inevitably force contradictions to the surface, will perhaps require us to fashion policies that promote human development over the lifespan? Those who believe in historical determinism may have a confident answer to this question, but I do not. The future still remains open, but the alternatives are already clear. The most gloomy scenario would see the aging society as a specter of decline with competition polarized along lines of age as different generations seek opposing interests. A growing aging population would mean stagnation and loss of creativity as each group seeks to protect its gains in a new war of all against all.

An alternative scenario would envision the aging society as a society where education and human development, at last, become a lifelong enterprise, where opportunities for social contribution are available to all age-groups. Instead of generations in opposition, the aging society would promise opportunities for young and old alike. The three boxes of life would give way to an ideal of human development extending over the entire life course. This ideal implies vast expansion of education and retraining for middle-aged and older adults, just as it calls for a new appraisal of nonmonetized contributions of all kinds. Instead of the idolatry of an economy based on the GNP, our public policy would be dedicated to what Lewis Mumford called the "economy of life."

The final difference between these two scenarios lies not so much in different economic forecasts about the future as it does in a fundamental question of values. Is the new abundance of life now produced by gains in longevity to be seen as a problem or an opportunity? Are younger and older generations simply interest groups, or are all generations bound in obligations toward a common good? To insist that the future remains open is to insist that human beings have in their power the capacity to act, on whatever scale, and to move toward an abundance of life shared by all generations.

Notes

2. The Specter of Decline

General Note

For a comprehensive treatment of population aging and the American future, the best single volume is Alan Pifer and Lydia Bronte, eds., *Our Aging Society: Paradox and Promise* (New York: Norton, 1986). For an overview of current demographic trends in aging, see Jacob Siegel and M. Davidson, "Demographic and Socioeconomic Aspects of Aging in the United States," in *Current Population Reports* (August 1984). On fears about the adverse consequences of population aging, see Michael Teitelbaum and Jay M. Winter, *The Fear of Population Decline* (New York: Academic Press, 1985).

One of the most distinguished and most pessimistic of demographers, who has written on this subject throughout his long career, is the French scholar Alfred Sauvy. His *Zero Growth* (New York: Praeger, 1976) is only one of many places where he expounds the specter of decline thesis. From the opposing side, one of the most optimistic and controversial projections is found in James Fries and Lawrence Crapo, *Vitality and Aging: Implications of the Rectangular Curve* (San Francisco: W. H. Freeman, 1981). On the economics of an aging society, see John L. Palmer and Stephanie G. Gould, "The Economic Consequences of an Aging Society," in Pifer and Bronte, *Our Aging Society*.

This chapter is concerned with alternative images of the future of an aging society. On this subject, see Sanford A. Lakoff, "The Future of Social Intervention," in Robert Binstock and Ethel Shanas, eds., *Handbook of Aging and the Social Sciences* (New York: Van Nostrand Reinhold, 1976); J. Fowles, *Handbook of Futures Research* (Dorsey, Ill.: Greenwood, 1978); and Willis Harman, *An Incomplete Guide to the Future* (San Francisco: San Francisco Book Publishing Co., 1976).

Other books relevant to themes in this chapter include: Fred Polak, *The Image of the Future* (New York: Elsevier, 1973); Hazel Henderson, *Creating Alternative Futures: The End of Economics* (New York: Windhover, 1978); Paul Hawken, James Ogilvy, and Peter Schwartz, *Seven Tomorrows: Toward a Voluntary History* (New York: Bantam, 1982); and Raymond Williams, *The Year 2000* (New York: Pantheon, 1983).

1. W. Andrew Achenbaum, "Images of America as an Aging Society," in Pifer and Bronte, *Our Aging Society*.

2. *Ibid.*, p. 19.

3. David Hackett Fischer, *Growing Old in America* (New York: Oxford University Press, 1978).

4. Barbara Tuchman, *A Distant Mirror: The Calamitous 14th Century* (New York: Knopf, 1978).

5. Brigitte Berger and Peter Berger, *The War Over the Family: Capturing the Middle Ground* (New York: Doubleday, 1983), p. 130.

6. John Lukacs, *Outgrowing Democracy: A History of the United States in the 20th Century* (New York: Doubleday, 1984), p. 189.

7. See "American Workers Don't Get Around Much Anymore," *Business Week* (October 28, 1985), pp. 94–95. On the Baby Boomers and their mobility, see Richard Easterlin, *Birth and Fortune: The Impact of Numbers on Personal Welfare* (New York: Basic Books, 1980); and Langdon Jones, *Great Expectations: America and the Baby Boom* (New York: Ballantine, 1980).

8. See Edward Walter, *The Immorality of Limiting Growth* (Albany, N.Y.: SUNY Press, 1981); and Julian Simon, *The Ultimate Resource* (Princeton, N.J.: Princeton University Press, 1981).

9. Sheldon Wolin, "From Progress to Modernization: The Conservative Turn," *Democracy* (Fall 1983) 3(4): 10. See also Ben Wattenberg, *The Good News Is the Bad News Is Wrong* (New York: Simon & Schuster, 1984).

10. Teitelbaum and Winter, *The Fear of Population Decline*. On population decline as a geopolitical threat to the West, see Ben Wattenberg and Karl Zinsmeister, eds., *Are World Population Trends A Problem?* (Washington, D.C.: American Enterprise Institute, 1986).

11. Sauvy, *Zero Growth*. See also R. G. Ridker, "The Effects of Slowing Population Growth on Long-Run Economic Growth in the U.S. During the Next Half Century," in T. J. Espenshade and W. J. Serow, eds., *The Economic Consequences of Slowing Population Growth* (New York: Academic Press, 1978).

12. See Robert L. Clark and Joseph J. Spengler, *The Economics of Individual and Population Aging* (New York: Cambridge University Press, 1980), pp. 4ff.

13. On the motif of the elderly as a "burden," note the British observation: ". . . for the mainstay purposes of the nation, whether production in peace-time or defence in war-time, I am afraid that nearly all of them (the old) must be rated as passengers, not crew. Therefore their enormous increase . . . makes it worse, since there is a much larger burden for the few shoulders to carry." Ensor (1950), p. 129, cited by Chris Phillipson, *Capitalism and the Construction of Old Age* (London: MacMillan, 1982), p. 168. The same theme would reappear in mass media in the 1980s, such as cover stories in magazines like *Newsweek* and *The Economist*, where younger generations are depicted being crushed by "Granny Power."

14. Phillipson, *Capitalism and the Construction of Old Age*, p. 7.

15. See Frank Notestein et al, *The Future Population of Europe and the Soviet Union,*

Population Projections 1940–1970 (Geneva, League of Nations, 1944); Royal Commission on Population, *Report* (London, 1949); and William Beveridge, *Full Employment in a Free Society* (New York: Norton, 1945)—all cited by Clark and Spengler, *The Economics of Individual and Population Aging.*

16. K. Thompson et al, *The Care of Old People* (London: Conservative Political Centre Discussion Series, Pamphlet No. 121), cited by Phillipson, *Capitalism and the Construction of Old Age,* p. 101.

17. On the call for "generational equity" and the specter of decline theme, see Phillip Longman, "Justice Between Generations," *Atlantic Monthly* (June 1985): 73–81; and Longman's book *Born To Pay* (Boston: Houghton, Mifflin, 1987). One of the most widely discussed articles on the same theme was Samuel H. Preston, "Children and the Elderly: Divergent Paths for America's Dependents," *Scientific American* (December 1984).

18. William Graebner, *A History of Retirement* (New Haven, Conn.: Yale University Press, 1980).

19. See National Resources Committee, *The Problems of a Changing Population* (Washington, D.C.: U.S. GPO, 1938).

20. For typical articles in the press in the late 1970s, see, for example, Steven V. Roberts, "Growing U.S. Expenditures for the Aged Cause Concern Among Policymakers," *New York Times* (December 27, 1978), B-8; R. J. Samuelson, "Busting the U.S. Budget: The Costs of an Aging America," *National Journal* (1978), 10(7): 256–60. By the mid-1980s, after the great Social Security crisis, many of the same themes surfaced again, this time under the rubric of generational equity. See, for example, Bill Neikirk, "The Graying of America: As the Nation Ages, New Battlefields Emerge," *Chicago Tribune* (December 15, 1985), pp. 1, 18; Paul Taylor, "The Coming Conflict as We Soak the Young to Enrich the Old," *Washington Post* (January 5, 1986), pp. D1, D4; and Terry Hartle, "Take from the Young, Give to the Old: Elderly Have the Political Clout, Get the Lion's Share of Benefits," *Los Angeles Times* (September 27, 1984), part 2, p. 7.

21. Sauvy, *Zero Growth,* p. 49.

22. Sauvy, cited in Clark and Spengler, *The Economics of Individual and Population Aging,* p. 41.

23. Alan Sweezy and Aaron Owens, "The Impact of Population Growth on Employment," *American Economic Review* (May 1974), 64(2):44–50. See also, Joseph J. Spengler, *Facing Zero Population Growth: Reactions and Interpretations, Past and Present* (Durham, N.C.: Duke University Press, 1978).

24. See the Work in American Institute, *The Future of Older Workers in America: New Options for an Extended Working Life* (Scarsdale, N.Y., 1980); and the report of the National Committee on Careers for Older Americans, *Older Americans: An Untapped Resource* (New York: Academy for Educational Development, 1979).

25. Lester Thurow, *The Zero-Sum Society* (New York: Basic Books, 1980).

26. Robert Binstock, "Interest-Group Liberalism and the Politics of Aging," *The Gerontologist* (1972), 12:265–80.

27. I am indebted to Robert Hudson for the metaphor and for his thinking on the evolution of aging policy.

28. Theodore Marmor, *The Politics of Medicare* (Chicago: Aldine, 1973). On the history of American aging policy, see W. Andrew Achenbaum, *Shades of Gray* (Boston: Little, Brown, 1982).

29. For a provocative attack on aging programs and age-based entitlements, see Phillip Longman, "Taking America to the Cleaners," *The Washington Monthly* (November 1982). Longman goes to excess and gets some of the facts wrong, but he is not wrong to emphasize the importance of "hidden" subsidies like mortgage interest rates and their impact on different age cohorts. For example, on the question of home ownership and generational equity, see Hal Kendig, "Housing Tenure and Generational Equity," *Ageing and Society* (1984), 4(3):249–72.

30. Carroll Estes, "Social Security: Construction of a Crisis," *Millbank Memorial Quarterly* (Summer 1983), 61:3. See also John F. Myles, "Conflict, Crisis and the Future of Old Age Security," *Millbank Memorial Quarterly* (Summer 1983), 61:3.

31. The Yankelovich survey data are reported in Alan Otten, "Young Professionals' Retirement May Be Brighter Than They Think," *Wall Street Journal* (December 10, 1985), p. 33. For complete analysis, see Yankelovich, Skelly, and White, Inc., *A 50-Year Report Card on the Social Security System: Attitudes of the American Public* (Washington, D.C., August 1985).

32. See Peter Laslett, *The World We Have Lost*, ed. 3 (New York, Scribners, 1983); and Peter Laslett, "Societal Development and Aging," in Robert H. Binstock and Ethel Shanas, eds., *Handbook of Aging and the Social Sciences* (New York: Van Nostrand Reinhold, 1983), pp. 202–4.

33. Peter Berger, Brigitte Berger, and Hansfired Kellner, *The Homeless Mind: Modernization and Consciousness* (New York: Random House, 1974), p. 185.

34. Gerald Gruman, "Cultural Origins of Present Day 'Age-ism:' The Modernization of the Life Cycle," in Stuart Spicker et al, eds., *Aging and the Elderly: Humanistic Perspectives in Gerontology* (Atlantic Highlands, N.J.: Humanities Press, 1978).

35. *New York Times*, May 31, 1983.

36. Roy L. Walford, *Maximum Life-Span* (New York: Norton, 1983), p. 61.

3. Aging in the Postindustrial Society

1. Mancur Olson, *The Rise and Decline of Nations: Economic Growth, Stagflation, and Social Rigidities* (New Haven, Conn.: Yale University Press, 1982), p. 40.

2. On bargaining between management and Swedish and Japanese unions, see Robert Kuttner, *The Economic Illusion: False Choices Between Prosperity and Justice* (Boston: Houghton, Mifflin, 1984).

3. M. Olson, *Rise and Decline of Nations*, p. 90.

4. Harold Wilensky, "Political Legitimacy and Consensus: Missing Variables in the Assessment of Social Policy," in S. Spiro and E. Yuchtman-Yar, eds., *Evaluating the Welfare State* (New York: Academic Press 1983).

5. Marc Porat, *The Information Economy* (Washington, D.C.: U.S. GPO, 1983).

6. Daniel Bell, *The Coming of Post-Industrial Society* (New York: Basic Books, 1973). See also Alain Touraine, *The Post-Industrial Society* (New York: Random House, 1971); Seymour Martin Lipset, ed., *The Third Century: America as a Post-Industrial Society* (Palo Alto, Calif.: Hoover Inst., 1979); and B. Gustaffson, ed., *Post-Industrial Society* (London: Croom Helm, 1979). In this discussion, I largely follow Bell's account.

7. On Kondratief's concept of long waves of economic growth, see C. Freeman, ed., *Long Waves in the World Economy* (Guildford, England: Butterworth, 1982); and

A. K. Graham and P. M. Senge, "A Long Wave Hypothesis of Innovation," *Technological Forecasting and Social Change* (1980), 17:4, 283–311.

8. Alvin Toffler, *The Third Wave* (New York: Morrow, 1980). Also, A. Toffler, *Previews and Premises* (New York: Morrow, 1983).

9. Toffler, *The Third Wave*, pp. 127–28.

10. Edward Cornish, "The Coming of an Information Society," *The Futurist* (April 1981); and N. Bjorn-Anderson et al, *Information Society: For Richer, For Poorer* (Amsterdam: North Holland, 1982).

11. See also Robert D. Hamrin "The Information Economy: Exploiting an Infinite Resource," *The Futurist* (August 1981), p. 66. See also Graham T. T. Molitor, "The Information Society: The Path to Post-Industrial Growth," *The Futurist* (April 1981); Fritz Machlup, *Knowledge Creation, Distribution, and Economic Significance* (Princeton, N.J.: Princeton University Press, 1980).

12. Jonathan Gershuny, *After Industrial Society? The Emerging Self-Service Economy* (Atlantic Highlands, N.J.: Humanities Press, 1978), p. 234.

13. Andre Gorz, *Farewell to the Working Class: An Essay on Post-Industrial Socialism*, trans. by Michael Sonenscher (Boston: South End Press, 1982).

14. Harry Braverman, *Labor and Monopoly Capital: The Degradation of Work in the 20th Century* (New York: Monthly Review Press, 1975).

15. "Many heavy industry jobs are being lost forever, and hurt the most will be many unskilled and semi-skilled workers with few chances of finding other satisfying jobs. 'Smokestack' communities are likely to be depressed indefinitely. Hopes for the 'reindustrialization' of America will be frustrated, even if the U.S. keeps its lead in some high-technology fields." Henry F. Myers, writing in the *Wall Street Journal*, cited by Michael Harrington, *The New American Poverty* (New York: Holt, Rinehart, and Winston, 1984), p. 56.

16. See Wassily Leontief and Faye Duchin, *The Future Impact of Automation on Workers* (New York: Oxford University Press, 1985). See also Harley Shaiken, *Work Transformed: Automation and Labor in the Computer Age* (New York: Holt, Rinehart, and Winston, 1985).

17. Gershuny, *After Industrial Society?* pp. 147–48.

18. Scott Burns, *The Household Economy* (Boston: Beacon Press, 1976).

19. Gershuny, *After Industrial Society?* p. 81.

20. Warren Johnson, *Muddling Toward Frugality: A Blueprint for Survival in the 1980s* (San Francisco: Sierra Club Books, 1978).

21. Gershuny, *After Industrial Society?* pp. 149–50. See also J. I. Gershuny, *Social Innovation and the Division of Labour* (New York: Oxford University Press, 1983).

22. Adapted from J. I. Gershuny and I. D. Miles, *The New Service Economy. The Transformation of Employment in Industrial Societies* (New York: Praeger, 1983), p. 2.

23. *Ibid.*, p. 6.

24. *Ibid.*, p. 255.

25. Robert Clark and John Menefee, "Federal Expenditures for the Elderly: Past and Future," *The Gerontologist* (1981), 21:132–37; Robert Hudson, "The Graying of the Federal Budget," *The Gerontologist* (October 1978), 18(5):428–40.

26. Claus Offe, *The Contradictions of the Welfare State* (Cambridge, Mass: MIT Press, 1984).

27. Gershuny and Miles, *The New Service Economy*, p. 89.

28. Lewis Mumford, *The Human Prospect* (Boston: Beacon Press, 1955). See especially the chapter "From a Money Economy to a Life Economy."

4. Late Life and The Uses of Time

1. On the uses of time in old age, see Nancy Osgood, *Life After Work: Retirement, Leisure, Recreation and the Elderly* (New York: Praeger, 1982); and Jaber Gubrium, ed., *Time, Roles, and Self in Old Age* (New York: Human Sciences Press, 1976).

2. On the lifetime allocation of work and leisure, see Juanita Kreps, *Lifetime Allocation of Work and Leisure* (Durham, N.C.: Duke University Press, 1971); and Fred Best et al., "Income-Time Tradeoff Preferences of US Workers: A Review of the Literature and Indicators," *Leisure Sciences* (Summer 1979), 2(2):119–41. See also Sar Levitan and Richard Belous, *Shorter Hours, Shorter Weeks: Spreading the Work to Reduce Unemployment* (Baltimore: The Johns Hopkins University Press, 1977).

3. The most sustained analysis of this theme is given by Fred Best in a series of publications: Fred Best, *Flexible Life Scheduling: Breaking the Education-Work-Retirement Lockstep* (New York, Praeger, 1980); Fred Best, "The Future of Retirement and the Lifetime Distribution of Work," *Aging and Work* (Summer 1979), pp. 173–81; Fred Best, "Preferences on Worklife Scheduling and Work-Leisure Tradeoffs," *Monthly Labor Review* (June 1978), pp. 31–37; Fred Best, "The Time of Our Lives: The Parameters of Lifetime Distribution of Education, Work, and Leisure," *Society and Leisure* (May 1978), 1(1):95–124; Fred Best and Barry Stern, "Education, Work, and Leisure—Must They Come in That Order?" *Monthly Labor Review* (July 1977), pp. 3–9.

4. The phrase is from Richard Bolles, *The Three Boxes of Life* (Berkeley, Calif.: Ten Speed Press, 1978).

5. E. P. Thompson, "Time, Work Discipline and Industrial Capitalism," *Past and Present* (December 1967), no. 38, p. 95.

6. Peter Stearns, *Old Age in European Society: The Case of France* (New York: Holmes and Meier, 1976).

7. M. Abrams, "Time and the Elderly," *New Society* (December 1978), nos. 21–28, pp. 685–86.

8. Daniel Bell, *The Cultural Contradictions of Capitalism* (New York: Basic Books, 1976).

9. John Myles, *Old Age in the Welfare State: The Political Economy of Public Pensions* (Boston: Little, Brown, 1983).

10. Sebastian de Grazia, *Of Time, Work and Leisure* (New York: Doubleday, 1964).

11. Matilda Riley, "Longevity and Social Structure: The Potential of the Added Years," in Alan Pifer and Lydia Bronte, eds., *Our Aging Society* (New York: Norton, 1986), pp. 53–78.

12. Data from *Aging in America: Trends & Projections*, a report prepared by the U.S. Senate Special Committee on Aging and AARP, Washington, D.C., 1985.

13. Benjamin K. Hunnicutt, "Aging and Leisure Politics," in Michael Teague et al, eds., *Perspectives on Leisure and Aging in a Changing Society* (Columbia, Mo.: University of Missouri Press, 1982), p. 78.

14. *Ibid.*, p. 97.

15. William Graebner, *A History of Retirement: Meaning and Function of an American Institution, 1885–1978* (New Haven, Conn.: Yale University Press, 1980). Graebner argues that Social Security's purpose was precisely to cope with the contradictions

and crisis of capitalism by removing older workers from the labor market. Others take a more complex view of the situation; for example, see W. Andrew Achenbaum, *Social Security: Visions and Revisions* (New York: Cambridge University Press, 1986).

16. See Richard Freeman, *The Overeducated American* (New York: Academic Press, 1976).

17. Cf. Seymour Sarason, *Work, Aging, and Social Change: Professionals and the One Life-One Career Imperative* (New York: Free Press, 1977).

18. Peter Townsend, "The Structured Dependency of the Elderly: Creation of Social Policy in the Twentieth Century," *Ageing and Society* (March 1981), 1(1):5–28; also, Alan Walker, "Towards a Political Economy of Old Age," *Ageing and Society* (March 1981), 1(1):73–94.

19. Willard Wirtz, *The Boundless Resource: A Prospect for an Education-Work Policy* (Washington, D.C.: New Republic Books, 1975).

20. On the role of the labor movement and the shifting balance of work and leisure in late capitalism, see Stanley Aronowitz, "Why Work?" *Social Text: Theory/Culture/Ideology* (Fall 1985), pp. 19–42.

21. Daniel Yankelovich, *New Rules: Searching for Self-Fulfillment in a World Turned Upside Down* (New York: Random House, 1981).

22. Robert W. Kleemeier, ed., *Aging and Leisure: A Research Perspective into the Meaningful Use of Time* (New York: Oxford University Press, 1961); and Andrea Fontana, *The Last Frontier: The Social Meaning of Growing Old* (Beverly Hills, Calif.: Sage, 1977).

23. See David Riesman, "Work and Leisure in Post-Industrial Society," in E. Larrabee and R. Meyersohn, eds., *Mass Leisure* (Glencoe, Ill.: Free Press, 1960); also, Robert McIver, *The Pursuit of Happiness* (New York: Simon & Schuster, 1955). On the fear of leisure, see James C. Charlesworth, ed., *Leisure in America: Blessing or Curse?* (Philadelphia: American Academy of Political and Social Science, 1964).

24. Ortega Y. Gasset, *The Revolt of the Masses* (New York: Norton, 1932); and Christopher Lasch, *The Culture of Narcissism* (New York: Norton, 1979).

25. J. Dumazedier, *Toward a Society of Leisure* (London: Collier-Macmillan, 1962); Kenneth Roberts, *Leisure* (London: Longmans, 1970); Josef Pieper, *Leisure: The Basis of Culture* (London: Faber & Faber, 1962).

26. Sandra Timmermann, "The Older Consumer in the 1980s: Implications for the Private Sector," *Journal of Institute for Socioeconomic Studies* (Winter 1981–82), 4(4):61–75. See "Discovering the Over-50 Set," *Business Week* (November 19, 1979); "Measuring Mature Markets," *American Demographics* (March 1981), vol. 3, no. 3; and Howard B. Schutz, Pamela Baird, and Glenn Hawkes, *Lifestyles and Consumer Behavior of Older Americans* (New York: Praeger, 1979).

27. Louis Sahagun, "Firms Aim at 'Graying' of Marketplace," *Los Angeles Times* (February 1, 1985), pp. 1–3.

28. Andre Gorz, *Farewell to the Working Class: An Essay on Post-Industrial Socialism* (Boston: South End Press, 1982), p. 52.

29. H. R. Moody, "Late Life Learning in the Information Society," in David Peterson et al, eds. *Education for Older Adults* (Englewood Cliffs, N.J.: Prentice-Hall, 1987).

5. Aging and Quality of Life

1. On public policy and quality of life, the concept of "social indicators" has been one example of an effort to anchor qualitative determinations in a more "objective" mode. For an introduction, see F. M. Andrews and S. B. Withey, *Social Indicators of Well-Being* (New York: Plenum Press, 1976).

2. On the public and private world in modern societies, see Hannah Arendt, *The Human Condition* (Chicago: University of Chicago Press, 1955).

3. John Naisbitt, *Megatrends: Ten Directions Transforming Our Lives* (New York: Warner, 1982).

4. Ronald Inglehart, *The Silent Revolution* (Princeton, N.J.: Princeton University Press, 1977).

5. Daniel Yankelovich, *New Rules: Searching for Self-Fulfillment in a World Turned Upside Down* (New York: Random House, 1981).

6. Daniel Bell, *The Coming of Post-Industrial Society* (New York: Basic Books, 1974). A similar positive forecast is offered by Rolf Dahrendorf, *The New Liberty* (London: Routledge & Kegan Paul, 1975).

7. Jean-Pierre Dupuy, "Myths of the Information Society," in Kathleen Woodward, ed., *The Myths of Information: Technology and Postindustrial Culture* (Madison, Wisc.: Coda Press, 1980), p. 4.

8. *Ibid.*, pp. 4–5.

9. In a different way, Fred Hirsch, too, in *The Social Limits of Growth*, raised critical questions about the economism of prevailing models. See Adrian Ellis and Krishan Kumar, *Dilemmas of Liberal Democracies: Studies in Fred Hirsch's Social Limits of Growth* (London: Tavistock Publications, 1983). For alternatives to the dominant economic model, see Mark Lutz and Kenneth Lux, *Humanistic Economics: Fundamentals and Applications* (Menlo Park, Calif.: Benjamin-Cummings, 1979).

10. Jurgen Habermas, "Introduction," in Habermas, ed., *Observations on 'The Spiritual Situation of the Age,'* (trans. by Andrew Buchwalter) (Cambridge, Mass: MIT Press, 1984), pp. 19–20.

11. Laura Katz Olson, *The Political Economy of Aging* (New York: Columbia University Press, 1982).

12. Burkhardt Strumpel, "Social Policy Evaluation and the Psychology of Stagnation," in S. Spiro and E. Yuchtman-Yaar, eds., *Evaluating the Welfare State: Social and Political Perspectives* (New York: Academic Press, 1983).

13. Harry Boyte, *Community is Possible* (New York: Harper & Row, 1984).

14. John Palmer and Isabel Sawhill, *The Reagan Record: An Assessment of America's Changing Domestic Priorities* (Cambridge, Mass: Balinger, 1984).

15. On the quality-of-life society, see Amitai Etzioni, *An Immodest Agenda: Rebuilding America Before the 21st Century* (New York: McGraw-Hill, 1983), pp. 259–60, 288–92. Etzioni does acknowledge that the shift to a quality-of-life society can be made possible by concentrating on culture and knowledge, thus making quality of life possible despite lower output or productivity. For future scenarios that explore such alternatives, see Paul Hawken, James Oglivy, and Peter Schwartz, *Seven Tomorrows: Toward a Voluntary History* (New York: Bantam, 1982).

16. D. Yankelavich, *New Rules.*

17. Thomas Peters and R. Waterman, *In Search of Excellence* (New York: Warner, 1982).

18. Paul Hawken, *The Next Economy* (New York: Holt, Rinehart, and Winston, 1983); and Robert Reich, *The Next American Frontier* (New York: Times Books, 1983).

19. On the importance of "cross-commitment" in policymaking, see Etzioni, *An Immodest Agenda*, pp. 301–3.

20. Robert Kuttner, *The Economic Illusion* (Boston: Houghton, Mifflin, 1984).

21. Stephen Crystal, *America's Old Age Crisis: Public Policy and the Two Worlds of Aging* (New York: Basic Books, 1982).

22. Ellen Langer, *The Psychology of Control* (Beverly Hills, Calif.: Sage, 1983).

23. A. N. Schwartz, "An Observation on Self-Esteem as the Linchpin of Quality of Life for the Aged: An Essay," *The Gerontologist* (1975), 15:470–72.

24. M. Bloom, *The Paradox of Helping: Introduction to the Philosophy of Scientific Practice* (New York: Wiley, 1975).

25. Linda K. George and Lucille B. Bearon, *Quality of Life in Older Persons: Meaning and Measurement* (New York: Human Sciences Press, 1980), pp. 8–10.

26. Bernice Neugarten, *Age Or Need?* (Beverly Hills, Calif.: Sage, 1982).

27. Harold Lewis, "Self-Determination: The Aged Client's Autonomy in Service Encounters" (unpublished paper given in Toronto, 1983), p. 9.

28. On "single vision" and alienation, see Theodore Roszak, *Where the Wasteland Ends: Politics and Transcendence in Postindustrial Society* (New York: Doubleday, 1973).

29. Richard Titmuss, *Essays on the Welfare State* (Boston: Beacon Press, 1969).

30. Robert Reich, *The Next American Frontier* (New York: Times Books, 1983), p. 201.

31. *Ibid.*, pp. 223–24.

32. *Ibid.*, p. 249.

33. See John Forester, "What Analysts Do," in William N. Dunn, ed., *Values, Ethics, and the Practice of Policy Analysis* (Lexington Mass.: Lexington Books, 1983). On the ideology of policy analysis, see Lawrence Tribe, "Policy Science: Analysis or Ideology?" *Philosophy and Public Affairs* (1972), vol. 2.

34. Robert Dahl, *Who Governs? Democracy and Power in an American City* (New Haven, Conn.: Yale University Press, 1961).

35. Forester, "What Analysts Do," p. 53.

36. Jean-Pierre Dupuy, "Myths of the Information Society," in Woodward, *The Myths of Information*, p. 4.

37. See Martin Murphy, "The Value of Non-Market Household Production: Opportunity Cost vs. Market Cost Estimates," *Review of Income and Wealth* (September 1978), 24:243–56; Reuben Gronau, "Leisure, Home Production & Work: The Theory of the Allocation of Time Revisited," *Journal of Political Economy* (December 1977), pp. 1099–1123.

38. The literature on "social indicators" proliferated during the 1960s and 1970s, as quality-of-life concerns came to the fore in social policy discussions. For an introduction, see A. Campbell, P. E. Converse, and W. L. Rodgers, *The Quality of American Life* (New York: Russell Sage Foundation, 1976). See also Angus Campbell and Robert L. Kahn, "Measuring the Quality of Life," in *Qualities of Life: Critical Choices for Americans*, vol. 7 (Lexington, Mass.: Lexington Books, 1976); Angus Campbell, *The Sense of Well-Being in America: Recent Patterns and Trends* (New York: McGraw-Hill, 1980).

1978); Jon H. Goldstein, *The Effectiveness of Manpower Training Programs: A Review of Research on the Impact on the Poor* (Washington, D.C.: GPO, 1972); Charles R. Perry et al., *The Impact of Government Manpower Programs* (Philadelphia: Wharton School, 1975).

21. Harold Lewis, "Self-Determination: The Aged Client's Autonomy in Service Encounters," unpublished paper given in Toronto, 1983. In that paper, Lewis enunciates a first ethical principle public policy for autonomy in old age: "To maximize opportunity for the disadvantaged older person to exercise self-determining action, emphasis should be given to efforts that promote motivation and capacity. This, in contrast to what should govern the provision of services to the disadvantaged non-aged—i.e., among whom motivation and capacity are likely to exceed opportunity" (p. 6).
The inverse relationships between motivation, capacity, and opportunity among young versus older people suggests an important reason why the simple equal opportunity criterion of traditional liberalism fails to provide an adequate criterion for social justice in an aging society.

22. Paul B. Baltes and Sherry L. Willis, "Life-span Developmental Psychology, Cognitive Functioning, and Social Policy," in Matilda W. Riley, ed., *Aging from Birth to Death: Interdisciplinary Perspectives*, Boulder, Colo.: Westview Press, 1979); J. L. Horn and G. Donaldson, "On the Myth of Intellectual Decline in Adulthood," *American Psychologist* (1976), 31:701–19.

23. J. Rodin and Ellen Langer, "Aging Labels: The Decline of Control and the Fall of Self-Esteem," *Journal of Social Issues* (1980), 36:12–29. See also R. Schulz, "Aging and Control," in J. Garger and M. E. P. Seligman, eds., *Human Helplessness: Theory and Applications* (New York: Academic Press, 1980).

24. A. Bandura, "Self-Efficacy in Human Agency," *American Psychologist* (1982), 37:122–47.

25. M. E. Lachman, "Personal Efficacy in Middle and Old Age: Differential and Normative Patterns of Change," in G. H. Elder, Jr., ed., *Life-course Dynamics, 1968 to the 1980s* (Ithaca, N.Y.: Cornell University Press, 1983).

26. Ellen Langer, "The Illusion of Incompetence," in L. Perlmutter and R. Monty eds., *Choice and Perceived Control* (Hillsdale, N.J.: Erlbaum 1979).

27. Andre Gorz, *Farewell to the Working Class: An Essay on Post-Industrial Socialism* (trans. by Michael Sonenscher) (Boston: South End Press, 1982), 1:4.

28. Rolf G. Heinze and Thomas Olk, "Development of the Informal Economy: A Strategy for Resolving the Crisis of the Welfare State," *Futures* (June 1982).

29. A. Gorz, *Farewell to the Working Class*, p. 5.

30. Amory Lovins, *Soft Energy Paths* (Harmondsworth, England: Penguin, 1977). See also Lester Brown, *Building a Sustainable Society* (New York: Norton, 1982); Warren Johnson, *Muddling Toward Frugality: A Blueprint for Survival in the 1980's* (San Francisco: Sierra Club Books, 1978).

7. Ideology and the Politics of Aging

1. For a typical example, see Ethel Shanas, "Social Myth as Hypothesis: The Case of the Family Relations of Old People," *Gerontologist* (1979), 19:3–9.

2. Erdman Palmore, "Attitudes Toward the Aged," *Research on Aging* (1982), 4(3):333–48.

3. Clark Tibbitts, "Can We Invalidate Negative Stereotypes of Aging?" *The Gerontologist* (1979), 4(3):10–20.

4. Thomas Cole, "The 'Enlightened' View of Aging: Victorian Morality in a New Key," *Hastings Center Report* (June 1983), 13(3):34–40.

5. Carroll Estes et al, "Dominant and Competing Paradigms in Gerontology: Towards a Political Economy of Ageing," *Ageing and Society* (1982), 2(2):285–98.

6. David Apter, *Ideology and Discontent* (New York: Free Press, 1964), p. 17. Apter admits that this way of putting the matter can be troublesome because "it extends our ordinary notions of ideology into new areas." The current chapter is an effort to extend this concept of ideology into the field of aging. On ideology, see also Everett Carl Ladd, *Ideology in America* (Ithaca, N.Y.: Cornell University Press, 1963); Irving Louis Horowitz, *Ideology and Utopia in the United States: 1956–1976* (New York, Oxford University Press, 1977).

7. Jurgen Habermas, *Knowledge and Human Interests* (trans. by Jeremy Schapiro) (Boston: Beacon Press, 1971).

8. See, for Karl Marx, *The German Ideology and Other Works*, Karl Marx and Fridrich Engels, *Basic Writings on Politics and Philosophy* Lewis S. Feuver, ed. (New York: Doubleday, 1959). On the Marxist concept of ideology, see George Lichtheim, *Marxism: An Historical and Critical Study* (London: 1961); and Martin Seliger, *The Marxist Conception of Ideology: A Critical Essay* (London, 1977).

9. Douglas W. Nelson, "The Meanings of Old Age for Public Policy," *National Forum*, (Fall 1982), 62(4):27.

10. Richard A. Kalish, "The New Ageism and the Failure Models: A Polemic," *The Gerontologist* (1979), 19:175–202.

11. Louis Harris and Associates, *The Myth and Reality of Aging in America* and *Aging in the Eighties* (Washington, D.C.: National Council on Aging, 1974 and 1981). The extraordinary gap between public perception and reality is discussed by Douglas McAdam, "Coping with Aging or Combating Ageism?" in Aliza Kolker and Paul I. Ahmed, eds., *Aging* (New York: Elsevier, 1982). McAdam, echoing Estes (*The Aging Enterprise*), seems to imply that large numbers of service personnel—including academic gerontologists—benefit from the "service strategy" linked to a liberal ideological view of old age. There is no question that such financial interests play a role in the budgets of aging advocacy organizations—of AARP or NCOA—just as government funding does for hospitals, physicians, insurance companies, and so on. But the history of the liberal ideological view of aging advocacy organizations long predates the availability of government grants and contracts. We do not really require such grossly material influences to explain the persistence of the ideology in any case. On the contrary, what demands explanation is the strength and persistence of such views among intellectuals and policy influentials who are potentially quite free of financial entanglements.

12. Nelson, "The Meanings of Old Age."

13. Nelson, "The Meanings of Old Age," p. 28.

14. Robert Butler, "Ageism: Another Form of Bigotry," *The Gerontologist* (1969), 19:243–46. See also Robert Butler, *Why Survive? Being Old in America* (New York: Harper & Row, 1975); and Erdman Palmore, "Are the Aged a Minority Group?" *Journal of the American Geriatrics Society* (May 1978), 26(5):214–17.

15. On the history of the Townsend Movement, see J. K. Putnam, *Old Age Politics in California* (Stanford, Calif.: Stanford University Press, 1971); and Roy Lubove, *The Struggle for Social Security, 1900–1935* (Cambridge, Mass.: Harvard University Press, 1968).

16. Clifford Geertz, "Ideology as a Cultural System," in David Apter, ed., *Ideology and Discontent* (New York: Free Press, 1964), pp. 63–64.

17. *Ibid.*, p. 55.

18. Carole Haber, "Mandatory Retirement in Nineteenth Century America: The Conceptual Basis for a New Work Cycle," *Journal of Social History* (1978), vol. 12; and C. Haber, *Beyond Sixty-Five* (New York: Cambridge University Press, 1983).

19. Henry J. Pratt, *The Gray Lobby* (Chicago: University of Chicago Press, 1976).

20. W. Andrew Achenbaum, *Shades of Grey* (Boston: Little, Brown, 1982), p. 116.

21. Donald Gelfand, *The Aging Network: Programs and Services*, ed. 2 (New York: Springer, 1983).

22. On political developments, see Robert B. Hudson, ed., *The Aging in Politics: Process and Policy* (Springfield, Ill.: Charles C Thomas, 1981).

23. Achenbaum, *Shades of Grey*, p. 128.

24. H. J. O'Gorman, "False Consciousness of Kind: Plualistic Ignorance Among the Aged," *Research on Aging* (1980), 2(1):105–28.

25. Samuel Preston, "Children and the Elderly in the U.S.," *Scientific American* (December 1984). Preston's analysis, like that of other proponents of generational equity, is controversial because of its reliance on statistics reflecting the official poverty rate as opposed to the near-poor (e.g., those up to 100% above the poverty line) and also because of failure to address the risk of impoverishment in old age due to catastrophic health expenses. Even apart from these qualifications, the question of measuring poverty among the old remains a matter of controversy. For a useful discussion of the role of ideological elements in shaping the way poverty is defined and measured among the elderly, see Lori Gershick and John Williamson, "The Politics of Measuring Poverty among the Elderly," *Policy Studies Journal* (March 1982), 10(3):483–99.

26. Peter Townsend, "The Structured Dependency of the Elderly: Creation of Social Policy in the Twentieth Century," *Ageing and Society* (March 1981), 1(1):5–28.

27. Chris Phillipson, *Capitalism and the Construction of Old Age* (London: MacMillan, 1982), p. 110.

28. *Ibid.*, p. 3.

29. Alvin Rabushka and Bruce Jacobs, *Old Folks at Home* (New York: Free Press, 1980).

30. Elizabeth Kutza, *The Benefits of Old Age: Social-Welfare Policy for the Elderly* (Chicago: University of Chicago Press, 1981). Kutza calls into question the historical liberal commitment to age-categorical entitlement programs. She suggests that more effective means-testing could allocate limited resources to those elderly in greatest need. Policy proposals along these lines continue to generate enormous controversy among aging advocates and gerontologists.

31. Peter Peterson, "A Reply to Critics," *New York Review of Books* (March 17, 1983), pp. 48–57.

32. Martha Derthick, *Policy Making in Social Security* (Washington, D.C.: Brookings Institution, 1979).

33. Randall Rothenberg, *The Neoliberals* (New York: Simon and Schuster, 1984), p. 16.

34. *Ibid.*, p. 44.

35. Lester Thurow, *The Zero-Sum Society* (New York: Basic Books, 1980).

36. On the political economy perspective in aging, see, for example, Laura Katz Olson, *The Political Economy of Aging* (New York: Columbia University Press, 1982); Alan Walker, "Towards a Political Economy of Old Age," *Ageing and Society* (March 1981), 1(1):73–94; John Myles, *Old Age in the Welfare State: The Political Economy of Pensions* (Boston: Little, Brown, 1982).

37. The doubtful claims by aging advocates to deliver the votes of the elderly amount to what Robert Binstock calls the "electoral bluff." Cf. Robert Binstock, "Interest-Group Liberalism and the Politics of Aging," *The Gerontologist* (1972), 12:265–80. Yet Binstock's view seems to overlook other ways in which "Gray Power" inhibits open consideration of policies that might threaten the interest of older voters.

38. See, for example, Eric Kingson, Barbara Hirschorn, and Jack Cornman, *Ties That Bind*, (Washington, D.C.: Seven Locks Press, 1986), a research monograph prepared by the Gerontological Society of America in order to refute proponents of generational equity.

39. James O'Conner, *The Fiscal Crisis of the State* (New York: St. Martin's Press, 1973).

8. Mediating Structures

General Note

The broad topic of mediating structures and aging policy has never been examined directly in the literature of gerontology or social policy. But specific topics, such as the family, are, of course, extensively treated. The broad sociological literature on what is now called "mediating structures" can be traced back to Ferdinand Toennies, *Community and Society* (trans. by Charles Loomis) (New York: Harper & Row, 1957, orig. 1887).

Contemporary policy analysis using the category "mediating structures" originates with Peter L. Berger, and Richard J. Neuhaus, *To Empower People: The Role of Mediating Structures in Public Policy* (Washington, D.C.: American Enterprise Institute, 1977). See also Peter Berger, "In Praise of Particularity: The Concept of Mediating Structures," *Review of Politics* (1976), 38:399–410; and P. Berger, "Mediating Structures: The Missing Link of Politics," *Commonsense* (Summer 1978), 1:1–9. For a critical discussion, see "Mediating Structures and Public Policy," a special issue of *Soundings* (Winter 1979), 52:4, including especially Theodore M. Kerrine, "Mediating Structures: Paradigm for Public Policy," *Soundings* (Winter 1979), 52(4):331–37; and David E. Price, "Community, 'Mediating Structures,' and Public Policy," pp. 369–94.

The literature on gerontology, social policy, and the professions is rich in discussions of the aged in family, neighborhood, and ethnicity, and each of these mediating structures has clear and powerful implications for the design and organization of formal services, discussed in more detail below. This chapter does not offer detailed discussion of voluntary organizations and religious groups as mediating structures, although both are important in old age and neither has received extensive analytical treatment in the literature of gerontology. For further inquiry into these areas, two specialized journals are helpful: the *Journal of Voluntary Action Research* and the *Journal of Religion and Aging*.

1. Peter Laslett, *The World We Have Lost* (New York: Scribners, 1971); and P. Laslett, *The World We Have Lost Further Explored* (New York: Scribners, 1984).

2. Peter L. Berger and Richard J. Neuhaus, *To Empower People: The Role of Mediating Structures in Public Policy* (Washington, D.C.: American Enterprise Institute, 1977).

3. The phrase is Peter Berger's. See Peter Berger, *Pyramids of Sacrifice*, (New York: Doubleday, 1974).

4. For an overview, see the chapter on the family in Ethel Shanas and Robert Binstock, eds., *Handbook of Aging and Social Sciences* (New York: Van Nostrand, 1985).

5. For an overview of bioethical dilemmas in aging, see "Ethics and Aging," special issue of *Generations* (Winter 1985).

6. See Jarold Kieffer, "The Older Volunteer Resource," in Institute of Medicine/National Research Council, *America's Aging: Productive Roles in an Older Society* (Washington, D.C.: National Academy Press, 1986); and Carol Jusenius, *Retirement and Older Americans' Participation in Volunteer Activities* (Washington, D.C.: National Commission for Employment Policy, 1983); R. A. Ward, "The Meaning of Voluntary Association Participation to Older People," *Journal of Gerontology* (1979), 34(3):438–45.

7. For the literature on informal support systems, see David Biegel et al., *Building Support Networks for the Elderly: Theory and Applications* (Beverly Hills, Calif.: Sage, 1984).

8. On modernization, see Donald O. Cowgill and Lowell D. Holmes, eds., *Aging and Modernization* (New York: Appleton-Century-Crofts, 1972); W. Andrew Achenbaum and Peter Stearns, "Old Age & Modernization," *The Gerontologist*, (June 1978), 18:307–12; J. Hendricks, "The Elderly in Society: Beyond Modernization Theory," *Social Science History* (Summer 1982), pp. 321–45. For a comprehensive recent treatment, see Donald Cowgill, *Aging Around the World* (Belmont, Calif.: Wadsworth, 1986).

9. On the life world, see Benita Luckmann, "The Small Life-Worlds of Modern Man," in Thomas Luckmann, ed., *Phenomenology and Sociology* (Harmondsworth, England: Penguin, 1970).

10. On this theme, see Marshall Berman, *All That Is Solid Melts Into Air: The Experience of Modernity* (New York: Simon & Schuster, 1982).

11. Robert N. Bellah et al., *Habits of the Heart: Individualism and Commitment in American Life* (Berkeley, Calif.: University of California Press, 1984).

12. For an analysis and critique of this conventional opposition, see Harry Boyte and Frank Riessman, *The New Populism: The Politics of Empowerment*, (Philadelphia: Temple University Press, 1986); and Harry Boyte et al., *Citizen Action and the New American Populism* (Philadelphia: Temple University Press), 1986.

13. Edward Cornish, *The Study of the Future* (New Brunswick, N.J.: Transaction Books, 1977), pp. 4, 49.

14. Theodore Caplow et al., *Middletown Families* (Minneapolis: University of Minnesota Press, 1982).

15. James C. Musselwhite, Jr. and Lester M. Salamon, "Social Welfare Policy and Privatization: Theory and Reality in Policymaking," in Mark Rosentraub, ed., *Urban Policy Problems* (New York: Praeger, 1986).

16. Michael P. Balzano, *Federalizing Meals-on-Wheels: Private Sector Loss or Gain?* (Washington, D.C.: American Enterprise Institute, 1979). Balzano argues that federal policy failed to take account of the distinctive contributions of mediating structures and has harmed them through bureaucratic heavy-handedness, even in well-meaning initiatives such as the Meals-on-Wheels Program for the aged.

17. Saul Alinsky, *Reveille for Radicals* (New York: Vintage, 1969).

18. See reference 12, above.

19. See reference 12, above.

20. On the populist-communitarian revival, see Harry Boyte, *The Backyard Revolution: Understanding the New Citizens' Movement* (Philadelphia: Temple University Press, 1979); and H. Boyte, *Community is Possible: Repairing America's Roots* (New York: Harper & Row, 1984).

21. The literature on aging and the family is vast. On the contemporary family, see Mary Jo Bane, *Here To Stay: American Families in the 20th Century* (New York: Basic Books, 1976); S. Kammerman and A. Kahn, eds., *Family Policy: Government and Families in Fourteen Countries* (New York: Columbia University Press, 1978).

For recent and past history of the family, see Tamara Hareven, *Transitions: The Family and the Life Course in Historical Perspective* (New York: Academic Press, 1978); Christopher Lasch, *Haven in a Heartless World* (New York: Norton, 1977); and Peter Laslett, *Household and Family in Past Time* (Cambridge, England: Cambridge University Press, 1972). See also John Demos, "Old Age in Early New England," in M. Gordon, ed., *The American Family in Social Historical Perspective* (New York: St. Martin's Press, 1978).

On the family and aging, see Matilda White Riley, "The Family in an Aging Society: A Matrix of Latent Relationships," in Robert W. Fogel, Elaine Hatfield, Sara Kiesler, and Ethel Shanas, eds., *Aging: Stability and Change in the Family* (New York: Academic Press, 1981); Gordon Streib and R. W. Beck, "Older Families: A Decade Review," *Journal of Marriage & Family* (1980), 42(4):937–58; Lillian E. Troll et al., *Families in Later Life*, (Belmont, Calif.: Wadsworth, 1979); Ethel Shanas and Marvin B. Sussman, eds., *Family, Bureaucracy, and the Elderly* (Durham, N.C.: Duke University Press, 1977).

22. Ethel Shanas, "Social Myth as Hypothesis: The Case of Family Relations of Old People," and "The Family as a Social Support System in Old Age," in *The Gerontologist* (1979), 19(2):3–9, 169–74.

23. Brigitte Berger and Peter L. Berger, *The War Over the Family: Capturing the Middle Ground* (New York: Doubleday, 1983), p. 20.

24. On the general issue of mediating structures and aging, as well as for the family in particular, we need to avoid false dichotomies and instead stress what Rose Dobrof calls the "shared function" of both formal and informal systems. See Eugene Litwak, *Helping the Elderly: Complementary Roles of Informal Networks and Formal Systems* (New York: Guilford Press, 1984); and Eugene Litwak and Stephen Kulis, "Changes in Helping Networks with Changes in the Health of Older People: Social Policy and Social Theory," in Shimon Spiro and Ephraim Yuchtman-Yaar, eds., *Evaluating the Welfare State: Social and Political Perspectives* (New York: Academic Press, 1983). Litwak and Kulus argue:

The policy of paying kin (to care for the aged) presents another problem. . . . If one introduces an economic incentive, will it destroy the primary group relationship which is based on affection and duty? . . . if one is talking about paying kin as full-time housekeepers, then the relationship between employer and employee might erode kinship ties. . . . The idea of paying primary group members raises yet another problem. Will such full-time pay open the flood gates for requests for payments from all kin for all services they provide? That could eventually bankrupt the society (p. 355).

For a more favorable view of direct cash subsidies, see "Direct Grants to Families for Care of the Elderly," *Aging* (January–February 1983), pp. 44–45; and Greg Arling and W. J. McCauley, "The Feasibility of Public Payments for Family Caregiving," *The Gerontologist* (June 1983), 23(3):43–69. See also D. L. Frankfather, M. J. Smith, and F. G. Caro, *Family Care of the Elderly*, (Lexington, Mass.: Lexington Books, 1981).

25. Cited in Berger and Berger, *The War Over the Family*, p. 77.

26. Of course we may never come to consensus on "family values" anyway; for a gloomy view on the subject, see Gilbert Steiner, *The Futility of Family Policy* (Washington, D.C., The Brookings Institution, 1973). For a useful summary of current trends and options in family care for the aged, see Pamela Doty, "Family Care of the Elderly: The Role of Public Policy," *Millbank Memorial Quarterly* (1986), 64(1):34–75.

27. Nathan Glazer and Daniel P. Moynihan, eds., *Ethnicity: Theory and Experience* (Cambridge, Mass.: Harvard University Press, 1975).

28. Daniel P. Moynihan et al., *Beyond the Melting Pot*, 2nd rev. ed. (Cambridge, Mass.: MIT Press, 1970).

29. See Peter Kong-Ming New, "Aging, Ethnicity and the Public: Policy Implications," *Journal of Applied Gerontology* (1985), 4(1):1–5. See also this entire special issue focusing on ethnicity and aging.

30. Donald E. Gelfand, *Aging: The Ethnic Factor* (Boston: Little, Brown, 1982), p. 2.

31. In this discussion, I take ethnic identification to refer to a distinctive sense of belonging, whether based on race, religion, language, or national origin. See M. Gordon, *Assimilation in American Life* (New York: Oxford University Press, 1964).

32. Gelfand, *Aging: The Ethnic Factor*, 65.

33. D. Gelfand and D. Fandetti, "Suburban and Urban White Ethnics: Attitudes toward Care of the Aged," *The Gerontologist* (1980), 20:588–94. See also John Stokesberry, "New Policy Issues in Black Aging: A State and National Perspective," *Journal of Applied Gerontology* (1985), 4(1):28–34.

34. Vern Bengston, "Ethnicity and Aging: Problems and Issues in Current Social Science Inquiry," in D. Gelfand and A. J. Kutzik, eds., *Ethnicity and Aging: Theory, Research, and Policy* (New York: Springer, 1979). The same attitudes were observed by B. Crouch, "Age and Institutional Support: Perceptions of Older Mexican-Americans," *Journal of Gerontology* 27 (1972), pp. 524–49.

35. Gelfand, *Aging: The Ethnic Factor*, p. 97. See Elizabeth Markson, "Ethnicity as a Factor in the Institutionalization of the Ethnic Elderly," in Gelfand.

36. Gelfand, *Aging: The Ethnic Factor*, p. 34.

37. J. Cuellar, "El Senior Citizens Club," in B. Myerhoff and A. Simic, eds., *Life's Career: Aging* (Beverly Hills, Calif.: Sage, 1978), p. 205.

38. Marshall Berman, *All That Is Solid Melts Into Air: The Experience of Modernity* (New York: Simon & Schuster, 1982), p. 317.

39. Barbara Myerhoff, *Number Our Days* (New York: Dutton, 1978), p. 7.

40. Marjorie H. Cantor, "Lifespace and the Social Support Systems of the Inner City Elderly in New York, *The Gerontologist* (1975), 15:23–27; and Marjorie H. Cantor, "Neighbors and Friends: An Overlooked Resource in the Informal Support System," *Research in Aging* (1979), 1:434–63.

41. Jane Jacobs, *The Death and Life of Great American Cities* (New York: Random House, 1961).

42. Marshall Berman, *All That Is Solid*, p. 324.

43. For a vivid evocation of those mediating structures, see Ronald Blythe, *The View in Winter* (New York: Harcourt, Brace, Javonovich, 1979).

44. David Biegel and W. Sherman, "Neighborhood Capacity Building and the Ethnic Elderly," in Gelfand and Kutzik, *Ethnicity and Aging*; Howard Hallman, *Neighborhoods: Their Place in Urban Life* (Beverly Hills, Calif.: Sage, 1984); L. Pollack and Robert J. Newcomer, "Neighborhoods and the Aged," in R. Newcomer, P. Lawton, and T. O. Byerts, eds., *Housing an Aging Society* (Stroudsberg, Penna.: Hutchinson Ross, 1984).

45. On revitalization, see James P. Zais and Thomas G. Thibodeau, *The Elderly and Urban Housing* (Washington, D.C.: Urban Institute Press, 1982); and Neil S. Mayer, *Neighborhood Organizations and Community Development* (Urban Institute Press, 1984).

46. Phyllis Myers, *Aging in Place: Strategies To Help the Elderly Stay in Revitalizing Neighborhoods* (Washington, D.C., The Conservation Foundation, 1982), p. 1.

47. *Ibid.* See also Shirley Laska and Daphne Spain, eds., *Back to the City: Issues in Neighborhood Renovation* (New York: Pergamon Press, 1980); Jeffrey Henig, "Gentrification and Displacement of the Elderly: An Empirical Analysis," *The Gerontologist* (March 1981), vol. 21, no. 1; James P. Zais, and T. Thibodeau, "Urban Revitalization and the Elderly" (Washington, D.C.: Urban Institute, 1981); Jeffrey Henig, "Community Organizations in Gentrifying Neighborhoods," *Journal of Community Action* (November, December 1981), vol. 1, no. 2.

48. Phyllis Myers, *Aging in Place*, p. 11.

49. *Ibid.*, p. 6.

50. My discussion has focused on old people in cities. For a parallel examination of issues in other geographic settings, see John R. Logan, "The Graying of the Suburbs," *Aging* (June–July 1984), pp. 4–8; and Michael Gutowski and Tracey Field, *The Graying of Suburbia* (Washington, D.C.: Urban Institute Press, 1979); and Raymond T. Coward and Gary R. Lee, eds., *The Elderly in Rural Society* (New York: Springer, 1985).

51. Harry C. Boyte, "Rebuilding the American Commonwealth," in Alan Gartner et al., eds., *Beyond Reagan: Alternatives for the Eighties* (New York: Harper and Row, 1984), p. 318.

52. *Ibid.*, p. 323.

9. Mutual Self-Help

The literature on self-help in the human services is vast and much of it is relevant to problems of the aging, for example, coping with chronic diseases. But a good deal of the literature consists of "how-to" approaches to the organization of mutual-aid groups for specific problems faced by the elderly: support groups for Alzheimer's families, self-care for arthritis patients, and so on. What is lacking is a conceptual argument that would locate self-help for older people in broader terms. As this chapter suggests, very little has been done to offer an analytical or policy framework for understanding the self-help approach in an aging society.

On the self-help ethos today, see Stuart Langton, ed., "Special Issue: Self-Help in America," *Citizen Participation* (January/February 1982), vol. 3, no. 3. Alfred H. Katz and Eugene I. Bender, *The Strength in Us: Self-Help Groups in the Modern World* (New York: New Viewpoints, 1976); Gerald Caplan and Maria Killilea. eds., *Support Systems and Mutual Help: Multi-Disciplinary Explorations* (New York: Grune & Stratton, 1976); Alan Gartner and Frank Riessman, *The Self-Help Revolution* (New York: Human Sciences Press, 1984); and Alan Gartner and Frank Riessman, *Self-Help in the Human Services* (San Francisco: Jossey-Bass, 1977); Phyllis Silverman, *Mutual Help Groups: Organization and Development* (Beverly Hills, Calif.: Sage, 1980); David Spiegel, "Self-Help and Mutual Support Groups: A Synthesis of the Recent Literature," in David Biegel and A. J. Naparstek, eds., *Community Support Systems and Mental Health: Practice, Policy & Research* (New York: Springer 1982).

For a useful theoretical framework, see David Biegel, B. Shore, and E. Gordon, *Building Support Networks for the Elderly: Theory and Applications* (Beverly Hills, Calif.: Sage, 1984). For a bibliography, see Rubin Todres, *Self-Help Groups: An Annotated Bibliography (1970–1982)* (New York: National Self-Help Clearinghouse, 1982).

For a policy perspective on self-help, see Audrey Gartner, "Self-Help/Self-Care: A Cost-Effective Strategy," *Social Policy* (Spring 1982); R. Hess, "Self-Help as a Service Delivery Strategy," *Prevention in Human Services* (1982), 1:1–2; Sol Tax, "Self-Help Groups: Thought on Public Policy," *Journal of Applied Behavioral Science* (1976), 12:3, 448–54; Ralph Tyler, "Social Policy and Self-Help Groups," *Journal of Applied Behavioral Science* (1976), 12:3,444–48.

On self-help and aging see Frank Riessman, H. R. Moody, and E. Worthy, "Self-Help and the Elderly," *Social Policy* (Spring 1984), 14:4; David Haber, "Promoting Mutual Help Groups among Older Persons," *The Gerontologist* (1983), 23:251–53; Robert N. Butler, Jessie S. Gertman, Dewayne L. Oberlander, and Lydia Schindler, "Self-Care, Self-Help and the Elderly, "*International Journal of Aging and Human Development* (1979), 10:95–117; Cala Michael et al., *The Older Person's Handbook: A Mutual Aid Project Handbook* (New York: Mutual Aid Project, 1978); Beth Hess, "Self-Help among the Aged," *Social Policy* (1976), 7:55–62.

1. Naisbitt, John, *Megatrends: Ten New Directions Transforming Our Lives* (New York: Warner, 1982).

2. On the "service strategy," see Carroll Estes, *The Aging Enterprise* (San Francisco: Jossey-Bass, 1979).

3. Alan Gartner and Frank Riessman, *Self-Help in the Human Services* (San Francisco: Jossey-Bass, 1977).

4. Diane Pancoast, *Rediscovering Self-Help* (Beverly Hills, Calif.: Sage, 1983). See also Alfred Katz and E. Bender, "Self-Help Groups in Western Society: History and Prospects," *Journal of Applied Behavioral Science* (1976), 12:265–82; and P. Gosden, *Self-Help: Voluntary Associations in the 19th Century* (London: Batsford, 1973).

5. (A) review of gerontological literature on self-help among the aged reveals a bleak picture. Few gerontologists seem to be aware of mutual self-help groups. When self-help among the elderly is discussed, it is viewed primarily within a limited context of professional control. This attitude of professional control and the implied de-

pendency of the elderly on the professional may be viewed as an example of the New Ageism.

Thomasina Borkman, "Where Are Older Persons in Mutual Self-Help Groups," in Aliza Kolker and Paul Ahmed, *Aging* (New York: Elsevier, 1982), p. 263. See also Thomasina Borkman, "Experiential Knowledge: A New Concept for the Analysis of Self-Help Groups," *Social Service Review,* 50:445–56.

6. M. Romaniuk and J. M. Priddy, "Widowhood Peer Counseling," *Counseling and Values* (1980), 24:195–203; Elizabeth A. Bankoff, "Widow Groups as an Alternative to Informal Social Support," in M. Lieberman and L. Borman, eds., *Self-Help Groups for Coping with Crisis* (San Francisco: Jossey-Bass, 1979); P. Silverman and A. Cooperband, "Mutual Help and the Elderly Widow," *Journal of Geriatric Psychiatry* (1975), 8:1, 9–27.

7. On self-help groups as a "haven in a professionalized world," see Alfred Katz, "Self-Help and Mutual Aid: An Emerging Social Movement," *Annual Review of Sociology* (1981), pp. 129–55. What is clearly needed is a collaborative approach to professional versus self-controlled human services. See Abraham Jefer et al., "Toward a Self-Help/Professional Collaborative Perspective in Mental Health," in Biegel and Naparstek, *Community Support Systems,* 1982.

8. William J. Arnone, "Mobilizing the Elderly in Neighborhood Anti-Crime Programs, *Aging* (March–April 1978), pp. 281–82; J. Goldsmith "Community Crime Prevention and the Elderly: A Segmental Approach," *Crime Prevention Review* (1975) 2:18–19. For the Oakland California Crime Patrol, see the *San Francisco Chronicle* (April 22, 1985), p. 1. See also George J. Washnis, *Citizen Involvement in Crime Prevention* (Lexington, Mass.: Lexington Books, 1976).

9. George Thabault, "Greenhouse for Seniors," *Gardens for All Newsmagazine* (May–June 1981), p. 42.

10. Judy Chaves, "4th Windiest City in US Gardens under Cover," *Gardens for All Newsmagazine* (August 1983), pp. 1, 2, 26.

11. J. H. Foegen, "Backyard Gardens: Homegrown Hope for the Hungry," *The Futurist* (June 1983), 17(3):37.

12. *Voluntary Action and Older Americans: A Catalogue of Program Profiles,* (Washington, D.C.: NCOA Policy Center, 1983). See also Eugene C. Durman et al., *Volunteers in Social Services: Consumer Assessment of Nursing Homes* (Washington, D.C.: Urban Institute Press, 1979).

13. Michael Walzer, "Politics in the Welfare State," in Irving Howe, ed., *Beyond the Welfare State* (New York: Schocken, 1982).

14. See Jerry Avorn, "Medicine: The Life and Death of Oliver Shay," in Alan Pifer and Lydia Bronte, *Our Aging Society: Paradox and Promise,* (New York: Norton, 1984); Dorothy Rice and Jacob Feldman, "Living Longer in the United States: Demographic Changes and Health Needs of the Elderly," *Millbank Memorial Fund Quarterly* (1983), 61:362–96; and John W. Rowe and Richard Besdine, *Health and Disease in Old Age* (Boston: Little, Brown, 1982).

15. On self-care and self-help in geriatric health promotion, see the comprehensive volume by Ken Dychtwald, ed., *Wellness and Health Promotion for the Elderly* (Rockville, Md.: Aspen Systems Corporation, 1985). For a discussion of the policy issues, see especially Carroll Estes, Sherry Fox, and Constance Mahoney, "Health Care and Social Policy: Health Promotion and the Elderly." On the programmatic side, see Stephanie FallCreek and M. Mettler, *A Healthy Old Age: A Sourcebook for Health Promotion with Older Adults* (New York: Haworth Press, 1983).

16. National Center for Health Statistics, "Survey of Chronic Conditions" (Survey Year 1979), reported in *Statistical Bulletin,* Metropolitan Life Foundation (January–March 1982), vol. 63, no. 1. See also US Comptroller General, Report to Congress, *The Well-Being of Older People in Cleveland, Ohio* (Washington, D.C.: GPO, April 1977).

17. Zachary Gussow and George W. Trace, "The Role of Self-Help Clubs in Adaptation to Chronic Illness and Disability," *Social Science and Medicine* (1976), 10:407–14; and Barry Stults, "Preventive Health Care for the Elderly," *The Western Journal of Medicine* (1984), 14(1):832–45.

18. Z. Gussow and G. W. Trace, "Self-Help Health Groups: A Grass Roots Response to the Need for Services," *Journal of Applied Behavioral Science* (1976), 12(3):381–82; David Robinson and S. Henry *Self-Help and Health: Mutual Aid for Modern Problems* (London: Martin Robertson, 1977); J. D. Williamson and K. Danaher, *Self-Care in Health* (London: Croom Helm, 1978).

19. Office of Technology Assessment, *Technology and Aging* (Washington, D.C.: U.S. GPO, 1985).

20. Louise Russell, *Preventive Health Care* (Washington, D.C.: Brookings Institution, 1985).

21. George S. Tracy and Z. Gussow, "Self-Help Health Groups: A Grass-Roots Response to the Need for Services," *Journal of Applied Behavioral Science* (1976), 12(3):381–82; Lowell Levin, A. H. Katz, and E. Holst, *Self-Care: Lay Initiatives in Health* (New York: Prodist, 1979). See also Lowell S. Levin and Ellen L. Idler, *The Hidden Healthcare System: Mediating Structures and Medicine* (Cambridge, Mass.: Ballinger, 1981).

22. Butler et al., "Self-Care, Self-Help."

23. L. F. Berkman and S. L. Syme, "Social Networks, Host Resistance and Mortality: A Nine-Year Follow Up Study of Alameda County Residents," *American Journal of Epidemiology* (1979). See also Marc Pilsuk and Meredith Minkler, "Supportive Networks: Life Ties for the Elderly," *Journal of Social Issues* (1980), 36(2):95–116.

24. K. Dunnell and A. Cartwright, *Medicine Takers, Prescribers, and Hoarders* (London: Routledge and Kegan Paul, 1972).

25. Stanley Wohl, *The Medical Industrial Complex* (New York: Crown, 1984).

26. Ivan Illich, *Medical Nemesis* (New York: Pantheon, 1976).

27. On cost-containment policy for health care, Samors and Sullivan argue for stronger market incentives but also offer the following cautionary remarks in conclusion:

> By reforming the current system of retrospective cost reimbursement, open-ended tax subsidies, and heavy reliance on planning and regulation, health cost increases might abate over time without jeopardizing the quality of care or access to it. But the growth in outlays will not be reduced immediately, while the increase in revenues may initially be minimal. Instead of a promising set of reforms, both the Reagan administration and its predecessors have offered a continuation of budget ceilings, rate caps, and cost shifting as they have striven for short-term savings. . . . These stopgap measures merely shift the costs of caring for the elderly and the indigent to patients, providers, and employers. This strategy allows the main cost of these programs to continue to rise while trimming their periphery and changing their form. In the end, this strategy leads to cutbacks in services to the groups in need and shifts from payment

through taxes to higher out-of-pocket expenses and higher health insurance premiums.

Patricia W. Samors and Sean Sullivan, "Containing Health Care Costs," in Jack Meyer, ed., *Meeting Human Needs* (Washington, D.C.: American Enterprise Institute, 1982), p. 381. Unfortunately, there is no assurance that cost-shifting will enhance self-help activities or promote higher levels of preventive care general health; indeed, the opposite may be true.

28. Carroll Estes et al., *Political Economy, Health and Aging* (Boston: Little, Brown, 1984).

29. Gibert Steiner, *The Futility of Family Policy* (Washington, D.C.: Brookings Institution, 1973).

30. H. Katz, "Self-Help Health Groups: Some Clarifications," *Ethics in Science & Medicine*, 5(2–4):109–14.

31. R. Brieff, L. G. Hiatt, M. Hager, and J. Horowitz, "Description of Self-Help Groups of Older People Meeting on Health Topics, with Special References to Professional Roles and Education Materials," in L. G. Hiatt, ed., *Uses of Self-Help in Compensating for Sensory Changes in Old Age. Final Grant Report*, vol. 1 (New York, American Foundation for the Blind, 1982).

32. Andre Gorz, *Farewell to the Working Class* (Boston: South End Press, 1982), p. 41.

33. James O'Conner, *The Fiscal Crisis of the State* (New York: St. Martin's Press, 1973), p. 15. But O'Conner is also hopeful that instead of being merely a "crisis cushion and ideology of austerity," communal self-help has the potential to become "a means or process of developing social individuality." See James O'Conner, *Accumulation Crisis* (New York: Basil Blackwell, 1984), pp. 248–49.

34. See David Selbourne, *Against Socialist Illusion: A Radical Argument* (New York: Schocken, 1985), pp. 130–32. See especially the entire chapter, "The Dilemmas of Public Provision."

10. Late-Life Education

General Note

Material from this chapter appears in two recent publications of mine: "Education in the Aging Society," *Daedelus* (Winter 1985) and also in Alan Pifer and Lydia Bronte, eds., *The Coming of the Aging Society* (New York: Norton, 1986); and in an edited monograph, *Education in an Aging Society*, (New York: Carnegie Corporation's Project on the Aging Society 1986).

The literature on older adult education has been growing rapidly since the initial publication of the journal *Educational Gerontology* in 1976. Two recent useful volumes are: James Birren, David Peterson, and James Thornton, eds., *Older Adult Education* (Englewood-Cliffs, N.J.: Prentice-Hall, 1987); and David A. Peterson, *Facilitating Education for Older Learners* (San Francisco: Jossey-Bass, 1983). See also Louis Lowy and Darlene O'Conner, *Why Education in the Later Years?* (Lexington, Mass.: D. C. Heath, 1986), for a wide-ranging and philosophical examination of a fundamental question treated in this chapter, namely, what is the rationale for public policy on behalf of late-life learning?

On lifespan development as the goal of adult education, see Robert J. Havighurst,

"Education Through the Adult Life Span," *Educational Gerontology* (1976), 1:41–51. See also Robert J. Havighurst, *Developmental Tasks and Education* (New York: McKay, 1952); R. J. Havighurst, "Life-span Developmental Psychology and Education," *Educational Researcher* (1980), 9:3–8; and James E. Birren and Diana S. Woodruff, "Human Development over the Life Span through Education," in P. B. Baltes and K. W. Schaie, eds., *Life Span Developmental Psychology: Personality and Socialization* (New York: Academic Press, 1973).

1. Gerald Gruman, "Origins of Age-ism: The Modernization of the Life Cycle," in Stuart Spicker et al., eds., *Aging and the Elderly: Humanistic Gerontology* (Atlantic Highlands, N.J.: Humanities Press, 1978).

2. Richard E. Peterson, *Lifelong Learning in America: An Overview of Current Practices* (San Francisco: Jossey-Bass, 1979).

3. Allen Tough, *The Adult's Learning Projects* (Austin, Texas: Learning Concepts, 1971).

4. Carol B. Aslanian and H. M. Bruckell, *Americans in Transition* (New York: College Entrance Examination Board, 1980).

5. Samuel B. Gould and K. Patricia Cross, *Explorations in Non-Traditional Study* (San Francisco: Jossey-Bass, 1972).

6. Catherine Ventura and Edmund Worthy, *Education for Older Adults: A Synthesis of Significant Data* (Washington, D.C.: National Council on the Aging, 1982). Much of these data are drawn from the regular surveys published under the title *Participation in Adult Education* from the National Center for Education Statistics (1969, 1972, 1975, 1978, and 1981). For earlier data on participation of older adults in education, see J. W. C. Johnstone and R. J. Rivera, *Volunteers for Learning* (Chicago: Aldine Press, 1965).

7. Louis Harris and Associates, *The Myth and Reality of Aging in America* (1974) and *Aging in the Eighties* (1981) (Washington, D.C.: National Council on the Aging).

8. Erdman Palmore, "The Future Status of the Aged," *The Gerontologist* (1976), 16:297–302.

9. Sherry L. Willis, "Towards an Educational Psychology of the Older Adult Learner: Intellectual and Cognitive Bases," in James Birren and Warner Schaie, eds., *Handbook of the Psychology of Aging* (New York: Van Nostrand Reinhold, 1985).

10. David A. Peterson, *Facilitating Education for Older Learners* (San Francisco: Jossey-Bass, 1983), p. 68.

11. I am indebted to Russell Edgerton of the American Association for Higher Education, for background on nontraditional learning and higher education. See also Fred Harvey Harrington, *The Future of Adult Education: New Responsibilities of Colleges and Universities* (San Francisco: Jossey-Bass, 1977).

12. On campus-based older adult education, see Ruth Weinstock, *The Graying of the Campus* (New York: Educational Facilities Laboratories, 1978). For community colleges, one of the most vital sectors of higher education offering opportunities for the elderly, see Roger DeCrow, *New Learning for Older Americans* (Washington, D.C.: American Association of Community and Junior Colleges); and Andrew S. Korim, *Older Americans and Community Colleges: An Overview* (Washington, D.C.: American Association of Community and Junior Colleges, 1974). All these sources are somewhat dated but still give the basic flavor of the enterprise.

13. Malcolm S. Knowles, *The Modern Practice of Adult Education*, ed. 2 (Chicago: Association Press, 1980). See also S. I. Meyer, "Andragogy and the Aging Adult

Learner," *Educational Gerontology* (1977), 2:115–22; Jacques Lebel, "Beyond Andragogy to Geragogy," *Lifelong Learning* (May 1978); and Gwen Yeo, "Eldergogy: A
Specialized Approach to Education for Elders," *Lifelong Learning* (1982), pp. 4–7.

14. H. R. Moody, "Education and the Life-Cycle: A Philosophy for Old Age," in
R. H. Sherron and D. B. Lumsden, eds., *Introduction to Educational Gerontology*
(Washington, D.C.: Hemisphere, 1978).

15. David Peterson, "A History of Education for Older Learners," in D. Barry
Lumsden, ed., *The Older Adult as Learner* (Washington, D.C.: Hemisphere, 1985).

16. H. R. Moody, "Philosophical Presuppositions of Education for Old Age," *Educational Gerontology* (1976), 1:1–16.

17. W. Andrew Achenbaum, "The Obsolescence of Old Age in America: 1865–
1974," *Journal of Social History* (1974).

18. Abraham Maslow, *Toward a Psychology of Being* (New York: Van Nostrand
Reinhold, 1968).

19. Leopold Rosenmayr, *Die Spaete Freiheit: Das Alter—ein Stueck bewusst gelebten
Lebens* (Berlin: Severin & Siedler, 1983).

20. *Lifelong Learning for Self-Sufficiency*, Report of the Mini-Conference on Education for the 1981 White House Conference on Aging (Washington, D.C.: U.S.
GPO, 1981).

See also Howard Y. McClusky, *Education: Background and Issues* (Technical Committee Report), available in the 1971 White House Conference Report, *Towards a
National Policy on Aging: Final Report*, vol. 2 (Washington, D.C.: U.S. GPO, 1971);
and Howard McClusky, "Education for Older Adults," in C. Eisdorfer et al. eds.,
Annual Review of Gerontology and Geriatrics (New York: Springer, 1982).

21. CONSERVA, Inc., *Education and Training for Older Persons* (Washington, D.C.:
U.S. GPO, 1981; and Julia R. French, *Education and Training for Middle-Aged and
Older Workers: Policy Issues and Options* (Washington, D.C.: National Institute for
Work and Learning, 1980). See also Nell Eurich, *Corporate Classrooms* (New York:
Carnegie Foundation, 1985).

22. Alan Gartner and Frank Riessman, *The Self-Help Revolution* (New York: Human Sciences Press, 1984).

23. On experiential learning and self-help, see Thomasina Borkman, "Where Are
Older Adults in Self-Help Groups?" in A. Kolker and P. I. Ahmed, *Aging* (New York:
Elsevier, 1982).

24. Catherine Ventura, *Education for Older Adult: A Catalogue of Program Profiles*
(Washington, D.C., National Council on the Aging, 1982), pp. 23–25. See also
B. Shannon and H. Smiciklas-Wright, "Nutrition Education in Relation to Needs of
the Elderly," *Journal of Nutrition Education* (1979), 11:85–89.

25. I am grateful to Cindy Marano of the National Displaced Homemakers Program for information on that program.

26. See M. A. Okun, ed., *New Directions for Continuing Education: Programs for
Older Adults*, no. 14 (San Francisco: Jossey-Bass, 1982); and "Higher Education and
the Older Learner" (special issue), *Journal of Nontraditional Studies* (Fall 1980), vol.
5, no. 1; H. C. Covey, "American Higher Education and Older People," *Educational
Gerontology* (1981), 6:373–90.

27. K. Patricia Cross, *Adults as Learners: Increasing Participation and Facilitating
Learning* (San Francisco: Jossey-Bass, 1981).

28. Charles Wedemeyer, *Learning at the Back Door: Reflections on Non-Traditional
Learning in the Lifespan* (Madison, Wisc.: University of Wisconsin Press, 1981). See

also Michael Newman, *The Poor Cousin: A Study in Adult Education* (London: Allen & Unwin, 1979).

29. James A. Thorson, "Future Trends in Education for Older Adults," in Ronald Sherron and D. Barry Lumsden, eds., *Introduction to Educational Gerontology* (Washington, D.C.: Hemisphere, 1978).

30. W. Perry, *Open University: History and Evaluation of a Dynamic Innovation in Higher Education* (London: Open University Press, 1976).

31. Max Kaplan, "Elderhostel: Using a Lifetime of Learning and Experience," *Change* (1981), 13:38–41; Jean Romaniuk and Michael Romaniuk, "Participation Motives of Older Adults in Higher Education: The Elderhostel Experience," *The Gerontologist* (1982), 22:364–68; Ron Winslow, "Elderhostel: A Growing Chain," *New York Times* (September 9, 1979), education section, p. 11.

32. K. A. Chelsvig and Sandra Timmermann, "Tuition Policies of Higher Educational Institutions and State Governments and the Older Learner." *Educational Gerontology* (1979), 4:147–59; H. B. Long and B. E. Rossing, "Tuition Waiver Plans for Older Americans in Post-Secondary Public Education Institutions," *Educational Gerontology* (1979), 4:161–74; H. B. Long, "Characteristics of Senior Citizens' Educational Tuition Waivers in 21 States: A Follow-Up Study," *Educational Gerontology* (1980), pp. 139–49.

33. Jean Romaniuk, "State Policies of Tuition-Waiver and Their Impact on Institutions of Higher Education" (1982), study for National Policy Center on Education, Leisure and Continuing Opportunities, National Council on the Aging. See also H. B. Long, "Analysis of Research Concerning Free and Reduced Tuition Programs for Senior Citizens," *Educational Gerontology* (1982), 8:575–84. On broader questions of financing adult education, see R. E. Anderson and E. S. Kasl, *The Cost and Financing of Adult Education and Training* (Lexington, Mass.: Lexington Books, 1982).

34. David Peterson, *Facilitating Education*, p. 249.

35. K. Patricia Cross, "Older Adults & Higher Education" (1982), study for National Policy Center on Education, Leisure and Continuing Opportunities, National Council on the Aging.

36. Hyman Hirsch, "Higher Education in Retirement: The Institute for Retired Professionals," *International Journal of Aging and Human Development* (1977–78), 8:367–74.

37. On the Universities of the Third Age, see A. M. Minvielle, "L'enseignement des universites du Troisieme Age en France," *Gerontologie et Societe* (1980), 13:74–77.

38. Howard R. Bowen, *The State of the Nation and the Agenda of Higher Education* (San Francisco: Jossey-Bass, 1980); Carnegie Council on Higher Education, *Three Thousand Futures: The Next 20 Years for Higher Education* (San Francisco: Jossey-Bass, 1980).

39. Robert Hutchins, *The Learning Society* (New York: Praeger, 1968). See also R. Glover, "Alternative Scenarios of the American Future: 1980–2000" (New York: Future Directions for a Learning Society, 1979); Carnegie Commission on Higher Education, *Toward a Learning Society* (New York: McGraw-Hill, 1973); Thorsten Husen, *The Learning Society* (London: Methuen, 1974).

40. Later published as W. Cross and Carol Florio, *You Are Never Too Old To Learn* (New York: McGraw-Hill, 1978).

41. Ann P. Parelius, "Lifelong Education and Age Stratification: Some Unex-

plored Relationships," in A. Foner, ed., *Age in Society* (Beverly Hills, Calif.: Sage, 1976).

42. Lee Kerschner and Paul Kerschner, "A Difference of Opinion on Higher Education and the Elderly," *Gerontology and Geriatrics Education* (1982), 3(2):121–28.

11. Retraining Older Workers

The issues discussed in this chapter have become matters of wide public debate, particularly in relation to unemployment and the coming of postindustrial society. A useful overview is found in E. Ginzberg, "The Mechanization of Work," *Scientific American* (September 1982), pp. 67–75. For a forecast, see H. N. Fullerton, Jr. and J. Tshetter, "The 1995 Labor Force: A Second Look," *Monthly Labor Review* (November 1983); Congressional Budget Office, *Displaced Workers: Issues and Federal Options* (Washington, D.C.: U.S. GPO, 1982).

For industrial gerontology, see *Older Workers: Prospects, Problems and Policies* (9th Annual Report) (Washington, D.C.: The National Commission for Employment Policy, 1985); *Human Resource Implications of an Aging Work Force* (New York: Carnegie Corporation Aging Society Project, 1984); and Malcolm Morrison, "Work and Retirement in an Older Society," in Alan Pifer and Lydia Bronte, eds., *Our Aging Society: Paradox and Promise* (New York: Norton, 1986); and Lois F. Cooperman and Frederick D. Keast, *Adjusting to An Aging Workforce* (New York: Van Nostrand Reinhold, 1983).

The literature on retraining older workers is much more modest. See S. Barkin, "Retraining and Job Redesign: Positive Approaches to Continued Employment of Older Persons," in H. Sheppard, ed., *Toward an Industrial Gerontology* (Cambridge, Mass.: Schenkman, 1970); *Job Redesign and Occupational Training for Older Workers* (Paris: Organization for Economic Cooperation and Development, 1965); and E. Weinberg, A. Tannenbaum, and G. Grenholm, *Industrial Training Programs for Technology Change: A Study of the Performance of Older Workers,* report prepared for the U.S. Dept. of Labor, (Washington, D.C.: U.S. GPO, 1963). See also the comprehensive study done by the Office of Technology Assessment, *Technology and Aging in America* (Washington, D.C.: U.S. GPO, 1985).

1. J. Sonnenfeld, "Dealing with the Aging Work Force," *Harvard Business Review* (1978), 56:80–90; and B. Rosen and T. H. Jerdee, "Too Old or Not Too Old," *Harvard Business Review* (1977), 59:261–66.

2. On retirement age, see R. Thomas Gillaspy, "Labor Force Participation of the Older Population," in Pauline Ragan, ed., *Work and Retirement: Policy Issues* (Los Angeles: University of Southern California Press, 1980); and S. Bould, "Unemployment as a Factor in Early Retirement Decisions," *American Journal of Economics and Sociology* (April 1980), 39(2):123–36. See also Robert L. Clark and David T. Barker, *Reversing the Trend Toward Early Retirement* (Washington, D.C.: American Enterprise Institute, 1981); and Harold L. Sheppard and Sara E. Rix, *The Graying of Working America: The Coming Crisis in Retirement Age Policy* (New York: Press Fress, 1977).

3. The "third quarter of life concept" is Alan Pifer's. See Pifer and Bronte, *The Aging Society.*

4. See Terry F. Buss and F. Stevens Redburn, *Shutdown in Youngstown: Public Policy for Mass Unemployment* (Albany, N.Y.: SUNY Press, 1983). For a more upbeat

picture of Youngstown, see Linda S. Hayes, "Youngstown Bounces Back," *Fortune* (December 17, 1979), pp. 102–6. For information on unemployment and initiatives for retraining older workers in Youngstown, Ohio, I am indebted to Prof. Carol Franken, Dept. of Sociology, Kent State University.

5. For research on why older workers are reluctant to move, see J. B. Lansing, *The Geographic Mobility of Labor* (Ann Arbor, Mich.: 1977); Michael J. Greenwood, "Research on Internal Migration in the United States: A Survey," *Journal of Economic Literature* (June 1975), 3(2):397–433. See also David Shapiro and Steven Sandell, *Age Discrimination and Labor Market Problems of Displaced Older Male Workers* (Washington, D.C.: National Commission for Employment Policy, 1983).

6. C. Mullen and L. Gorman, "Facilitating Adaptation to Change: A Case Study in Retraining Middle-Aged and Older Workers at Aer Lingus," *Industrial Gerontology* (1972), 15:23–29.

7. Philadelphia Area Takes on New Identity for Robust, Post-Industrial Era," *New York Times* (November 24, 1985), p. 50; and "Northeast Prospers, But New Obstacles May Rise," *New York Times* (September 21, 1986), p. 54.

8. Barry Bluestone and Bennett Harrison, *The Deindustrialization of America: Plant Closings, Community Abandonment, and the Dismantling of Basic Industry* (New York: Basic Books, 1983), p. 12. See also Samuel Bowles et al., *Beyond the Waste Land: An Alternative to Economic Decline* (New York: Doubleday, 1983); J. P. Gordus, P. Jarley, and L. A. Ferman, *Plant Closings and Economic Dislocation* (Kalamazoo, Mich.: W. E. Upjohn Institute for Employment Research, 1981).

9. See Jarold A. Kieffer, *Gaining the Dividends of Longer Life: New Roles for Older Workers* (Boulder, Colo.: Westview Press, 1983).

10. Michael Harrington, *The New American Poverty* (New York: Holt, Rinehart and Winston, 1984), p. 59.

11. Eunice Belbin and M. Meredith Belvin, *Problems in Adult Retraining* (London: Heinemann, 1972), p. 2. See also "The Discovery Method in Training Older Workers," H. Sheppard, *Toward an Industrial Gerontology.*

12. Mancur Olson, *Rise and Decline of Nations* (New Haven, Conn.: Yale University Press, 1982).

13. Randall Rothenberg, *The Neoliberals: Creating the New American Politics* (New York: Simon & Schuster, 1984).

14. Felix Rohatyn, "Reconstructing America," *New York Review of Books* (Feb. 5, 1981); Felix Rohatyn, "The Disaster Facing the North," *New York Review of Books* (Jan. 22, 1981).

15. Lester Thurow, "Reindustrialization and Jobs," *Working Papers* (November–December 1980), vol. 7, no. 6. See also Lester Thurow, *Zero Sum Solution: Building a World Class American Economy* (New York: Simon & Schuster, 1985).

16. Robert B. Reich, *The Next American Frontier* (New York: Times Books, 1983).

17. E. Clague, B. Palli, and L. Kramer, *The Aging Worker and the Union* (New York: Praeger, 1971).

18. Douglas A. Fraser, former president of the United Automobile Workers, commented bluntly: "The biggest problem in all this is in retraining workers in new skills and then not having jobs for them to fill at the end of the line." *New York Times* (February 27, 1983). See also "A.F.L.-C.I.O. Pushes Retraining Funds," *New York Times* (February 27, 1983).

19. Herbert S. Parnes and Randy King, "Middle-Aged Job Losers," *Industrial Ger-*

ontology (Spring 1977), 4(2):77–95. See also H. S. Parnes, ed., *Work and Retirement: A Longitudinal Study of Men* (Cambridge, Mass.: MIT Press, 1981).

20. See Wassily Leontief, *The Future Impact of Automation on Workers* (New York: Oxford University Press, 1985).

21. Data from Bureau of Labor Statistics, *New York Times*, "Fifth of U.S. Workers Hold Only Part-Time Jobs, Out of Necessity or Desire" (August 14, 1983), p. 22.

22. Bluestone and Harrison, *Deindustrialization of America*, p. 59.

23. *Ibid.*, pp. 97–98.

24. *Ibid.*, p. 81.

25. See the discussion of the Swedish model in Robert Kuttner, *The Economic Illusion: False Choices between Prosperity and Justice* (Boston: Houghton, Mifflin, 1984).

26. Victor R. Fuchs, *How We Live* (Cambridge, Mass.: Harvard University Press, 1983), pp. 193–94.

27. Robert B. Reich, *The Next American Frontier* (New York: Times Books, 1983), p. 210.

28. *Ibid.*, p. 207.

29. For more on patterns of collaboration between business and higher education, see Nell Eurich, *Corporate Classrooms* (New York: Carnegie Foundation for the Advancement of Teaching, 1985).

30. R. Reich, *The Next American Frontier*, p. 209.

31. Paul Barton, *Worklife Transitions: The Adult Learning Connection* (New York: McGraw-Hill, 1982), p. 25.

32. On CETA and older workers, see specifically C. J. Reesman, K. Rupp, and R. Mantovani, *Coordination and Cooperation between SCSEP and CETA Operations* (Washington, D.C.: National Commission for Employment Policy, 1983).

33. P. Barton, *Worklife Transitions*, p. 82.

34. On the Trade Adjustment Act, see Reich, *The Next American Frontier*, p. 211. See also General Accounting Office, *Restricting Trade Act Benefits to Import-Affected Workers Who Cannot Find a Job Can Save Millions* (Washington, D.C.: U.S. GPO, 1980).

35. Barton, *Worklife Transitions*, p. 85.

36. Work in America Institute, *The Future of Older Workers in America: New Options for an Extended Working Life* (Scarsdale, N.Y.: Work in America Institute, Inc., 1980). On work-life extension, see also National Committee on Careers for Older Americans, *Older Americans: An Untapped Resource* (New York: Academy for Educational Development, 1979).

37. Barton, *Worklife Transitions*, p. 44.

38. David Birch, "Who Creates Jobs?" *The Public Interest* (Fall 1981). Examining records of 6 million businesses in the United States, Birch argues that job growth in any geographical region has little to do with firms moving in or out of the region. The key is not the demise of firms but the rate at which successful new businesses are formed. Birch's approach is that of microeconomics, not the macro approach of mainstream liberalism. In 1982 the Brookings Institution, a bastion of traditional liberalism, released a study challenging some of Birch's conclusions, but the importance of job creation seems well established.

39. Studies have consistently shown that older workers tend to have stronger personal commitment to their employers and show lower rates of turnover. See D. B. Newsham, "The Challenge of Change to the Older Trainee," *Industrial Gerontology*

(October 1969), pp. 32–33 and C. H. Kelleher and D. A. Quirk, "Age, Functional Capacity and Work: An Annotated Bibliography," Industrial Gerontology (Fall 1973), pp. 80–98.

Despite the ambiguity of turnover costs, there is a real issue to be faced here in the area of pension policy. If an older worker (say, aged fifty-five) is hired and works long enough to become vested in a pension plan, then the company will acquire a pension liability at the point of retirement. By contrast, there is an *advantage* of high turnover of younger workers is that many younger workers will leave the company before pension rights are vested, thus reducing the company's total pension liabilities. Any advantage of recouping a training investment by lower turnover may be offset by higher pension and medical costs for older workers. Retraining, in short, is only one element in the cost mix.

40. "Investing in Jobs," Ford Foundation Letter (April 1, 1984), 16(2):1.

41. See Bryna Shore Fraser, Gerard G. Gold, John Rankin, Lois Rudick, and Ronnie C. Ward, Industry-Education-Labor Collaboration: The Literature of Collaborative Councils (Washington, D.C.: National Institute for Work and Learning, 1981). For some successful regional models, see John Hoy and Melvin Bernstein, New England's Vital Resource: The Labor Force (American Council on Education); and John Hoy and Melvin Bernstein, Business and Academia: Partners in New England's Economic Renewal (Hanover, N.H.: University Press of New England, 1981).

42. L. S. Root and L. H. Zarrugh, "Innovative Employment Practices for Older Americans" (Ann Arbor, Mich.: University of Michigan, 1983), pp. 71–72.

43. Ibid., pp. 68–69.

44. Ibid., p. 71.

45. Sally Coberly, "Retraining the Older Worker for Changing Technology: Programs and Practices," paper presented at annual meeting of the Gerontology Society of America, 1984, p. 10.

46. R. Reich, The Next American Frontier, p. 220. On worker retraining in other advanced industrialized countries, see Klaus von Dohnany, Education and Youth Employment in the Federal Republic of Germany (Washington, D.C.: Carnegie Council on Policy Studies in Higher Education, 1978); Richard Peterson et al., Adult Education Opportunities in Nine Industrialized Countries (Princeton, N.J.: Educational Testing Service, 1980); and P. Andrews et al., The German Vocational System: Comparative Papers in Further Education (Bristol, England: The Further Education Staff College, 1979).

47. R. A. Kasschau, R. Lachman, and K. R. Laughery, eds., Information Technology and Psychology: Prospects for the Future (New York: Praeger, 1982); Harvey L. Sterns and M. Patchett, "Technology and the Aging Adult: Career Development and Training," in Pauline Robinson and James Birren, eds., Aging and Technology (New York: Plenum Press, 1984).

48. Harvey Sterns, "Training and Retraining Adult and Older Adult Workers," in James Birren, ed., Aging, Work, and Health (Englewood Cliffs, N.J.: Prentice-Hall, 1985).

49. K. N. Wexley, "Personnel Training," Annual Review of Psychology (1984), 35:519–51; Herbert L. Selesnick, "Changing Worker Values and Worker Utilization of Industrial Skills Training," in Peter B. Doeringer, ed., Workplace Perspectives on Education and Training (Boston: Martinus Nijhoff, 1981), pp. 75–76.

50. On the current Job Training Partnership Act (JTPA), a 1985 study by the National Alliance of Business surveyed nearly all of the 593 service delivery areas

established to administer the program and reported that older workers were among the most difficult to enroll in the program.

Both problems and opportunities of retraining older workers were highlighted in a study issued in 1985 by the National Commission for Employment Policy, *Older Worker Employment Comes of Age: Practice and Potential.* The study points to the special difficulties faced by displaced homemakers and workers with obsolescent skills. Significantly, the report observes that the payback for investment in retraining older workers may actually be greater than for training younger ones.

51. R. Reich, *The Next American Frontier,* p. 206.

52. Isabel V. Sawhill, "Human Resources," in G. William Miller, ed., *Regrowing the American Economy* (The American Assembly) (Englewood Cliffs, N.J.: Prentice-Hall, 1983), p. 119.

12. Culture, Leisure, and Lifespan Development

The discussion in this chapter explores theoretical, as well as programmatic and policy, issues, but very few works cover this entire range or relate program design to broad questions of policy or theory. For a general overview, see John Balkema, *The Creative Spirit: An Annotated Bibliography on the Arts, Humanities and Aging* (Washington, D.C.: National Council on the Aging, 1986), including my introductory essay, "The Humanities, Arts, and Aging: A Decade in Review." Two useful periodicals that cover the field of culture and aging are *Collage,* a newsletter published by the National Council on the Aging (600 Maryland Avenue, Washington, D.C.) and *The Journal of Human Values and Aging* (New York: Springer Publishing Company).

1. Stanley Aronowitz, *False Promises: The Shaping of American Working Class Consciousness* (New York: McGraw-Hill, 1973), p. 16.

2. Christopher Lasch, *The Culture of Narcissism* (New York: Norton, 1979).

3. Josef Piper, *Leisure, the Basis of Culture* (New York: Pantheon, 1964).

4. H. R. Moody, "The Meaning of Life and the Meaning of Old Age," in Thomas Cole and Sally Gadow, eds., *Meaning and Aging: Views from the Humanities* (Durham, N.C., Duke University Press, 1986).

5. This tie between "generativity" and ego-integrity, on the one hand, and cultural continuity with the larger world beyond the self is a point repeatedly emphasized in the work of Erik Erikson. See *The Life Cycle Completed* (New York: Norton, 1982).

6. For two prominent examples of this "activist" prescription for old age, see Simone de Beauvoir, *The Coming of Age* (New York: Putnam, 1972); and Alex Comfort, *A Good Age* (New York: Crown, 1976).

7. Peter Clecak, *America's Quest for the Ideal Self* (New York: Oxford University Press, 1983), pp. 289–96.

8. My own approach to aging and mass culture is heavily influenced by the perspective of Critical Theory. For an approach inspired by Critical Theory and the analysis of ideological dimensions of domination, see Oskar Negt, "Mass Media: Tools of Domination or Instruments of Emancipation? Aspects of the Frankfurt School's Communications Analysis," and Andreas Huyssen, "The Hidden Dialectic: The Avant Garde—Technology—Mass Culture," both in Kathleen Woodward, ed., *The Myths of Information: Technology and Postindustrial Culture* (Madison, Wis.: Coda Press, 1980). For the seminal text of the Frankfurt School on these issues, see Max Horkheimer

and T. W. Adorno, *Dialectic of Enlightenment* (trans. by John Cumming) (New York: Herder & Herder, 1972). See especially the chapter on "The Culture Industry: Enlightenment as Mass Deception."

9. Stanley Aronowitz, *False Promises*, p. 100.

10. Alan Jabbour, "Some Thoughts from a Folk Cultural Perspective," in P. W. Johnson, ed., *Perspectives on Aging: Exploding the Myths* (Cambridge, Mass., Ballinger, 1981).

11. For the general lines of such a critique of television, see H. M. Enzensberger, *The Consciousness Industry* (New York: Seabury Press, 1974); Raymond Williams, *Television: Technology and Cultural Form* (New York: Columbia University Press, 1961); Stuart Ewen, *Captains of Consciousness: Advertising and the Social Roots of the Consumer Culture* (New York: McGraw-Hill, 1976); and Michael Real, *Mass-Mediated Culture* (Englewood Cliffs, N.J.: Prentice-Hall, 1977).

12. R. Hemming and K. Ellis, "How Fair Is TV's Image of Older Americans?" *Retirement Living* (April 1976), pp. 21–24; S. J. Francher, "It's the Pepsi Generation . . . .," *International Journal of Aging and Human Development* (1973), 4:245–55; R. W. Kubey, "Television and Aging: Past, Present, and Future," The *Gerontologist* (1980), 20:16–35; A. Harris and J. F. Feinberg, "Television and Aging," *The Gerontologist* (1977), 17:464–69. U.S. House of Representatives, Select Committee on Aging, *Age Stereotyping and Television* (Washington, D.C.: U.S. GPO, 1977).

13. Bradley Greenberg, Felipe Korzenny, and Charles Atkin, "The Portrayal of the Aging: Trends on Commercial Television," *Research on Aging* (Sept. 1979), 1(3):319–34. See also C. Aronoff, "Old Age in Prime Time," *Journal of Communication* (1974), 24:86–87; and M. Petersen, "The Visibility and Image of Old People on Television," *Journalism Quarterly* (1973), 50:569–73.

14. Neil Postman, *The Disappearance of Childhood* (New York: Delacorte, 1982), p. 117. For a more general critique, see Joshua Meyrowitz, *No Sense of Place: The Impact of Electronic Media on Social Behavior* (New York: Oxford University Press, 1985).

15. N. Postman, *The Disappearance of Childhood*, p. 133. Postman's point was anticipated by Dwight Macdonald. Speaking of our "homogenized" media culture, Macdonald suggests how this homogenization brings about an erosion of distinctions between age groups. Mass media, particularly television, require an immense homogeneous audience whose tastes can be shaped by the architects of mass culture. This homogenization means an erosion of distinctions between children and adults, thus entailing: "(1) infantile regression of (adults), who, unable to cope with the strains and complexities of modern life, escape via kitsch (which, in turn, confirms and enhances their infantilism); (2) 'over-stimulation' of (children), who grow up too fast." Dwight Macdonald, "Theory of Mass Culture," in Bernard Rosenberg and David Manning White, eds., *Mass Culture* (New York: Free Press, 1964), p. 66.

16. Postman, *The Disappearance of Childhood*, pp. 105–6.

17. On the dialectic between mass culture and popular culture, see Juan Flores, "Reinstating Popular Culture: Responses to Christopher Lasch," *Social Text: Theory/Culture/Ideology* (Fall 1985), pp. 113–23.

18. Alvin Toffler, *The Third Wave* (New York: Morrow, 1980).

19. Gerald Straka, "Television and the Elderly: From Broadcasting to Narrowcasting," and H. R. Moody, "Late Life Learning in the Information Society," both

in J. E. Birren, D. Peterson, and J. Thornton, eds., *Education and Aging* (Englewood Cliffs, N.J.: Prentice-Hall, 1987).

20. Ivan Illich, *Tools for Conviviality* (New York: Harper & Row, 1973).

21. Michael Real, H. L. Anderson, and M. H. Harrington, "Television Access for Older Adults," *Journal of Communication* (1980), 30:81–88.

22. Jacqueline Sunderland, ed., *Education: An Arts/Aging Answer* (Washington, D.C.: National Council on the Aging, 1979); Jean Ellen Jones, ed., *Educational Gerontology* (March–April 1982), vol. 8, no. 2 (entire issue on arts and aging).

23. Naida Weisberg and Rosilyn Wilder, eds., *Creative Arts with Older Adults: A Source Book* (New York: Human Sciences Press, 1984).

24. D. Hoffman, *Pursuit of Arts Activities with Older Adults: An Administrative and Programmatic Handbook* (Washington, D.C. and Lexington, Ky.: National Council on the Aging and Center for Professional Development, University of Kentucky, 1980).

25. Jean Ellen Jones, "On Teaching Art to the Elderly: Research & Practice," *Educational Gerontology* (1980), 5(1):17–31.

26. See "Art Museums and Older Adults," *Museum News* (1981), 59(5):30–35; I. Heffernan and S. Schnee, *Art, the Elderly, and a Museum* (Brooklyn, N.Y.: Brooklyn Museum, 1980).

27. Isabel Burger, *Creative Drama for Senior Adults* (Wilton, Conn.: Morehouse-Barlow, 1980); and A. H. Thurman and C. A. Piggins, *Drama Activities with Older Adults: A Handbook for Leaders* (New York: Haworth, 1982).

28. Marc Kaminsky, *What's Inside You It Shines Out of You* (New York: Horizon Press, 1974); and Kenneth Koch, *I Never Told Anybody: Teaching Poetry Writing in a Nursing Home* (New York: Random House, 1977).

29. Marc Kaminsky, *The Uses of Reminiscence* (New York: Haworth, 1984).

30. E. Caplow-Lindner, L. Harpaz, and S. Samberg, *Therapeutic Dance Movement: Expressive Activities for Older Adults* (New York: Human Sciences Press, 1979).

31. Ruth Bright, *Music in Geriatric Care* (New York: Belwin-Mills, 1980).

32. Lauraine L. Kartman, "The Use of Music as a Program Tool with Regressed Geriatric Patients," *Journal of Gerontological Nursing* (1977), 3(4):38–42.

33. P. Hessing, "Naive Painting: An Occupation of One in Old Age," *Leonardo* (U.K.), 12(4):306–7.

34. Joan Phillips, "The Art of Grandma Layton: An Art Therapy Tool with the Elderly," *Activities, Adaptation, and Aging* (1981), 2(1):3–10.

35. Leslie Lieberman and Leonard Lieberman, "Second Careers in Arts and Craft Fairs," *The Gerontologist* (1983), 23(3):266–72.

36. Patricia McFate, ed., *Paying for Culture, The Annals of the American Academy of Political and Social Science* (January 1984), vol. 471 (entire issue).

37. See Edward C. Banfield, *The Democratic Muse: Visual Arts and the Public Interest* (New York: Basic Books, 1984). The Reagan Administration policy was given in Charles L. Heatherly, ed., *Mandate for Leadership: Policy Management in a Conservative Administration* (Washington, D.C.: Heritage Foundation, 1981). For a more reasonable, though conservative defense of a public cultural policy, particularly concerning the humanities, see Ronald Berman, *Culture and Politics* (Washington, D.C.: University Press of America, 1984). These different works encompass a split in conservative thinking: on the one hand, conservatives who want to do away with all public culture in favor of the private sector (Banfield); on the other hand, those who want cultural policy to uphold high standards for both public and private support of

cultural activities (Berman). The latter point is directly relevant to aging policy, as in the controversy between elite and popular culture.

38. On these broader debates about cultural policy, see Kevin V. Mulcahy and C. Richard Swaim, *Public Policy and the Arts* (Boulder, Colo.: Westview Press, 1982). See also Kingsley Amis, "An Arts Policy," *Policy Review* (Fall 1980), 12:82–94; Margaret J. Wyszomirski, "Arts Policy-making and Interest-Group Policies," *Journal of Aesthetic Education,* (October 1980) vol. 14; Joseph Wesley Zeigler, "Centrality Without Philosophy: The Crisis in the Arts," *New York Affairs* (1978), p. 4.

39. National Endowment for the Arts, *Summary of Activities Relating to Older Americans,* Fiscal Year 1982.

40. House Select Committee on Aging, "The Arts and Older Americans" Hearing (Feb. 7, 1980), House Subcommittee on Human Services (Washington, D.C.: U.S. GPO, 1980.

41. These survey data are discussed by Carolyn Setlow in "Older Americans and the Arts: Analysis of Current Survey Findings," in the National Council on the Aging, *The Arts, the Humanities, and Older Americans: A Policy Symposium* (February 1981), pp. 79–104.

42. Priscilla McCutcheon and Cathryn Wolf, *The Resource Guide to People, Places and Programs in Arts and Aging* (Washington, D.C.: National Council on the Aging, 1985).

43. But see Richard C. Swaim, "Educational and Cultural Programs for the Older Person: A Caveat," *Gerontology and Geriatrics Education* (1983), 3(3):193–99.

44. National Endowment for the Arts, *Summary of Activities Relating to Older Americans,* Fiscal Year 1982. (Washington, D.C.: The Council).

45. Dick Netzer, *The Subsidized Muse* (Cambridge, Mass., Cambridge University Press, 1980).

46. Paul Di Maggio and Michael Useem, "Cultural Policy and Public Policy: Emerging Tensions on Government Support for the Arts," *Social Research* (Summer 1978), p. 45.

47. Bernice Neugarten, *Age or Need?* (Beverly Hills, Calif.: Sage, 1983).

48. Susan Kline, "Humanities Enrichment Is Road to Self-Discovery," *Perspective on Aging* (1978), 7(2):11–13; Lee Mulane, "Age for Enrichment," *American Education* (1978), 14(6):13–17; Arthur Hillman, "Elders Respond to the Humanities," *Aging* (January–February 1982).

49. Jurgen Habermas, ed., *Observations on 'The Spiritual Situation of the Age'* (trans. by Andrew Buchwalter) (Cambridge, Mass.: MIT Press, 1984), p. 7.

50. On late-life creativity, see Hugo Munsterberg, *The Crown of Life: Creativity in Old Age* (San Diego: Harcourt, Brace, Javonovic, 1983).

51. See Walter Benjamin, "The Storyteller," in his volume of essays, Hannah Arendt, ed., *Illuminations* (New York: Harcourt, Brace, 1968). See also H. R. Moody, "Late Life Learning in the Information Society," in J. E. Birren, D. Peterson, and J. Thornton, eds., *Education and Aging* (Englewood-Cliffs, N.J.: Prentice-Hall, 1987).

52. For a philosophical overview of recent work on aging and narrative, see C. G. Prado, *Rethinking How We Age: A New View of the Aging Mind* (London: Greenwood Press, 1986).

53. Dwight Macdonald, "Theory of Mass Culture," in Bernard Rosenberg and David Manning White, eds., *Mass Culture* (New York: Free Press, 1964), p. 60.

54. See H. R. Moody, *An Evaluation of the Senior Center Humanities Program* (Washington, D.C.: National Council on the Aging, 1982).

Index